The Floating Brothel

the Floating Brothel

The Extraordinary True Story of
an Eighteenth-Century Ship
and Its Cargo of Female Convicts

SIÂN REES

AN IMPRINT OF HYPERION
NEW YORK

Library of Congress Cataloging-in-Publication Data

Rees, Siân
    The floating brothel : the extraordinary true story of an eighteenth-century ship and its cargo of female convicts / Siân Rees.— 1st ed.
        p. cm
    Includes bibliographical references and index.
    ISBN 0-7868-6787-6
        1. Prisoners, Transportation of—Great Britain—History—18th century. 2. Penal colonies—Great Britain—History—18th century. 3. Penal colonies—Australia—New South Wales—History—18th century. 4. Women prisoners—Great Britain—History—18th century. 5. Female offenders— Great Britain—History—18th century. 6. Lady Juliana (Ship) I. Title.

HV8950.N6 R46 2002
365'.6—dc21
                                                                                2001046338

Original book design by Casey Hampton

Hyperion books are available for special promotions and premiums. For details contact Hyperion Special Markets, 77 West 66th Street, 11th floor, New York, New York 10023–6298, or call 212-456-0133.

FIRST PAPERBACK EDITION

PAPERBACK ISBN: 0-7868-8674-9

10 9 8 7 6 5 4 3 2 1

Dedicated to John Rees, 1934–2000,
and my Australian family

ACKNOWLEDGMENTS

Tom, Jeanne and Christopher Rees; Pat Patterson and Michael Snowling for sharing their knowledge of navigation with me; Marion Bloxsome for sharing her research with me; Isobel Dixon and her colleagues at Blake Friedmann, London; Doug Young and Jo Roberts-Miller at Headline UK; Lisa Highton at Hodder Headline Australia; Tristan Palmer; Martin Banfield for hospitality in Sydney; the staff at the Public Records Office in Kew, the Corporation of London Records Office and the Plymouth Records Office; the guides at Old Government House and Elizabeth Farm, Parramatta.

CONTENTS

The Floating Brothel

Representation of the Transports going from

Newgate to take water at Blackfriars.

FOREWORD

Sydney, Australia: the gleam of the Opera House, the line of the Harbour Bridge, the glitter of sun on sea on glass, the blue of the water, the brown of surfers' skin. It is a city built in one of the world's most beautiful locations—sophisticated, wealthy, and confident. But just over two hundred years ago, Sydney was a collection of dirty huts around a ragged waterline where people were dying from hunger and disease. They had been sent from Britain, 13,000 miles away, to establish the first European settlement on the continent which would become known as Australia.

In the seventeenth and eighteenth centuries, many European states used transportation to overseas colonies as a means of ridding the home country of criminals and, at the same time, consolidating their hold on foreign land, cultivating it, defending it and settling it. For decades, the British off-loaded undesirables in America but when the American colonies defeated British soldiers and tax collectors, they also stopped accepting British criminals. By 1783, therefore, Britain had to find somewhere else in the world to transport its criminals. After a few unsuccessful attempts in Africa, the British government decided on New South Wales, Australia, and an advance party of just over a thousand people was sent out in 1787. Eight months after leaving Britain, they landed in a small bay on the other side of the world and named it Sydney Cove. The vast majority of the men and women on this First Fleet were British convicts, sentenced to transportation for seven years, fourteen years and, in some cases, the term of their natural lives.

Two years later, the colonists were in a dire situation. They had been expecting relief from Britain—ships bringing more people, more food, more tools and more materials—but none arrived. Crops would not grow. Disease swept the camp. The colonial experiment named Sydney Cove seemed destined to fail and its people to die, forgotten. Then, in June 1790, a Second Fleet of four ships from England arrived and saved the colony. One of them was the *Lady Julian*, which brought a cargo of fertile female convicts to populate Sydney Cove.

The convicts aboard the *Lady Julian* were ordinary women who, by a caprice of fate, found themselves in extraordinary circumstances: rounded up on the streets of Britain, shipped across the world and landed at a dirt camp in an alien continent. They had been sent into exile to a New World which some regarded as a terrifying unknown but others saw as an escape from a wretchedness inescapable in their own country. Some of the women who arrived as frightened teenage criminals would become the founding mothers of Australia, settling into respectability and prosperity. Others would be lost along the way, recreating in the New World the misery they had left in the Old.

This is the story of their journey from the Old World to the New: the quirks of fate in Britain which decided their exile, their long voyage across the world aboard the *Lady Julian* and their reception in the struggling settlement on the other side.

1

DISORDERLY GIRLS

*W*inter 1788, London. At the bottom of the Mall, outside the royal stables, a 26-year-old Scots prostitute staked out her space and began the night's work.

Matilda Johnson already knew William McPherson by sight as a fellow Scot. As he passed through the mews on his way from Westminster to Oxford Street, he said she stopped him, "pressed me close against the wall and asked me what I would give her." Wise to the ways of prostitutes, McPherson felt for his watch to move it into his waistcoat pocket but it was already up her sleeve. He remonstrated; Matilda flirted and would not give it back. First, she wanted a gin in Orange Street. Next, she wanted a plate of salmon around the corner. He refused, refused again, told her nicely he was not interested that night and wanted his watch. Matilda was confident or drunk enough to assume he would bargain it back and disappeared into a pawnshop in St. Martin's Lane where she announced her countryman would pawn his watch to buy her a petticoat. McPherson was now late and exasperated and asked Pawnbroker Crouch to search her. Realizing he meant it, Matilda finally produced the watch from beneath her petticoats.

It was the pawnbroker who insisted on calling in the constable, hoping for part of the reward. McPherson said afterward that Matilda, now crying, "begged me to take the watch, and I wished to have taken it." By now defender rather than prosecutor, he even accompanied Matilda and the constable to the watchhouse[1] and there "begged the clerk and the constable to discharge her." They refused. Still pleading with McPherson to rescue her, Matilda was shackled, hoisted onto a cart and within hours was in Newgate Gaol as "prisoner for law," awaiting trial at the Old Bailey.

A few days later, Charlotte Marsh and her mother Ann Clapton were out shoplifting among the linendrapers of Holborn. They entered Edward Bowerbank's drapery on Newgate Street as the afternoon light was fading and went through to the back shop. They asked the assistant to show them some aprons and launched into the four-step sequence of eighteenth-century shoplifting. Step one was to "tumble the muslins" on the counter. Step two was to divert the shopman by sending him off for scissors or change. Step three was to stuff a piece of cloth up your skirt and step four, to leave the premises unhurriedly and without ungainly lumps. Every shoplifter did it and every linendraper was watching out for it. Skillfully packaged, up to 60 yards of material could disappear beneath a woman's petticoats.

Charlotte Marsh was fussy in her choice and there were a dozen aprons out before she chose one, paid and asked the assistant to change half a crown. He had no change, he said, and called for Mr. Bowerbank. This was a prearranged signal that something suspicious was going on and, sure enough, the moment the shopman turned his head, Mrs. Clapton plucked an apron from the counter and hid it under her cloak. Mr. Bowerbank stepped lithely across the shop and got to the door before her, told her "she had something she should not have" and "wished her to produce it."

Both women were outraged. They had taken nothing. The apron in Mrs. Clapton's inside pocket? She had wanted to see it by the door

---

[1] The "watchhouse" and the "compter" were both premises from which peace officers worked.

in the light. But Mr. Bowerbank had now cast a professional draper's eye over the messy bundle under Charlotte Marsh's arm. When he unrolled a bundle of stolen cloth, both women gave in, bargaining that they would not only buy several expensive items from Mr. Bowerbank's shop but even sell him some lengths of hot calico. This might have been their mistake: the honest drapers of Holborn stuck together. Bowerbank sent one assistant for the peace officer[2] and another to knock on doors in Holborn, Snow Hill and Newgate Street to identify the shopmark on the stolen cloth. When the man from whose shop the women had earlier taken 11 yards of printed calico arrived, Ann Clapton pretended to swoon. The men remained stony faced. She summoned the last of her resources, jumped back on her feet, pointed at her daughter and swore, "It was not me, it was her!" They were both taken in to Wood Street Compter.

A classier heist was being carried out in Soho. Ann Gallant presented herself at Mrs. Underhill's apartment house as a superior sort of maidservant to a superior sort of employer. She had been sent, she said, to inquire for a lodging on behalf of a French lady and gentleman. Rooms were inspected and approved. The following day, Ann came back with a French interpreter to supervise personally the airing of the apartments, the making of the beds and the arrangement of knickknacks for Madame and Monsieur. The interpreter bowed over Mrs. Underhill's hand and spoke with a charming accent. Ann Gallant ordered coal and checked the inventory of linen and plate Mrs. Underhill had sat up the night before to prepare.

Madame moved in with two more servants the next day. For four days, all went well. The foreigners kept to themselves, Mrs. Underhill had found herself a tenant with some cachet (even if the tenant had not actually paid yet) and the interpreter continued to lisp and bow. So it was a rude shock when Ann Gallant woke her on Monday morning, apparently worried that neither Madame nor the interpreter had

---

[2] Forerunner of the police officer.

The magistrate's court in Bow Street, near Covent Garden, where Ann Gallant and Francis Bunting were taken in November 1788. (Rowlandson and Pugin, Guildhall Library, Corporation of London, UK/Bridgeman Art Library)

returned the previous night. A peace officer arrived from Litchfield Street Compter, Ann Gallant was searched and before the end of the day she was up before a magistrate on a charge which could carry a capital sentence. Alone, unable to contact her accomplices and threatened with the noose, she confessed to being the insider on the job.

The charming interpreter was a plain Englishman, Francis Bunting. He would be found, said Ann, in the French coffeehouse in Jermyn Street or at the French hairdresser in Peter Street. Taken by surprise by the Litchfield Street officers, Bunting pretended he could neither speak nor understand English. Was this not strange for an interpreter, they asked and took him the rounds of the usual dodgy pawnbrokers of Golden Square and Brewer Street, where he redeemed a few Underhill sheets, then before a Bow Street magistrate, Bunting still protesting he spoke no English. The magistrate managed to work out more or less what had gone on in this whole confusing story and ordered both Bunting and Ann Gallant be detained until "the other woman" be found. She never was.

By the first week in December 1788, all these "disorderly women" (and Francis Bunting) were awaiting trial in Newgate Gaol, London, part of a turbulent population of seven hundred accused or convicted prisoners. The situation in the cells inside was a reflection of the crisis on the streets outside, for this was the most crowded gaol in the most crowded city of England. There had been a huge growth in population over two generations, increased mobility throughout the country, particularly in and out of the hub of London, and a sudden rise in unemployment. The nation was gripped by royal paralysis at the top and racked by too rapid a change at the bottom. Caught in between, magistrates, parish councils and peace officers struggled to apply old rules to communities which did not conform to old patterns. The forces of law and order were overstretched.

In 1783, overcrowding had worsened acutely when a disbanded army of monstrous size came home from the wars. About 130,000 males were discharged when the American colonies defeated King George's British and German forces. London alone had to house and employ tens of thousands of ex-soldiers. The streets filled with war cripples begging halfpennies and thousands of women began to find themselves "out of a place" and out on the streets. It is a familiar post-war story: male unemployment could be solved by giving women's jobs to men and sending women back to the home—except that in the urban world of 1780s England, many had no home to go to. Throughout the decade, the unemployed veterans and amputees were joined by ex-shopgirls, ex-milkmaids, ex-laborers, and ex-maidservants, now "disorderly girls" living off gin and plates of fatty meat, scraping by on pennies supplemented wherever possible by stealing from someone marginally better off. "A few years ago," said the *Times*, "[such women] had arrangements in shops; it is now different; needles, ribbons and the most trifling article must be supplied by a fellow 6 foot high or the shop is thought of no account . . ." and suggested a tax on shopmen working in drapers, milliners, perfumers and haberdashers, all of which had previously been regular employers of women.

In London, the authorities turned to repression. One evening in November 1785, City peace officers arrived en masse at St. Paul's, on the outskirts of the City, and began an orchestrated expulsion of prostitutes from the City into Westminster. The same evening, Westminster peace officers turned up with the intention of driving the same women away from Westminster—and into the City. "In consequence of these moral proceedings," wrote the *Times*, "these wretched women must seek an asylum in the arms of old Father Thames or starve in their wretched hovels."

The same year, Prime Minister Pitt proposed a tax on maidservants over the age of 15. This was, Lord Surrey told the House of Lords, deeply unfair to women "who had no other mode of obtaining a subsistence but by their domestic labour." He, too, proposed a tax on men "who trespassed on the natural employment of women, such as men-milliners, haberdashers, staymakers &co, &co." The *Times* was behind him. "Fifteen is a most dangerous time for the female sex; that thousands will be turned out of employment at that age, there is everything to be dreaded . . . when poverty and want have no relief but from the wages of prostitution." The tax was approved nevertheless. By July 1786, the *Times* estimated that "upon a very modest calculation, not less than 10,000 have been added to the number of common prostitutes by Mr. Pitt's tax on maidservants." By October, it despaired. "The height to which female prostitution is carried," it wrote, "and is likely to increase in this capital is truly alarming . . . there are in London and its environs 50,000 common women."

It was acknowledged that unemployed maidservants were "one of the grand sources which furnish this town with prostitutes." Some sought desperately to avoid this fate. Twenty-year-old Mary Anderson had been sentenced to seven years' Transportation to Parts Beyond the Seas at a brief and pathetic trial following a brief and pathetic theft. Mary Anderson was from Bristol and had come to London to find work, perhaps because some misadventure had sullied her name in her home parish, perhaps because there was no work there anyway. Alone in the capital, she could find no place and, when her money was gone, she snatched a bundle of clothes and household linen from a lodging house in Shadwell and was seen leaving with a bulge under her apron. The woman who caught her told the judge, "she cried and said, if I would let her go, she would not come near the house any more." Mary Anderson's defense was equally artless: "my friends live in Bristol; I did take the things . . . I thought I had better do that than be a common prostitute."

Society of the time did sometimes acknowledge that the cause of her crime might lie outside a female's control but could not yet make the leap to accepting this as mitigation of her guilt. Deserving of charity, yes; compassion, certainly; some minor change in the enforcement, wording and even aim of legislation to curb sentencing—but rehabilitation, no. Disgraced females found "their character is utterly gone" and "may never be retrieved," whereas disgraced males might "reform, and be admitted into that same society and meet with a cordial reception as before." It was regrettable—but there it was: nature's way, God's will, human nature. When the number of women offending rose, as it did in the 1780s, there was neither sufficient gaol space to accommodate them nor the means to absorb them back into society. Among their own kind, more prosaic attitudes to disorderly women prevailed. But it was society which judged them and recorded its judgments.

The problem of how to regard female offenses lurked in the background in December 1788. More important was finding some way to prevent them but nobody seemed to know how to do this. It was not that the authorities were unaware of the problem. At every level, their workload increased. Lowly peace officers were recording the effects of postwar maladjustment in laborious longhand entries in their Compter Books each night. At Poultry Compter, one disorderly girl after another was taken up for "wandering abroad crying in the Open Air," "having no visible way of living and lying in the Open Air on the streets," "running away with a Watchman's Lantern," "making use of approbrious language," and once, with greater spirit, "chasing a Bullock down Poultry." When the Compter Books, with their miserable record of disorderly lives, were brought into court promptly at eleven o'clock each morning, it was the turn of the magistrates to deal with the pickpockets, shoplifters, prostitutes and bag snatchers who each told some pathetic and predictable story of want suffered and opportunity seized. And when the magistrates had sifted the misdemeanors from the felonies, responsibility passed to the High Court judges who would have to decide how to punish this endless stream of petty criminals, with their numbingly similar stories of life lived in unremitting insecurity.

Among the women who passed each month through the courts, some had lived with family, friends or some other human connection which anchored them to a place and a social group. But many, like Mary Anderson, had lived alone and by their wits, drifting from city to city and place to place, single and cunning, left by or leaving whatever family they had, passing through friendships and partnerships which lasted a night or a week until one or the other wandered off, often picking her partner's pocket as she went. London was full of "common lodging houses"—a combination of inn, flophouse and brothel—packed with drunks, nursing mothers, thieves, immigrants, out-of-work servants and thousands of other unfortunates on the margins of city life. They slept in dormitories, sheds, stables, lean-tos and even the privies in the yard. Beds were let by the night to singles, couples, triples or however many it took to come up with the bed rent, sleeping head to toe in garrets on mattresses of damp straw beneath windows stuffed with rags to keep out the cold and keep in an air rank with foul breath, farts and copulation. A bed in a dormitory might cost 6d (pence), 4d a head if sharing. Downstairs in the yard, it cost 3d to sleep in the straw next to the privies—the sort of money the cheapest prostitutes were backing themselves against the wall for.

Sleepers in such houses were prey to cold, damp, disease and the depredations of fellow lodgers. Elizabeth Ayres, 28, and her friend

Ann Wood, 23, had a casual lodging arrangement one night in 1787 in Goldsmith Alley. They allowed one James Roach, laborer, to share their bed for the night for one shilling. He assured the court this was for sleeping purposes only. The women waited until he was asleep, took his clothes and ran. Around the corner, Ann Wood paused to pull his breeches on under her skirt and ran on with his coat over her arm. They got as far as Plumtree Street where Constable Cornelius Harrigan appeared and asked why they were running with a man's coat. It is my husband's coat, Ann told him, and claimed she was taking it to the tailor to be mended. What did her husband do? He was a hackney coachman. Surely hackney coachmen did not wear that sort of coat? Constable Harrigan marched them both to the nearest compter where the constable of the night examined the coat and decided both tailors and hackney coachmen were irrelevant as it did not need mending. Then he examined the women and discovered Ann Wood's breeches. Both women were sentenced to Transportation to Parts Beyond the Seas.

Sleeping arrangements such as these were normal and it was not only the possessions of men brought back to rented beds which went missing in the night. One petty thief commonly stole from another and a woman who had just relieved her bedmate of his watch and seals might stuff them under the pillow and find someone else had removed them in her turn by morning. It was hard for a woman who lived from bed to bed to keep even the clothes she wore safe from the gentle fingers of a stranger sharing her mattress. Coins were sewn into seams or swallowed for safety, then retrieved with a good laxative, graphically known as an "opening medicine." One Welsh magistrate recalled another hiding place "in the hair . . . where decency forbids to name." He knew of a woman who had stored thirty gold sovereigns there. But not everything could be swallowed or inserted and necklaces were taken from around necks, coins unsewn, shoe buckles sliced off with razors, shifts, shoes and aprons undone and removed by strangers in the night.

One step up from this squalor were the "private lodging houses" where thousands of slightly better off transients rented furnished bed-sits at four or five shillings a week. Most private lodging houses were the homes of tradesmen, shopkeepers or widows earning a second income by taking in lodgers. The ground floor was commonly taken up with trading premises and the "one pair of stairs" (first floor) occu-pied by the tradesman's family. Above and below this, the house was stuffed with tenants, each floor and room let at a graded rent and attracting a minutely differentiated clientele. A huge volume of human traffic passed through these places and new faces were con-stantly seen on stairs and landings. Petty opportunistic theft by lodgers was rife, from landladies or from each other: the single lady eking out a pension and sharing the one pair of stairs with her land-lady might find the box beneath her bed broken into as she slept; the servants doubling up for a week in the garret while looking for work might find the cloak hung on a hook overnight had gone in the morning; the washerwomen in the cellars opened their trapdoors for ventilation and did not notice the thief sneaking down from the pave-ment to raid the laundry line. Women newly out of work, or newly arrived in the city, would commonly take rooms in these houses, exhaust their savings, start pawning the landlady's furniture to meet the rent and fall into ever more hopeless debt. Their stories were heard every month at the Old Bailey.

Widow Ryan was a typical landlady. She lived on the one pair of stairs in her dwelling house at Seven Dials and rented out the other rooms by the week. Elizabeth Gosling took a room there in August 1787 at three shillings a week. It was not a good month to find work: many wealthy families were in their summer lodgings in Bath or Cheltenham. By mid-September, she was unable to meet her rent and pawned first a quilt worth 18d, then a sheet worth 6d. She did not deny this to the constable who arrested her, to the magistrate or even to the Old Bailey judge. "I never gave up my apartment til she took me to the office," she told the court, under the common but mistaken belief that this exonerated her. She was in Newgate Gaol for a year, awaiting Transportation to Parts Beyond the Seas.

Another Seven Dials landlady, Mrs. Martha Davis, had prose-cuted a woman now sharing the cells with Elizabeth Gosling for the same offense a few months earlier. Mary Stewart claimed Mrs. Davis had said she could pawn what she liked as long as everything was there when she left. This was common in the Davis' house, she claimed—"there is not one [room] which has got a pair of sheets"—and Mrs. Davis connived at the system: "[she] takes in the things her-self; the things were pledged to pay her the rent." Mrs. Davis denied it. It may have been that she was fed up with lodgers selling her mov-able goods and then pleading innocence. Some landladies were only a few steps up from the poverty of their tenants and could not afford to lose a flatiron or a pair of curtains every time a room changed hands. Certainly, not all lodgers were down on their luck but had good intentions for the future. Elizabeth Kearnon alias Price moved into Mrs. Davis' house just before Mary Stewart and within forty-eight hours had pawned an iron frying pan, a flatiron, three blankets, a pair of linen sheets, a bed quilt, a copper saucepan—as the landlady testi-fied, "everything in the room but the chairs and tables." When caught, she used the same excuse as Gosling and Stewart. All three were awaiting Transportation to Parts Beyond the Seas.

Both common and private lodging houses were regularly used by prostitutes, turning tricks among the sleeping clientele. Any woman could rent a bed or a room for the night and share it with others, turn and turn about as the customers came through the night. A prostitute with a customer and nowhere to go might displace a friend from a rented bed for half an hour in return for part of the fee—or, notori-ously, in return for part of the profit made by stealing and pawning his watch or breeches. Stories of prostitutes emptying the pockets of their clients and passing the contents to a friend in the shadows were as common in the Old Bailey as stories of lodgers pawning the quilt.

Nimrod Blampin admitted openly in court that he had picked up Rachel Hoddy on the "cooing seats" of St. James Park when drunk and gone back with her to her lodging on Gravel Lane for a supper of beer and salmon before sex. Shortly afterward, he turned his face to

The "cooing seats" in St. James Park where Rachel Hoddy picked up Nimrod
Blampin in June 1788. (Guildhall Library, Corporation of London)

the wall and slept it all off—until seven o'clock in the morning, when
he awoke to find himself naked, locked in from the outside and
robbed of all his clothes and money. It was June—the situation was
embarrassing rather than critical. Naked, he smashed down the door
with a poker and persuaded a soldier lodging below to lend him some
clothes. By the time he got to the nearest compter, an alert officer of
the night had already taken up Rachel's fellow lodger, Ann Hardiman, on her way to the pawnshop with Nimrod's shirt over her arm.
She had already placed clothes with three different pawnbrokers
along Fleet Street which, she confessed, were Blampin's, passed on by
Rachel during the night but that "the things were given [Rachel] in
lieu of cash."

Nimrod Blampin escaped with some damage to his dignity but
none to his person. In the rougher parts of town, however, a prostitute with one hand in a man's pocket often used the other to punch
him in the head or summon a partner to do it for her. Then, it was
known as "assault on the king's highway"; now, as mugging. The area
most notorious for this was the Ratcliff Highway, a long, straight
road leading east from the City to Limehouse, packed with lodging
houses which sheltered gangs of prostitutes and muggers. Picking up

a woman here was known to be a risky business, especially if a man were alone and drink fuddled. The whisk of dirty skirts around a corner, down an alley and into a court where a dozen vicious slum dwellers waited to defend their own was a common experience. A prudent man would cut his losses and back away.

A "Report on Common Lodging Houses" of 1788 went into some details on traps for the unwary punter. In particular, it described a situation repeated nightly up and down the Ratcliff Highway: "when a prostitute has decoyed a man and robbed him, the mistress of the house has half the pay and the plunder." In October 1788, Mary Anson decoyed Benjamin Solomon into a house owned by Elizabeth Underhill. Underhill was a woman to make a man tremble, although Solomon, without his breeches and ready for love, was particularly vulnerable. Not only did she have the muscle to threaten him physically, she had the imagination to make her threat truly foul. Twenty-three-year-old Mary must have been more alluring, at least in the dark streets of Shoreditch, where she picked up Solomon on his way home from a convivial evening in Hoxton Square. First he gave her a penny for a candle, next he laid out a shilling to buy her a drink and by the time they reached St. Paul's Alley, he was committed. Solomon made the grave mistake of being the first to undress. When naked from the waist down, his jingling breeches were snatched from his hand, pretty Mary disappeared, and in her place was Mrs. Underhill. She "demanded to know what I wanted there," he told the judge and then threatened magnificently to "smother me, if I talked, under 6 or 7 load of nightsoil . . . emptied from the necessaries . . ." Faced with death by sewage, Solomon agreed to silence. His breeches, no longer jingling, reappeared and he was shown the door, loose about the knees because his buckles had been part of the price of freedom.

Cowed, but not to the point of complete capitulation, he flapped away to find the patrol. Mary Anson was tried at the Old Bailey and sentenced to seven years' Transportation to Parts Beyond the Seas. Mrs. Underhill was held over for later trial as "accessory to the fact." Both were in Newgate Gaol.

Another East End twosome in the Newgate cells under the same sentence were Poll Randall and Mary Butler. These two had committed an even more audacious raid on Joseph Clark at a lodging house or brothel in Cable Street apparently owned by Elizabeth Sully. On the night of 10 November 1787, Clark was strolling down Cable Street with the extraordinarily incautious sum of £40 in his pocket and half a cheese on his head. When he found himself seized from behind by Poll Randall and Mary Butler and dragged into a house it was, he explained to a bemused court, care for his cheese which prevented his putting up any resistance. Inside, his cheese was snatched and this, he went on, was why he could not leave. A wiser man might have abandoned a few shillings' worth of cheese and saved £40 in cash.

Joseph Clark held out for his cheese during half a pint of gin, a game of cards, a further half of gin and a convivial supper, although when supper was suggested, he did object that "I only want my cheese and to go home." But suddenly the mood changed. Poll and Mary hauled him upstairs—"you could not resist at all?" asked an incredulous judge—and forcibly undressed him—"she threw me on the bed!" he defended himself. "I cried out, for God's sake do not use me ill!" It was only when Poll demanded the banknotes in his pocket that Clark realized they were not just after his cheese. Even at this dramatic point, they all had another round of beef and gin but then Poll Randall ran out of patience: "she took both my hands and put them behind me; I was afraid to make any resistance!" Both Poll Randall and Mary Butler were 13. Five months later, they were joined in the cells of Newgate by Mother Sully, owner of the house, and another of her brood of teenage chicks, convicted of robbing another Cable Street punter of his silver watch.

The overcrowded city of London was a curious place in the 1780s. Grandeur overlapped squalor and in middling districts common lodging houses existed side by side with the respectable households of tradesmen, clerks and smaller merchants. The servant maid down on her luck in a Seven Dials flophouse might, with a stroke of good fortune, be maid of all work to a respectable butcher in Smithfield next week. A shopkeeper's widow on a small pension might lodge next door to a pickpocket. People lived in constant, intimate contact with strangers. Charles Marsh arose early one morning to go to work and "heard a woman's voice in the necessary." This was Esther Curtis, 18 years old and thoroughly drunk. She had fallen over the night before, she said, slept on his steps and was relieving herself before moving on. Marsh let her go about her business but discovered later she had robbed him of twenty shillings' worth of clothes. He would have forgotten her had not Esther, once more blind drunk, turned up again in his lavatory the following night. This time he went for the watch and Esther swiftly found herself in Newgate Gaol.

Even away from the lodging houses, people lived tightly packed together in all but the very grandest households. This gave rise to another of the commonest stories of female felony heard in the Old Bailey: the maidservant who pinched the silver.

"The offence of servants, in general, robbing their masters . . . is a crime which so entirely cuts up every bond of civil society that it is the duty of the Courts of Justice, at all times to punish it with severity." These were the words of the recorder of London, James Adair, who had sentenced many of the women in Newgate Gaol to Transportation to Parts Beyond the Seas in his capacity as Old Bailey judge. His view of servant-employer relationships bore less and less relation to reality. Amid Georgian concerns about the number of people out of a place, there are glimpses of an almost Elizabethan fear of masterless men. However, insistence on the old bonds of duty and obedience to master and mistress, with financial and moral protection as quid pro quo, was becoming obsolete in this shifting world of casual employment. Few family retainers passed through the courts; the stories heard in the Old Bailey came from a world where people moved from job to job with their possessions in a box on their back, looking constantly for an extra sixpence a week, a warmer bed or better food. In this world, strangers were taken on as servants with a

minimum of preliminaries and given intimate access to a household—and dismissed again with the same lack of thought, replaced
by other floating unknowns as necessary.

The most usual time for a maidservant to be "turned off" was late
spring, when wealthy households prepared to move to summer lodgings out of London. Employers knew it would be easy to restock the
attics with maids when they returned in the autumn. They also knew
the few days between dismissal and departure was a time to keep a
close eye on the family valuables. There was little surprise in
Grosvenor Square in April 1788 when a local pawnbroker knocked at
the door of Sir Henry George Little, baronet, with a crested silver
tablespoon and a description of the skivvy who had been turned off
the day before. The butler, who deposed, could not tell the court why
Catherine Hounsam had been dismissed. One can almost detect the
lift of his eyebrows at the suggestion he should be familiar with the
affairs of a kitchen maid. Catherine comes across in her testimony as
slightly simpleminded. She had taken a valuable and easily identified
spoon to a pawnbroker just around the corner and told him it had
fallen off the back of a dust cart. Off the back of a dust cart? Yes, off
the back of a dust cart and the dustmen told me, "I might have it to
eat my porridge with." Even the jury thought her a little lacking. The
value and circumstances of the theft required the death sentence be
passed, but the jury humbly recommended her for mercy "being very
young and ignorant." In fact, she was 30 and proved more canny in
later life than one might suspect from the ineptitude of her crime.

Catherine had probably grabbed the spoon to tide her over until
she found another place scrubbing out the scullery, and the situation
in which she and thousands like her found themselves was well
understood. Elizabeth Gale did the same. She had been maidservant
to Alexander Annersely for sixteen months and was "going away the
day after the robbery." That night, Gale herself woke the family and
called the watch. The officers found "the sideboard stripped" and,
damningly, "a neighbor's coachman under the prisoner's bed." In her
box was 9d worth of children's clothing and during her interrogation

she admitted to having let four other men sleep under her bed during her time in service. The theft of the silver, worth £17, could not be pinned on her but the 9d worth of clothing was enough to sentence her to seven years' transportation.

There was some sympathy for a maidservant in Catherine Houn-sam's position, as there was for shopgirls replaced by returning soldiers. However, she was tarred by the brush of both irredeemable female and thieving servant, for there were many other servants out there stealing not because they had to but because they could. Employers who forgot to lock the tea chest or the parlor door were considered fair game and pilfering was endemic in households of all sizes.

Elizabeth Parry was 21 and claimed to be freshly down from Lancashire when she went knocking on doors around the fields north of City Road in May 1787, looking for work "in the milk business." She struck lucky with Mrs. Attewell, who took her on as cow keeper, and she moved into the Attewell house as soon as the deal was made. During the eight days she spent there, she never milked an Attewell cow or dirtied her boots in an Attewell field, as within two days she had fallen sick and taken to her bed. Mrs. Attewell attended the girl in her room, paid for the attentions of an apothecary—including bleeding at thruppence the time—then came home and found Elizabeth gone, her desk robbed and the money set aside for the other cow keepers' wages stolen. Susanna Attewell might have been a poor judge of character but was experienced enough to know that if she did not get a constable to Elizabeth Parry within hours, the girl would disappear into the sea of bonnets and brown cotton gowns which swirled up and down the City Road. She moved swiftly and within a couple of hours Elizabeth had been taken up. In court, she was feisty, interrupting Mrs. Attewell's testimony with "I never said any such thing!," pointing out that her mistress had also gone out the day before and the things could have been taken then and making a defiant final defense: "The things are my own and as for money, the prosecutrix had none!"

Elizabeth Parry was a girl on the make, Catherine Hounsam a woman in distress, Elizabeth Gale somewhere in between. The story of another servant in Newgate Gaol was more ambiguous. Twenty-seven-year-old Rachel Turner had worked for Cleophas Comber, a wax and tallow chandler in the parish of St. Martin's. He was prosperous enough to employ Rachel, two menservants and, during his wife's confinement, a nurse as well. It was when the nurse came to live in that certain clothes, linen and sauceboats went missing. Comber suspected Rachel but did not wish to confront her himself and so sent for Officer Parsley. Mr. Parsley listened to the master's suspicions then questioned the maidservant and insisted on seeing her box. Inside were the silver sauceboats.

Rachel had enough savings to employ a well-known counsel, Mr. Garrow, and his principal line of defense was attack. Rachel, he said, had been framed. Harassed by accusations from his wife that he was sleeping with Rachel, Comber had hit upon this solution for getting rid of the girl. She had worked blamelessly for Mrs. Comber over six months and the "curtain lectures" to Cleophas had begun only when "the good woman was in the straw" (and, being pregnant, inclined to hysterical fancies) and the nurse ("always a gossip") arrived and began insinuating that the master was getting up to no good with the maid in the back parlor. Did Mr. Garrow invent this entire story or did something that Rachel Turner told him put it in his mind? Nothing clear emerges from Cleophas Comber's version of events but he is a rather shamefaced figure in Rachel's downfall. It would not be the first time a husband went knocking on a maidservant's door one night and tried to buy her off with a hasty gift off the mantelpiece the next morning.

2

FAIR BRITISH NYMPHS

One of the most popular characters in late-eighteenth-century liter-
ature was the fallen woman. The girl of good family seduced and
betrayed by a plausible villain was particularly fascinating. "Chapbooks"—collections of *True Stories!* with a historical or moral twist—
were the staple reading material of the literate lower middle classes
and used the fallen woman as their single most frequent character.

The fictional story of Louisa Harewood was affectingly recounted
in one chapbook in the form of a confessional letter to her parents on
the eve of her departure for Botany Bay and followed by a little verse:

> *ye fair British nymphs of beauty and fame too*
> *listen to my story, beware of my fate too*
> *once like you I was happy, like you I was blest,*
> *though now I am wretched with sorrow oppresst*
> *oh! pity my sorrows! ah, me, well-a-day*
> *as a convict I'm forced now to Botany Bay!*

. . . And all because of a chance meeting with Lieutenant Henry Harris at the home of the local squire. One thing led to another with the
handsome lieutenant and "one fatal evening I resigned, with my

virgin innocence, the peace of my soul, your care and protection and intailed a series of lasting miseries on myself," when Lieutenant Henry persuaded her to elope. After only a few blissful weeks, he was called to his ship at Portsmouth and left, swearing "eternal constancy" and a promise to "transmit me money . . . which, alas! he never fulfilled." Louisa spent her last money on the coach to Portsmouth, found lodgings and sent word to Henry. They had another two days together before she learned his ship was under way, a shock which sent her into a decline from which she emerged "mistress of only four guineas." Forced to pawn her clothes and then "(though with the utmost regret) to make free with the furniture of my lodgings," she was prosecuted and sentenced to seven years in Botany Bay.

It is easy to mock moralistic tales like Louisa Harewood's, bursting with repressed sexual excitement—so easy that it is a shock to realize how closely they could conform to the truth. One young girl who could have been the model for Louise Harewood was in gaol 250 miles from London. Mary Rose, and another girl who was to become her best friend, Sarah Whitelam, were both natives of Lincolnshire, a long, flat, marshy county in eastern England. They were among a handful of disorderly girls sentenced to Transportation to Parts Beyond the Seas by the judges of the Norfolk Circuit in 1787.

In 1788, Lincolnshire had achieved an unusual claim to fame. The doctor attending mad King George III was a Lincolnshire man. Dr. Willis, however, was of low birth. Premier Lincolnshire bigwig of the age was Sir Joseph Banks of Revesby Hall, President of the Royal Society, sponsor to botanical missions all over the globe and, two decades before, gentleman passenger on Captain Cook's voyage of exploration and discovery, which took him to New Holland.[3]

Neither Dr. Willis nor Sir Joseph had ever heard of Sarah Whitelam, 18 years old, recorded only as "spinster of Tealby" at her trial in

---

[3] Until the British established a colony in New South Wales, it was most commonly known as New Holland, as the Dutch were thought to be the first Europeans to have landed there.

April 1787 and now in a country gaol. She had been convicted of stealing "with force and arms" an enormous haul, including "One Raven Grey Conventry Gown, One white Ground Cotton Gown with Red and laylock Stripes, One Norwich Crape Gown, one pink quilted pettycoat, 7 yards of Black Calomanco, 1 pair of Women's Stays, One Black Sattin Cloak, One Red Duffin Cloak, 1 Fine White Lawn Apron, One Chocoloate Ground Silk Handkerchief, One red and black silk handkerchief, One Black Silk handkerchief, One Women's Black Silk hat, three White Linen aprons, two Check'd Linen and Cotton Aprons, one pair of leather Shoes and one Pair of Plaited Shoebuckles," worth a total of fifty-one shillings. Any records illuminating the circumstances in which she stole have not been found. Not much can be inferred from "force and arms": this covered anything from pushing someone out of the way to get to the door to wielding an ax. She cannot have been carrying anything very threatening or this, combined with the fact that she had stolen to a value over thirty-nine shillings, would have brought a death sentence.

In the City of Lincoln, Mary Rose—aged 16 according to some records and 20 according to others—was preparing to spend her second Christmas in gaol. Her situation was rather different from Sarah Whitelam's for, by December 1788, Sir Joseph Banks was taking a personal interest in her case. He had been alerted to it by other local worthies, all, it seems, distressed by the plight of this real-life Louisa Harewood with the pretty face, the romantic name and the story of love betrayed.

In the *Lincoln, Rutland and Stamford Mercury* of 26 December 1788, an extraordinary poem was published.

"On MARY ROSE, a young girl of about 16 or 17 years of age, a prisoner in Lincoln City Gaol . . . for a petty offence," it began, thundered along for a few execrable stanzas and finished:

> 'Twas then my wandering thoughts did bend
> To Lincoln prison-dreary cell
> Where weeks and months, without a friend
> A ROSE, distress'd is forc'd to dwell

Alas, poor girl, thy lot is hard
On straw to rest, from year to year.
The cheerful sun from thee is barr'd
Thy only solace is a tear
Thy prison-seat, a cold, damp stone
Thy dwelling-place, a murky cave
Give me, kind fate, a better home.
That place of rest—a silent grave.

Until her mid or late teens, it seems Mary Rose had lived a blameless life at home with her parents, part of a close family of middling income working the land, destined for marriage to a son off a neighboring farm and a tranquil life similar to the one her mother and grandmother had led. This all changed when she met an officer temporarily stationed in the county.

For some reason, marriage was not possible. She may still have been under 16. It could be that her family disapproved or thought her too young. More probably, it was his family or senior officers who disapproved of a match between a young gentleman and a farmer's daughter. Perhaps the question of marriage was never raised at all if the social differences between them were too great but Mary was persuaded nevertheless that her officer would look after her. They (or at least she) fell in love and one night she eloped from the family farm to lodgings in the city of Lincoln.

Her parents woke to find her gone. Whatever they did on discovering her absence, they had to do it immediately—within hours, their little girl would be an irredeemably fallen woman and the family disgraced. Mary Rose was not a penniless maidservant with tuppence and a spare shift to her name. With a personal income of £20 when she turned 21, she represented some considerable property and a respected local name. The family must already have known of the officer's existence. They had probably invited him to family meals and musical entertainments in their own parlor and seen him at the more genteel inns of Lincoln on market day. It cannot have taken long to guess what Mary had done.

Only immediate capture or immediate marriage would save her from scandal and neither of these happened. Within days, possibly hours, of leaving her parents' house, Mary Rose had shared her officer's bed. Perhaps he truly meant to marry her and her flight was a way of forcing her father's hand; possibly he had always meant to abandon her later. Either way, his own hand was now forced by events as, within weeks, his regiment was posted overseas and he left his teenage mistress in lodgings to await his return. It seems he behaved decently, leaving money with the landlady to cover the expense of Mary's board and lodging until he should return. The officer emerges ambiguous but with his honor more or less intact but the landlady turns out to be a real villain.

However Mary and her lover had passed themselves off to the landlady, Anne Kestleby, she soon summed the situation up. Mrs. Kestleby's behavior toward Mary when her officer had left reveals how much consideration could be expected by a girl who threw away respectability for love. As far as the landlady was concerned, Mary had forfeited her right to the protection of her family, had chosen to become a moral outcast and, with her only male protector on his way to France, would have to take what was coming to her. Mrs. Kestleby had her eyes on the cash the officer had left behind and what easier way of getting rid of the girl than accusing her of stealing from her lodgings? Mary Rose was charged and taken before a magistrate who, faced with Mrs. Kestleby's sworn testimony that a felony had taken place, had no choice but to hold her over for trial by a High Court judge at the next assizes of the Norfolk Circuit. She went into the cells of Lincoln City Gaol to wait.

The frequency with which this plotline is used in everything from chapbooks to the novels of Jane Austen indicates the fascination exerted by sexual downfall. The Bennet family of *Pride and Prejudice* was, crucially to the plot, blessed by Mr. Darcy, who beat

up the caddish Wickham and saved the day. No one collared Mary
Rose's officer and forced him to retrieve his bride from Lincoln City
Gaol.

Justice Heath entered the city of Lincoln late one afternoon in
May 1787, escorted by the sheriff's men in full livery. He was wel-
comed by Sheriff Theophilus Buckworth, accommodated in an inn
and called upon by the good and great of the county. The Lent assizes
opened the following day with the usual pomp. There were only ten
accused felons to be tried in the Lincoln courthouse but the ritual of
calling the names of every member of the commission of the peace,
followed by the names of every mayor, coroner, steward, bailiff and
constable took place in Lincoln with the same heavy dignity as in the
Old Bailey. The members of the grand jury filed in, those lumpen
middle-aged men of property on whose disinterest and intelligence
the entire system ultimately relied. They were charged and sworn in, the
judge intoned some rambling generic homily on the greatness of the
English constitution, the common law, George III, liberty, property
and morality, and then they filed back out into a private chamber to
hear the sessions clerk read the bills of indictment.

This was all rather dull for the audience assembled on rickety
benches in the public galleries. "The weather being fine, drew a
greater number of people to this assize than has been known for many
years," the *Lincoln Mercury* reported. They fidgeted and passed
refreshments. If there was a man of consequence on the grand jury,
some handsome landowner or young squire the middling sort rarely
got a look at, this enlivened the tedious early hours of the assize, but
what they were really waiting for was the thrill of seeing felons in
irons stumble up from the gaol and tell their stories. It may not have
been the fine weather which drew such a crowd to the Lent assizes but
rather the particularly juicy selection due to stand at the bar: two
murderers and one fallen female of good family.

The prosecutors and witnesses to each case were now summoned
before Justice Heath to be sworn and then led into the grand jury's
room, where they gave their evidence away from the public. Finally,

the ten accused felons from the City and Castle gaols were all brought in together. The public galleries sat up straight and commented on their appearance and prospects. Any whose indictments the grand jury had already dismissed were removed. The rest stepped forward one by one, raised their hands to acknowledge their names, were asked how they pled and replied.

"How will you be tried?" the clerk asked William Rawby.

"By God and by my country." It was the only possible answer.

"How will you be tried?" he asked Mary Rose, John Lee and John Thompson.

"By God and by my country."

Now a petty jury of twelve men was assembled and sworn and finally the public galleries stopped chatting as the sad, compelling stories of the prisoners were told. It was the high point of the day, but brief: hearings were conducted at a cracking pace and if the accused were in the slightest slow-witted, she would be pronounced innocent or guilty before she realized her case was being heard. Anne Kestleby, the spiteful landlady, told her story, the jury went into a brief huddle, emerged, was asked its verdict and pronounced Mary Rose guilty. The public buzzed. She was removed from the courtroom. If this assize followed the normal pattern, when the verdict had been pronounced on all ten cases, Justice Heath left the bench and was entertained at dinner by the sheriff. They discussed the affairs of the county and its notables, the health of the king and probably the state of the county's finances with reference to how many felons it could afford to keep in its gaols. After pudding, the judge reentered the courtroom, belched, and passed sentence.

"Can you offer any reason that judgment should not be passed upon you?"

"No," they replied.

Sentences followed. John Lee and John Thompson, housebreakers, and Mary Rose, thief: seven years' Transportation to Parts Beyond the Seas. William Rawby, murderer of his maidservant, execution on the morrow.

By four o'clock, it was all over. Justice Heath left town to judge the felons of Nottingham and Stafford and the farmers in from the villages got back in their carts and drove home. Mary Rose was taken back to the cells of the Lower Gaol, four decaying cells in a basement next door to the Guildhall where she would spend the next twenty months. Her only light came from small grated windows through which people outside could kneel on the pavement and hand in food and liquor. Mary was probably alone for much of her first months in gaol. Female felons here were few. It gave her a little more space; it meant the bucket in the corner contained no one's waste but hers but it also meant loneliness and time to dwell on her future. The fact she had not employed a counsel at her trial, nor did she appear to have anyone "to her character," indicates that at this stage her family was not able or did not want to help her.

Two months before Mary Rose and Sarah Whitelam were incarcerated in Lincolnshire gaols, several other prisons in the country had expelled a part of their long-term population. Felons sentenced to Transportation to Parts Beyond the Seas had been taken south for embarkation on the First Fleet to Botany Bay in New South Wales, the latest savage isle approved for the exile of British convicts. Mary and Sarah had missed the boat by weeks.

During their first months in gaol, the two girls may have been glad of it. A week after Mary Rose's trial, the *Lincoln Mercury* published a cheerful passage:

> The ships bound to Botany Bay have carried off near 1,000 felons.... This mode of transportation is to take place once a year, when all felons convicted within the period will be assembled and sent off together.... The transportation to Botany Bay has the advantage of the former mode of Transportation to America, in securing the kingdom from the dread of being again infected with these pernicious members of society. From the mortality which has already taken place on the transports, it is supposed not more than 1

in 5 will survive the voyage; and should the remainder live to the
expiration of their sentence, they can never pay the expence of a passage home.

It would become clear during the dreary eighteen months which
Mary Rose and Sarah Whitelam spent in gaol that this tidy plan for
annual expulsions was not going to work. In November 1787, the
Mercury still believed all was proceeding smoothly with the next fleet.
"The ships bound for Botany Bay," it reported, "are expected to sail
at the latter end of next month." In February, the ships had still not
sailed but seven male felons from Lincoln Castle Gaol had been conveyed in prison wagons to Portsmouth to embark. In mid-June 1788,
five more men joined them from Oakham, another Lincolnshire
town, but by December 1788, the ships for Botany Bay were still in
the yards of Deptford, the felons taken south in February and June
were living aboard prison ships in Portsmouth and Mary Rose and
Sarah Whitelam had served eighteen months of a seven-year transportation sentence without leaving Lincolnshire.

Sarah's family lived locally and had not abandoned their daughter.
They would have brought her gifts of food, clean linen, small things
to palliate the discomfort of her communal cell. Women in country
gaols like Sarah's were let out on parole during the summer to help
with the harvest on local farms, returning to the cells or the custody
of a trusted farmer each night. No records of any petition for remission of her sentence have been found and it is unlikely any was made.
She had been found guilty of a crime which carried the death penalty
and sentenced only to transportation. She would not receive more
clemency than this.

Mary Rose was suffering badly. Botany Bay had been a dreadful
prospect in spring 1787 but by December 1788 it had apparently
become preferable to life in the city gaol. Something of Mary's des-
peration can be imagined. Her family seemed to have abandoned her;
her officer was clearly not coming back; in eighteen months she had

had no fresh air or exercise beyond what a cell no larger than 13 square feet allowed; she was a girl with a sexual history, a natural target for sexual insult and possibly attack by the turnkeys. However, Mary was a determined lass or a lucky one as, during 1788, she collected sponsors. Possibly her family or someone else from her former, relatively privileged life had decided she was deserving of help and by December, Sir Joseph Banks had taken up her cause.

Sir Joseph Banks had been closely involved in the establishment of the New South Wales colony. As a young and ambitious man, he had spent three years with Captain Cook as botanist on a voyage which took him to the islands of the South Seas, New Zealand and then the strange southern continent which went by a variety of names. The explorers named the eastern part of this continent New South Wales and claimed it for Britain. The voyage, and the hugely popular exhibitions of fauna and flora which followed the explorers' return in 1771, had made Banks' name, and since then he had vigorously promoted himself as an expert on antipodean affairs. It had been partly upon his recommendation that the Secretary of State for Home and Colonial Affairs, Lord Sydney, plumped fifteen years later for New South Wales as a suitable place for felons sentenced to Transportation to Parts Beyond the Seas.

In 1786, the Banks-Sydney project for a penal colony in New South Wales was approved and the same month that Mary Rose and Sarah Whitelam were convicted in Lincolnshire, eleven ships left Portsmouth for New South Wales with the first batch of convict labor aboard. By the time Sir Joseph took up Mary's cause, a second fleet should already have joined the first but still no lists of names had been drawn up and only one transport had been commissioned. The inclusion of some Lincolnshire felons among those on the next ship out, with a little behind-the-scenes pushing from Sir Joseph, might relieve county finances and a Mr. Vanniel was sent by the mayor of Lincoln to visit Mary Rose in gaol. She seemed eager to go to Botany Bay, he reported back, indeed "she is very willing to go any where sooner than remain in that horrid place." A week or so later, her case was discussed at a parish or city council meeting. Mentions of Sir Joseph and Botany Bay were probably made, with hints at the desirability of using local influence to get some of their felons off parish expenses and on to national ones. The other side pointed out that getting the girl to London for embarkation would alone cost the parish £10 12s for the coach and the services of a turnkey to accompany her. Someone mentioned darkly that, according to his information, Mary Rose was "a bad one." All this was reported back to Banks, who overrode objections by offering personally to contribute to the cost of Mary's transport to London. By February, the decision was made and the Lincoln council was waiting for the official order from Lord Sydney to bring her south on the first leg of her voyage from Lincolnshire to New South Wales. Meanwhile, "a trifle of pocket money" was being raised for her.

Meanwhile, 13,000 miles away, those convicts who had left Lincoln in March 1787 had arrived in New South Wales with the rest of the First Fleet in January 1788. Nobody back in England yet knew it, but their camp was not at Botany Bay, for the land there had been found barren and exposed. Instead, the colonists had settled around a small bay a few miles down a river which had been spotted during Cook's 1770 voyage. They named it Sydney Cove. Here, the soil seemed more fertile, the waters of the creek at the head of the cove were plentiful and clean and the sea shelved sharply away from the land, which would allow future ships to come close in to a future wharf.

By December 1788, Sydney Cove was a British garrison town at the edge of an aboriginal continent, a labor camp worked by convicts, guarded by a military presence of 250 men, governed by a handful of civil appointments reporting to Britain's newest colonial governor, Arthur Phillip. From their base camp, some of the settlers had penetrated 15 miles inland and founded a village at the head of the river called Rose Hill. Others had sailed 1,000 miles northeast into the Pacific to found another on Norfolk Island, also noted by Captain

Cook and Sir Joseph eighteen years earlier. A 5,000-mile round trip separated them from their nearest European neighbors, the Dutch, who had trading settlements at Batavia[4] to the north and Cape Town to the west. Unknown thousands of miles of earth stretched north of them. No more isolated European settlement existed on the globe.

The First Fleet to Botany Bay had left England with food supplies calculated for six months at sea and one year after arrival, a promise from Secretary Sydney that relief would arrive within that year and the expectation that before then they would have reached some measure of self-sufficiency. They had brought livestock with them to breed but many animals became sick between Cape Town and Sydney Cove or disappeared into the bush. They had also brought seed from the Cape, but this germinated at sea and was useless on arrival. The soil among their little huts on the slopes of Sydney Cove was infertile and earth on the adjoining headlands and islands could not be made to produce enough greens to keep the camp healthy. The land around them lacked natural fertility and could only have been made fertile with buckets of manure, for which they needed animals and, indeed, buckets, and plows, hoes, axes, cart horses, carts, gardeners and agricultural laborers, people with some knowledge of horticulture and husbandry, people who could yoke a horse and knew what use to make of its dung. Governor Phillip had none of these. He had gangs of male city dwellers who had picked pockets in Covent Garden or stolen the furniture from lodgings in Bristol, now yoked into carts made of green wood with wheels imperfectly round, bumping along dirt tracks around the cove. He had gangs of female city dwellers who had grabbed from shops in Holborn or stolen the mistress' silver in Liverpool, now grubbing along the shoreline for bits of oyster shell to grind into lime to hold their huts together. He had squads of sullen military who squabbled among themselves over questions of precedence and honor and considered the duties of camp guard beneath their dignity.

---

[4] Now Jakarta.

The little colony at Sydney Cove was the latest in a series of camps manned by unsuitably dressed Europeans beating their way into the bush of an unknown continent. European governments had been sending colonial advance parties overseas for more than two centuries, to encourage trade, rid the home country of undesirables and prevent another country from getting there first. Sydney Cove was established for these three classic reasons and, by December 1788, it was suffering the problems of all young, male-dominated colonies far from home.

When the settlement was first promoted in the 1770s, officials had to calculate how to keep the place supplied until it became self-supporting. Discussions were not limited to seed, cattle and bricks. Provision of women was also vital to keep up numbers and safeguard against dangerous urges. "Without a sufficient proportion of that sex, it is well-known that it would be impossible to preserve the settlement from gross irregularities," wrote a prim functionary. Governor Phillip took a ferocious view of potential irregularities. He thought that anyone caught pants down in the act of sodomy should be given to the Maori to eat. "The very small proportion of females," he wrote in one of his first dispatches home, "makes the sending out of an additional number absolutely necessary."

The difficulty of finding sufficient females was debated with some imagination. In 1786, advisers to Lord Sydney had suggested they be obtained from the Friendly Islands[5] and New Caledonia, "from whence any number may be procured without difficulty." Both Sydney and Phillip had originally agreed this would be the happiest arrangement to keep the colony pure in deed and the plan was incorporated into Phillip's official instructions (although with the proviso that no "compulsive measures and fallacious pretences" be used to obtain them). However, when Phillip sent his first letters home from Sydney Cove in 1788, he had changed his mind: "to send for women from the Islands, in our present situation, would answer no purpose

---

[5] Now Tonga.

than that of bringing them to pine away in misery." Sydney Cove was
not the tropical paradise suitable for girls in grass skirts which had
been optimistically assumed in London.

Of the 1,079 people on the First Fleet to New South Wales, 259
were officials or marines, 35 of them accompanied by their wives, and
193 were women convicts, a number insufficient to prevent irregularities among the governing classes, let alone to iron them out among
the convicts. If the settlement were to grow, male emigrants and
emancipated convicts had to take a long-term interest in its future
and, if this were to happen, females had to be available. It was not a
new problem, nor a difficult one to solve. The transportation of
women felons was the traditional answer. Steady supplies had been
crossing the Atlantic and Indian Oceans to the Americas and the East
Indies for decades, through established routes and dealers. Some
60,000 men and women from the British Isles had already left the
mother country as felons to these plantations and trading stations
before New South Wales was established. It would be easy to transfer
the old system to the new colony. Once there, women would provide
the essential stabilizing influence of femininity. The new colonial
government in Sydney Cove was quite clear on their role. It would
not be long before some of the male convicts there would be emancipated. To keep them in the colony, and productive, they would
require land, assistance in tilling it, assigned labor from other convicts
and wives. It had been decided, therefore, that a married man would
be entitled to 50 acres of ground, with 10 extra for each child born,
whereas a single man would be eligible only for 30. As a plan to
ensure steady growth, it was sensible—but it required a stock of pli-
ant potential wives.

It was not planned that all incoming females become certified
wives. There was a place for the unmarried mate in the colony. Lord
Sydney had estimated that 200 women from the islands would "suf-
fice as companions for the men" and by "the men" he meant other
ranks, not convicts. An alternative source had now to be found. What
seems an astonishing piece of Georgian hypocrisy was all utterly nor-

mal to men like Sydney and Phillip, versed in the ways and needs of young colonies and familiar with the warped colonial version of the household. The role of colonial comfort women was so well established that many observers would refer to them, especially to those appointed to service men of rank, as "wives"—which, a visitor to Sydney Cove would write in five years' time, "every officer, settler and soldier is entitled to and few are without." Sydney Cove had immediately followed the social model of colonial garrison towns elsewhere in the world, of encouraging unions which neither partner expected to be permanent. Already there was scarcely a marine in the colony who did not have his "wife," nor officer, clerk, surgeon, surgeon's assistant or man in any other position which carried privilege. The only exception seems to have been the governor himself and this may be due to gaps in the records rather than chastity in the big house.

Governor Phillip believed that encouraging convicts to marry among themselves would be conducive to decency and good order in the lowest section of society. However, he was aware that marriage would not mop up all the sexual energy of a male-dominated colony and, before setting off from London, he suggested to Lord Sydney that he create a whores' ghetto staffed by "the most abandoned" where they would be "permitted to receive the visits of the convicts in the limits allotted to them and under certain restrictions." This would allow the rest of the women, strictly virtuous, to be kept under wraps pending marriage or concubinage with the military.

Letters from Governor Phillip outlining the colony's breeding prospects and other matters for Sydney's attention were, in December 1788, aboard two separate convoys returning from New South Wales to England. In them, he described baldly the state of the colony and less baldly his fears that it would have to be closed down unless it were better supported in this earliest and most vulnerable stage of its development. Phillip was a believer in New South Wales: he believed the soil would yield, the timber would fall, the savages would become friends, the seas would give up fish and turtle and that British men-of-war and traders would within a very few years be nestling side by

The camp at Sydney Cove (now Circular Quay) a few months after the arrival of the First Fleet in 1788. (Mary Evans Picture Library)

side in Sydney Cove. But he knew these ambitions would not be realized using the material supplied by the British government when it filled the holds and decks of the First Fleet in May 1787. His dispatches state over and over again his basic needs: more food, more skilled men and more females, in that order.

3

GAOL FEVER

$\mathcal{B}$y December 1788, 151 female convicts in Newgate Gaol were living in three cells built to house a maximum of 70. They lived on rations fixed for that theoretical maximum and not the number actually confined. Each cell had one window opening onto an interior wall. There were no beds; a ramp at one end of the room with a wooden beam fixed to its top end served as mattress and pillow. To sleep on the ramp and beam was a privilege, to be paid for weekly. To rent a blanket woven of raw hemp cost extra. Those who could afford neither curled up together on stone slabs awash with saliva and urine. Before the cells were opened each morning, turnkeys would drink a glass of spirits to keep them from fainting, for the "putrid stream or myasma" was enough to knock them off their feet.

The population of Newgate was malnourished, debilitated, cold, inadequately clothed and infested with disease-bearing lice. Its cells were a happy home for typhus. For some time, Mr. Simpson, surgeon to the gaol, had been personally augmenting gaol funds to pay for medicines and employ extra apothecaries. There was nothing new about this in the 1780s: the gaols went into crisis each winter and generally staggered through until spring, providing nothing terrible

Newgate Gaol to the left, fronting onto the Old Bailey alleyway, with the Sessions House adjoining on the right. (Guildhall Library, Corporation of London)

happened. But the winter of 1788 was exceptionally severe; the gaols were hopelessly crowded and there were not enough funds in the pot to pay for food, let alone medicine.

One morning in November 1788, Surgeon Simpson was summoned. A prisoner was displaying unmistakable signs of "the fever." Given conditions in the gaol, he knew he could have an epidemic on his hands.

During November and early December, while gaol staff struggled to contain the fever among the prisoners already in the cells, a total of 141 new "prisoners for law" were being brought in by harassed peace officers from compters all over London. Ann Clapton and Charlotte Marsh came in on the Wood Street Compter wagon on 5 December. Mary Arnold, caught picking pockets among the livery stables of Long Acre, and Mary Oakley, caught doing the same thing on Holborn, came in from Poultry. Esther Curtis, who had got drunk in the privies, arrived from Tothill. Fraudsters Ann Gallant and Francis Bunting were brought in with dozens of other petty criminals from all over London, "cast for law" at the December sessions at the Old Bailey.

They joined 306 convicted felons already there: 18 awaiting execution, 1 sentenced to Transportation to the Americas, 4 to Transportation to Africa, 4 to Transportation to New South Wales, and 270 to Transportation to Parts Beyond the Seas. The new prisoners, along with the long-term debtors who made up more than half of the gaol's long-term population, brought the total number in the cells up to over 800, exceeding the number for which it had been built ten years previously by over 300 percent. The situation was unmanageable and still the disorderly girls, the debtors, the petty thieves and muggers arrived each day, requiring space, bedding, food and air.

It was in these alarming conditions that the last sessions of 1788 opened at the Old Bailey. The courts backed directly on to Newgate Gaol. These two institutions ran the entire length of the Old Bailey, the north-south alleyway which connects Holborn and Ludgate Hill at the ancient boundary of the City of London. The gaol was connected to the court by Dead Man's Walk, an underground passageway down which prisoners were led to the bar. Yards from the courtrooms, at the other end of this passageway, the fever was rampant. Over four days, in the worst of the winter weather, judges, jurors, witnesses and court officials sat or stood in courtrooms whose doors and windows were kept wide open to the snow and pelting rain for fear of infection from the prisoners brought up from the cells. The courtrooms had been washed with wine and vinegar, and herbs were burned throughout the day on open braziers. Small amounts of sulphur and tobacco were exploded into the rooms. Juries, counsel and judges chewed on garlic, citrus peel, cardamom and caraway to prevent infection from the prisoners' breath.

The first day of the December sessions was raw. Prisoners for law huddled and coughed on the stairs leading up from Dead Man's Walk where a Bible, prayerbook and candlestick were chained to the walls. At nine in the morning, the lord mayor, in robe, hat and chain, was driven from the Mansion House to the Old Bailey, attended by the recorder of the City of London, the sergeant at arms, the sword bearer, and the city marshal. At the Old Bailey, they were ceremoniously received by Mr. Bloxham, sheriff of the City of London, and escorted inside. The lord mayor entered Courtroom One, the largest of the three courtrooms, and arranged himself beneath the sword of justice. The other two judges were taken by the aldermen and sheriffs to Courtrooms Two and Three. Juries were sworn and penned into wooden enclosures.

When the courts finally opened for business, justice was brisk. Matilda Johnson, Mary Oakley and Mary Arnold, for privy theft—transportation; Esther Curtis, for theft of clothes—transportation; Charlotte Thomas Marsh and Ann William Clapton, for theft of calico on Snow Hill—transportation; Ann Gallant, for theft in a dwelling house in Soho—transportation. Back into the cells they went, for the clerks to transcribe their names onto a different list.

The penal code of the late eighteenth century was an inadequate and crude instrument by which to regulate the country's affairs, even in the view of contemporaries. It had been built up haphazardly, with sudden splurges of lawmaking whenever there was a crime wave. Theoretically, capital crimes, as formally summarized in the written report on each Old Bailey session, were as follows:

> Arson, Burglary, Beast Stealing, Coining, Forgery, Highway Robbery, House-Breaking, Horse-Stealing, Murder, Manslaughter, Privately stealing, Rape, Robbery in a Dwelling-House, Robbing the Mails, Robbing the Post Office, Rioters, Stealing in a Dwelling-House, Shop-Lifting, Sheep-Stealing, Stealing on board a Ship or Barge, Treason, Unlawfully shooting.

However, it was not as simple as this. Most thefts came under the heading of single felony but became double felonies in certain circumstances regarding value and location of the offense. These had been decided on by previous generations and bore diminishing relation to conditions and values current in the 1780s. In most cases, "stealing to above the value of 39 shillings" was a capital offense. This was true, for example, of "stealing privily" in a private house, which covered theft by servants, theft by lodgers and some theft in shops. In some cases, the value could be lower than thirty-nine shillings but the theft would nevertheless be a capital offense because of other aggravating circumstances. Housebreaking (breaking and entering) was a double felony, whatever the value of goods taken. When "stealing privily" meant picking pockets, as was the case for nearly all prostitutes, theft of anything to a value of more than one shilling became a capital crime.

This legislation was unworkable. Juries, judges and prosecutors were no longer prepared to send people to the gallows for a theft of a few pence. With the connivance of the whole courtroom, women indicted of a double felony were routinely found guilty of a single felony and sentenced to transportation instead of death. Even when a death sentence could not be avoided, female offenders were rarely hanged. A petition for pardon would be drawn up by the sentencing judge and the sentence commuted to Transportation to "Parts Beyond the Seas," that vague name given to the rest of the world by the Elizabethan Transportation Act when the world was less known and unnamed continents lurked at the edges of charts. If the judges had been sticklers in sentencing according to the evidence, many of the women who ended up in Sydney Cove would have been hanged in England.

It would be a shock to those Australian observers who comment with smug horror on the barbarism with which the British treated their convicts to discover how their European neighbors regarded the British judicial system. Prussian Baron Johann von Archenholz wrote with perplexity in his "Picture of the Life and Manners of England" that in England "an infraction of [the laws] . . . is punished without respect to the rank or fortune of the culprit" and even "if the chief magistrate should depart from the line of conduct prescribed to him by the laws, he is obliged to submit to justice like one of the meanest citizens." To a European aristocrat, this was an outrageously democratic way to run a country. "Nothing is more astonishing than the mildness and humanity with which criminals are treated, whether they be thieves, murderers or incendiaries," he went on. "Even if their guilt is evident, the bar, the jury and the judges all seem to conspire for the acquittal; the counsel defend the culprit with zeal and the witnesses against him are questioned with much strictness and sometimes with much severity. His own confession is never demanded . . . a strange contrast to the practice of those tribunals of which torture is the grand resource."

Although merciful compared to the death sentences which could have been handed down had the law been strictly enforced, the frequency with which the judges resorted to the one-size-fits-all sentence of Transportation to Parts Beyond the Seas for women felons illustrates the severe limitations on sentencing. Even had they wanted to hand down something more lenient, they could not: there was nothing else to hand down. For this reason there appear cruel anomalies. Elizabeth Sully ran a pack of teenage prostitutes in Cable Street and routinely robbed the men they picked up. She got seven years. Esther Curtis got drunk in the privies—and got the same sentence. Justice was a blunt stick.

The English social reformer Jonas Hanway described the situation which had provoked admiration in von Archenholz from a different angle and put his finger on the problem this "leniety" created. "The punishments now in use are not equal to the evil," he wrote, noting that brutal corporal punishments were no longer used in England as "the gentler spirit of modern times has softened these rigors . . . whipping is in few cases deemed politic . . . and we do not think it a right measure to put all such persons to death . . . as have forfeited their lives to the laws. What then shall we do?" It was a question asked by all those connected with the gaols of Britain.

There were two blocks in Newgate Gaol, the Common Side, where most of the 151 women felons were held, and the Master's Side, which offered more comfortable accommodation for those who could afford the half crown a week rent. A single week's rent on the Master's Side was beyond most women, let alone the many half crowns which would be necessary during the months, sometimes years, which elapsed between conviction and discharge. The few who could afford the Master's rates were, apart from one, high-class shoplifters who had clearly stashed away a good few pounds before being caught. For those prepared to play for high stakes but with no training in specialist trades such as forgery—a very high earner—shoplifting was the crime of choice. Alice Haynes had been convicted of stealing lace in a Fleet Street haberdashery; clearly, previous crimes had been more successful as she was now paying her way on the Master's Side. Thirty-year-old Mary Higgins, eight months pregnant when she moved in in January 1789, stole blue lute string from Cranbourn Passage worth £7—roughly the equivalent of a maidservant's annual wage.

The cleverest of the women on the Master's Side was forger and businesswoman Nelly Kerwin. She was tried as Eleanor Kirwin alias Karavan, widow, who had for several years run "a house of entertainment for sailors, not in the public but in the private line" in Gosport, near Portsmouth. She was a familiar figure on board ships in Gosport Harbour. Her principal line of business was "bomb boating," extending credit to cash-hungry sailors against prize money or wages due. She also acted as informal employment agent for captains who were ready to sail but lacked a full complement of crew. Her story in court was that she had procured fourteen or fifteen seamen for a Captain Urmiston in 1781. Among them was Samuel Druce, for whom Nelly had already paid several pounds' worth of lodging and entertainment, in cash. He may have been a boyfriend who became a sponger. She arranged a job for him with Urmiston and, before he went, wanted a will made out to her which she would hold in security against his wages to repay the money she had spent on him. However, when Druce went aboard he signed up on the muster under an alias, under which he also drew up his will, witnessed in all innocence by the captain. This left wages and any prize money to his mother. The Admiralty would issue money according to whichever will conformed to the ship's muster and Nelly had been cheated. The implication of the case for the prosecution was that she decided to forge the will she had been promised, and, if Druce died overseas, would then disprove the legitimacy of the will he had drawn up under a false name.

It took the jury about an hour to decide Nelly's guilt on the counts of which she was indicted: first, of forging or causing to be forged the will; and second, of "uttering the will, with intention to defraud our Lord the King." She was found guilty of the second and sentenced to death.

If Nelly was the cleverest, the most flamboyant of the Master's ladies were Elizabeth Barnsley and her partner, Ann Wheeler. Among the shoplifters, these two were queens: Barnsley had the pedigree and Wheeler had the class. Even the officers of the court referred to them, apparently without irony, as "ladies," and Elizabeth Barnsley would, in future months, leave no one in doubt as to her rights and privileges.

Ann and Elizabeth stole from the best addresses: the 18 yards of muslin Wheeler tried to hide beneath her "white silk cloak, trimmed with furr" and behind her "large muff" came from Hodgkinson, Warrener and Percival of Bond Street. Like Mary Higgins, they were uninterested in thefts worth shillings and pence. That muslin was worth £6 and Wheeler proffered a £10 note in payment for her piece of Irish linen. The first part was beautifully performed but one or other of them fumbled the vital act of whipping the cloth off the counter, shoving it up her dress and sailing out with a confusing rustle of skirts. As the ladies turned to leave, they were challenged by a brave shopman. His courage did not fail even before their outrage at his impertinence. Wheeler inquired frostily if he did not recognize her as a lady who patronized the establishment regularly for both her own and her servants' needs and was, clinchingly, an intimate of Lady Spencer. Elizabeth Barnsley backed her up, but the shopman refused to back down and the ladies were bundled off to Newgate, protesting their connections. Both had been receiving visitors in their Master's Side apartments since they were sentenced to seven years' transportation in February.

The presence of 15-year-old Sarah Roberts is more of a mystery. Her theft of calico on Holborn Hill had neither yielded great value nor been carried out with great flair; moreover she, too, was in the early months of pregnancy. Some anonymous benefactor was paying to keep her in the relative comfort of the Master's Side, which was run more like an upmarket lodging house (with certain unusual restrictions) than a block of gaol cells. The same degree of comfort could be obtained in apartments on the Master's Side of Newgate Gaol as in Mayfair, with the difference being only that the locks were on the outside of the doors. Living conditions were substantially different for Elizabeth Barnsley et al. than for Matilda Johnson and her cellmates on the Common Side.

There was easy communication between the Master's Side and the Common Side of Newgate Gaol. In fact, in the second half of 1788, there was too much communication for the authorities' liking, for mutiny was rumbling. In August, discipline in the women's cells had all but broken down under the seditious influence of a man living in the Master's Side near Mrs. Barnsley, Mrs. Higgins and Mrs. Haynes. Lord George Gordon was the embodiment of fin de siècle radical chic, godson to the king himself but also darling of the London mob. He lived in style, attended by his own footman in rooms furnished with sofas, carpets and a soft bed, reading books brought from his own library and drinking wine brought from his own cellar.

Lord George had been imprisoned in 1787, convicted of stirring up mutiny among the convicts about to sail on the fleet to Botany Bay. He (or, rather, his footman) had distributed a pamphlet among the prisoners of Newgate which, it was said at his trial, "excites the subject [felons condemned to transportation or death] to rise in defence of those whose lives and liberties are forfeited." In Newgate Gaol, he immediately set himself to become Prisoners' Friend or, in the eyes of the authorities, to make trouble among the convicts sentenced to sail on the next fleet. He was daily to be seen in the cells on the Common Side, discussing cases, advising on petitions and distributing food and money. Gordon's ability to spin publicity for himself and his protegées was fearsome. So was his following among convicts, sailors, pro-Americans and other dangerous elements for whom his support was not restricted to encouraging words. Favored prisoners were given a "pension," which they came to collect from his apartments on the Master's Side each week. It may well have been Lord George who paid for Sarah Roberts' accommodation. Fifteen years old, pregnant and under sentence of transportation, she was a natural object of compassion. His appeal was a dangerous mixture of fanaticism, charisma and money, and the governor and sheriff considered him a serious threat to stability within the gaol.

His Majesty had recently been called on by his cabinet to speak against the increase of crime on the streets, of heavy drinking, gambling, prostitution, failure to observe the Sabbath and general moral decline. The proclamation had been published throughout Britain. Already one of the most famous speeches of the year, it became even more so when the women of Newgate, under Gordon's influence, attempted to turn it to their own advantage. That summer, petty thief Arabella Stewart astonished the Old Bailey with the uppity claim that God's Holy Law, as referred to by the king himself, required that "for all manner of trespass . . . whom the judges shall condemn . . . shall pay double unto his neighbour." Therefore, she said, she should pay back double what she had stolen but to banish her to Botany Bay would be to go against the word of the Lord. She was hanged.

Arabella was only the first of Lord George's convict friends to use this line. It bubbled beneath letters and petitions leaving the gaol through the summer. In August 1788, the *Times* reported a mass petition to His Majesty, claiming again that transportation was contrary to Holy Law as defined by His Majesty's own proclamation. It was signed by eighty-two women; all eighty-two were among the women who would be sent to New South Wales on the first ship out.

4

GALLEONS REACH

*I*n Britain, far-fetched plans had been promoted for several years to deal with the pile-up of felons in the gaols. They could be presented to the Empress Catherine of Russia, currently failing to persuade her own subjects to inhabit colonies in the "dreary, inhospitable regions" of the Caucasus, from which "escape is impossible." They could be eliminated by sending them to "Algiers, Tripoly and Tunis and exchanging them for unfortunate Christian slaves, in the hands of those Barbarians." They could be employed as galley slaves, as in France; as slave labor, as in the German states; or as miners, as in Sweden and Denmark.

These European methods of dealing with an overabundant lowlife did not appeal to the British government, which, after years of successful American and East Indian experience, continued to favor a penal colony over all other solutions. Even after America declared its independence, the British government clung to the idea that somewhere in the New World, someone would accept British felons. New World dumps were attempted further north but by now even American loyalists no longer wanted convict labor from the Old Country. In November 1785, it was reported that Halifax, Nova Scotia, had started to turn back British transport ships.

Five years after the American Wars, a Transportation to America list still existed in Newgate, the one convict under this sentence duly reentered each week. A list also existed for Transportation to Africa, which kept coming back as a penal option, and kept failing. In 1782, an advance party of 200 had been reduced to 50 in under a month on the West African coast. In 1783, another bunch landed "naked and diseased on the sandy shore" and had to be rescued later in the year. In 1785, the Portsmouth prison hulk *Ceres* was set aside specifically to hold convicts awaiting transportation to a privately run settlement on the River Gambia. The recorder of London had confidently told the city aldermen in February of that year that a ship "formerly employed in the Guinea trade"[6] was being fitted out at Deptford "to carry over some felons to the coast of Africa." The courts latched on to this option as in 1787 they would latch on to Botany Bay and in 1789 to Sydney Cove. The ship never sailed. A last, feeble attempt to set up a penal colony in Africa occurred in 1786, when the Bay of Das Voltas received and soon repelled a group of British surveyors— but not before the government at home had once again jumped the gun and promised a thousand convicts would be shipped off to the new African prison camp.

Judges had continued to sentence Transportation to Africa, *faute de mieux*, apparently reserving this option for felons of a peculiarly depraved nature. Frightful descriptions were made of the horrors they would meet. "The country on either side the [Gambia] river," wrote the *Times*, "is peopled by warlike tribes, who sacrifice to their idol deities, such white men as fall into their hands and whose bodies they devour . . ." In 1786, transportation of felons to the new colony for the Black Poor in Sierra Leone was suggested, with a bizarre twist. Those sent over "would be slaves for life," ran this extraordinary plan, "to attend upon black masters . . . which, it is thought, will be a greater punishment than death." This plan also failed.

Africa could not accept convicts, America would not and, worse

---

[6] That is, the slave trade.

still, nothing had been heard of Commodore Phillip's fleet to Botany Bay for over a year. As far as anyone knew in Britain, his ships had last been seen by Europeans leaving Cape Town in November 1787. As the *Times* said in August 1788—and then hastily denied—"it is probable we may never hear more from our Botany Bay convicts." The islands of the southern seas were littered with the bones of unfortunate mariners and, as the months passed, gloomy suspicions grew that those of Phillip's fleet were among them.

One last, halfhearted attempt at Transportation to Parts Beyond the Seas was made in the summer of 1788. This time, the destination was Quebec, where transported felons would undertake "menial and Laborious offices." If the convicts could be swiftly embarked, there was still time to get the ships across the Atlantic and up the St. Lawrence River before it froze over for the winter. Prison wagons rumbled off to Gosport but, by the time the Quebec fleet was ready, the last date at which the weather would allow a safe passage had passed. Some small relief was gained temporarily by the London gaols, at the expense of the prison hulks in Portsmouth Harbour, where the convicts spent most of the next year in conditions of utter squalor.

There were men in the Home Department and the Admiralty who knew that Commodore Phillip's fleet had been ill conceived, planned and equipped. They did not know whether he had even arrived in Botany Bay, let alone managed to survive once there, but, by late 1788, New South Wales seemed their only remaining transportation option.

And so ". . . regarding the affecting state of the Gaol of Newgate," wrote Lord Sydney on 20 December 1788, "I find . . . the Ship in which they are to be embarked is now nearly, if not altogether ready for their reception . . . I am led to suspect that 150 of the Convicts will be taken away, which will give great relief to the Goal [*sic*] . . . as to prevent the spreading of the dreadful Disorder which . . . has made its appearance." In this way, before anyone knew whether the men and women who had sailed with Phillip to establish the first European settlement in New South Wales were still alive, the officials of courts and gaols up and down the country were informed that a second fleet would be sent out to join them.

The ship hastily commissioned by the Admiralty to convey felons to New South Wales was the *Lady Julian*, "a fine, river-built vessel, the first ship that was taken by the Americans on her passage from Jamaica to London and was afterwards retaken by a man-of-war and conveyed to England." She was "barque-built," three masted and two decked. Her specification does not survive as she was built before the underwriters of Lloyds began their Green Book, recording tonnage and dimensions of new ships. However, the specification does survive of the *Scarborough*, the two-decked three-master which had been fitted at the same dock two years previously as part of Commodore Phillip's fleet. The *Scarborough* was of the same dimensions as the *Lady Julian* to within 10 registered tons—411 to the *Lady Julian*'s 401.

She was 100 feet long and 30 feet wide at her widest point, with a height between her decks of about 4 foot 5 inches. She carried square sails on the main and foremasts and was fore and aft rigged on the mizzen. Stay sails hung between each mast. At the bow, one, two or three foresails could be attached and a bowsprit projected some 25 feet. The sternmost part of her deck, the quarterdeck, was raised above the rest. It was enclosed by a rail and was the preserve of officers only, whose accommodation was built into the area below. The foremost part of the ship, between the mainmast and the bow, was known as the forecastle. The accommodation of the ordinary seamen—the "ship's company"—was built into a raised area on this which mirrored the officers' quarters at the stern. The bottom deck of the ship was the orlop, usually reserved for well-insulated cargo. This was where Deptford carpenters were currently at work to turn the *Lady Julian* into a prison ship. Partitions were erected to create three self-contained areas on the orlop deck. Forward and aft were stores and the middle section, anywhere between 1,500 and 2,000 square feet, was allotted to the 250 expected felons. The hatches which led into this space were fitted with gratings which could be bolted down from above. Wide shelves, sleeping four to six each, were attached to either side of the hull.

By December 1788, the *Lady Julian* was at Galleons Reach in the River Thames. She was now intended to carry over 150 female convicts and 100 male marines to New South Wales on an Admiralty contract, then sail north to Canton and bring home a cargo of tea for the East India Company. Captain Aitken, of whom little is known, had been appointed to command the ship. He was a less colorful character, and had less direct impact on the women who would come aboard, than Lieutenant Thomas Edgar, who had been appointed to the double role of master and government agent. Edgar was better known as "Little Bassey"—"Little" for his stature, "Bassey" for the speech impediment which had his favorite curse—"Blast 'ee"—emerge thus. He took up his post at Galleons Reach early in 1789.

A seaman who accompanied Thomas Edgar on his first commission after the *Lady Julian,* in 1794, described him with some affection as a "strange and unaccountable being . . . a good sailor and navigator, or rather had been, for he drank very hard, so as to entirely ruin his constitution." By 1794, he had been sadly brought down by liquor and spent the voyage getting steadily drunker, forgetting to carry out orders. "Edgar, you are drunk," the long-suffering captain would say. "No sir, bass me if I am," Edgar would reply.

In 1776, Edgar had been a bright young officer appointed to the commission of a lifetime as master of the *Discovery*, one of two ships which sailed on a four-year voyage to the Antipodes and back by way of Cape Horn and the South Seas, under command of the greatest seaman of the age, Captain James Cook. The other of the ships on this third and last of Cook's great voyages of exploration and discovery was commanded by William Bligh.

Thomas Edgar's part in the fracas in which Captain Cook died is unclear. He emerges not dishonorable but impetuous. It was partly his actions, the day before Cook was clubbed over the head on Hawaii in February 1779, that created the ill feeling between seamen and islanders which would break into violence. Tools from the *Dis-*

covery were snatched by an islander visiting on board and Edgar set off after the thief's canoe. He failed miserably to catch the giggling Hawaiians, who slipped into the palm banks and led him in circles. When the tools were handed back by a third party at the end of the day, an exasperated Edgar tried again to seize the thief's canoe and a scuffle broke out. In revenge, the islanders stole the *Discovery*'s cutter early the next morning and when Cook went ashore to demand it back, there was a far more serious fight in which the captain was killed.

Edgar had been lieutenant then, in 1779, and he was still lieutenant a decade later. Others among Cook's officers had been promoted through a series of commissions. William Bligh had been chosen to command the latest Cook-like voyage of trade and exploration, sponsored by Sir Joseph Banks. He was aboard HMS *Bounty*, on his way to investigate the possibility of collecting breadfruit in Tahiti to feed slaves on the Caribbean plantations. Nevertheless, Edgar's experience in navigating long Pacific voyages made him an obvious candidate for the post of master of the *Lady Julian* and, given their shared connection to Cook, he may have been recommended by Sir Joseph Banks.

Edgar's appointment as government agent was administrative rather than technical. The appointment of a decent man as agent was of prime importance to the convicts. Their well-being during the voyage to New South Wales depended on the honesty and humanity of this officer more than any other on board. It was he who would ensure—or not—that the shipping agent supplied in full all convicts' rations specified in his contract with the government. It was he who would ensure—or not—that the captain and crew allowed the convicts sufficient fresh air and exercise on deck while at sea. It was he who would ensure—or not—that the surgeon would perform his medical and surgical duties and the sailors and officers would not mistreat the convicts.

It is tempting to think that Lieutenant Edgar sought refuge in the bottle from guilt over his part in Cook's death and frustration from the brake this put on a promising career. In truth, however, he seems to have been a carefree chap: a fat, jolly, wheezy little man who drank for the pleasure of it rather than to escape his ghosts. Still a competent seaman in 1789, he was able to make decisions when necessary and his honesty and care for the convicts in his charge were exemplary. He was one of the few agents whose knee-jerk reaction to his powers was not to defraud the Naval Board and skim a private profit from the rations meant for the convicts but to ensure that those rations were of good quality. His steward on the *Lady Julian* described Edgar as a "decent, kindly man" and he performed his duties well.

Another *Lady Julian* appointment made at the beginning of 1789 was that of the surgeon, Richard Alley. The character of the surgeon would have almost as much effect on the health of the convicts as that of the agent. On those ships where an agent was cruel or negligent, it fell to the surgeon to defend the convicts' right to decent food and enough exercise. On ships where neither agent nor surgeon gave consideration to the sufferings of the orlop, the consequences were dreadful. Naval surgeons were popularly portrayed as incompetents and drunks. A First Fleet marine recalled one surgeon who "left the Ship for Drunk-ed" before they had left England. The drunkenness of the surgeon who had left the year before with William Bligh would be cited in the captain's explanation of the mutiny aboard his ship. Alley does not seem to have suffered from drunkenness and his treatment of the convicts was such that the government would promote him to agent on a later transport ship and send him out to New South Wales again. Whether these men were appointed because they were known to be of good character is unknown but the women of the *Lady Julian* were fortunate in having decent men occupying both positions which most influenced their living conditions on board ship.

It was part of the plan for colonial development that all convicts should, before being sent on board ship, undergo a cursory medical examination to test their survival prospects for the voyage and their ability to contribute to life in the colony. These examinations, depending on which doctor made them and how much pressure there was to get convicts out of the gaols, could easily allow the sick and the frail to slip through the net. There would be three women aged over 60 on board the *Lady Julian* who could not reasonably be expected to aid the colony either by producing babies or by hard labor. Almost half the women would come on board straight from a gaol crawling with typhus and many of them must already have had the pox. It was impossible to eliminate all women infected with some form of sexually transmitted disease. According to the most respected writer on syphilis and gonorrhea, Dr. William Buchan, "there is one class of society among whom this disease may be said to have its stronghold: I mean that description of females commonly called women of the town . . . very few of this class of patients ever get thoroughly well." It would not have made much difference to the colony anyway. Although no one in England knew it, Sydney Cove was already riddled with the clap.

Several members of the crew came on board the ship at Galleons Reach and at least one of the ship's tradesmen. This was 34-year-old John Nicol, who would act as both steward and cooper.[7] The only known firsthand account of the voyage of the *Lady Julian* is in John Nicol's memoirs, dictated over thirty years later to an Edinburgh journalist. Nicol had already spent twenty years at sea and traveled most of the known world since leaving his home in the Scottish Lowlands.

John Nicol had been on board in the river for three or four months when a ship homeward bound from Canton sailed slowly up the Thames in the first week of March 1789. She was the *Prince of Wales*, the first ship home from New South Wales. The destination of convicts in gaols all over the country was finally confirmed. Sydney Cove, Port Jackson, was in the news, accounts of the colony appeared in the press, papers authorizing the movements of prisoners piled up and the inky fingers of prison clerks struggled to keep records up to date. Within days, dazed women who had been sentenced to Trans-

---

[7] The steward was the officers' servant; the cooper was in charge of making and mending barrels in which provisions were stored and, usually, for other odd jobs involving carpentry and blacksmithing.

portation to Parts Beyond the Seas were being shunted across the country to London, the River Thames and the *Lady Julian*.

A coach arrived from Lincoln one day in the charge of a Castle Gaol turnkey. He was familiar with the procedure: he had brought down eleven felons and a baby three years before for embarkation on the previous fleet. This time, fourteen exhausted women were roped to the outside seats. The irons riveted around their wrists in Lincoln Gaol remained in place throughout the journey south. Here they had sat for thirty-six hours, exposed to an English March and the curiosity of every groom and potboy aroused by fallen womanhood in chains. Among them were Sarah Whitelam and Mary Rose. When finally they were rowed across the Thames and aboard the *Lady Julian*, the women were dirty, wet and weak from cold and hunger. It was John Nicol who pulled them and their few belongings over the side.

Despite these sordid circumstances, the attraction was immediate—at least on his side. Even in the lamentable condition in which the authorities had delivered Sarah Whitelam on board, she was still sufficiently personable to make an impact. The first thing Nicol did was free the hateful manacles from around the women's wrists, paying the Lincoln turnkey his half crown a head fee. The exhausted women lined up obediently in front of his anvil and held out their hands, Sarah among them. "I first fixed my fancy on her the moment I knocked the rivet from her irons upon my anvil," wrote Nicol. It was an unusual way to start a courtship.

As Sarah recovered from the coach journey in the relative warmth and safety of the ship, she recounted her story bit by bit to the besotted steward. It seemed to go something like this: she had been living in the village of Kesteven before her trial, sharing her lodgings with other young women. As was normal among girlfriends, they would freely have used each other's clothes and possessions, none having enough money to dress herself with the variety she would have liked and filling the gaps in her toilette with items borrowed from the others' boxes. All had gone well for some time. She had made a decent living and lived a decent life. Then she had borrowed a mantle from

one of the circle of friends and returned it the next day—nothing
unusual there. But for some reason, she was accused a couple of days
later of having taken it without permission. At first, she thought that
she must have given offense unknowingly; perhaps she had stained or
torn the mantle without realizing and upset her friend by not offering
to repair or replace it. But the friend would not listen to reason and
Sarah found herself being accused of an offense which from day to
day grew from abuse of friendship into felony, for now the other girl
was accusing her of deliberately stealing the mantle. She was thus
caught in the dreadful situation of being prosecuted by this "false
friend," as she defined her to John Nicol, pronounced guilty of a
crime she had not committed and sentenced to seven years in Parts
Beyond the Seas.

At 17, her life lay around her in ruins. Her family apparently
could not help her. From being a lively lass with good prospects, she
had become a convicted felon sleeping in rancid straw in a country
gaol, destined for exile. This was the story John apparently got out of
her during her first weeks on the river, recovering from the rigors of
Kesteven Gaol, and the one he remembered thirty years later.
Appalled by the tragedy which had befallen her, entranced by her
prettiness, determined to alleviate her distress, the ship's steward fell
hopelessly in love with this "girl of a modest, reserved turn, as kind
and true a creature as ever lived." Still a teenager and sentenced for a
crime she had not committed to the thieves' colony in the company
of rogues, she seemed worthy of Nicol's deepest compassion. And he
was the first man Sarah had known in two years who had not disbe-
lieved her, despised her or known the truth about her offense. So she
reciprocated—more slowly, but nevertheless with increasing trust and
affection. "I courted her for upward of a week," wrote Nicol. He
clearly considered this an unusually long courtship, but, long before
the ship left Galleons Reach, Sarah had left the convict quarters on
the orlop and was sleeping in the comfort and privacy of Nicol's bunk
on the 'tween deck. By the end of April, she was pregnant.

5

LIFE IN THE RIVER

The Lady Julian was now home to over 150 women with more arriving each week, sent from gaols throughout England for "a colony in great want of women." Plans that she should carry a cargo of male and female convicts, or females accompanied by a marine corps battalion to relieve the garrison in Sydney Cove, were both dropped. It was decided she should carry a full complement of women.

By far the largest group came out of Newgate Gaol. On 12 March 1789, 108 women and two infants were brought out of the gaol at dawn, loaded into lighters[8] at Blackfriars Bridge and rowed down the Thames to Galleons Reach.

Even at this early hour of the morning, the river was crowded. The Port of London was one of the busiest in the world. The City, anxious to preserve its huge income from licenses, refused to allow the construction of wharves and docks further east for another decade, despite huge congestion in the Pool of London. With as many as ten tall-masted ships there at one time, side by side, it was an obstacle course for the lightermen. For miles to the east, ships milled

---

[8] Small boats.

Felons being taken from Newgate Gaol to Blackfriars en route for the transport ships and prison hulks in the Thames. (Mary Evans Picture Library)

about for days waiting for a berth to become vacant. A haze of coal dust from the colliers hung over the docks.

Their route took the women along the north banks of the Thames where half the *Lady Julian*'s cargo had lived and worked among those they had robbed and assaulted. In Fishstreet Hill, 13-year-old Mary Cavenor had attempted to snatch a piece of cloth from the doorway of a drapery. On the other side of the Monument, in Lombard Court, Mary Hook had raided her mistress' bureau and stolen the household's wages when she should have been boiling lobsters in the kitchen. Bett Farrell had run into a constable in Blue Anchor yard, just past the Tower, who, "knowing her, stopt her and asked her what she had in her apron"; it proved to be stolen laundry. "Bett, this is £40 for me," he told her, and turned her in. A little further down, Mary Anderson had robbed a house because she did not want to be a common prostitute. And behind the house she had robbed, Mary Butler and Poll Randall had enticed Joseph Clark and his cheese into bed and Elizabeth Sully had kept a house of teenage whores. Just east in Whitechapel High Street, Elizabeth Jones had picked up a lighterman and stolen his knee buckles in the night.

The Ratcliff Highway almost touched the bank at the curve in the river between Wapping and Limehouse. It had been home to many in the lighters. Sophia Sarah Ann Brown had worked "in Mrs. Foy's house as a girl, an unfortunate girl" on the highway and robbed her drunken client of nine guineas, three shillings and a watch. Jane Walters had robbed her client here, also drunk, just two months ago when he fell asleep in a room rented by the hour. Ann Morgan had picked up an inn porter here with the words "come along with me, Ned," picked his breeches pocket in the first clinch and told him "she would poke my bloody eye out . . . though she was a woman she had fought a better man than I" when he tried to get his half guinea back.

As the lighters turned south down Limehouse Reach, they came into less familiar waters. Where the wharves of the City ended, ship-fitting and shipbuilding basins began. At the southern end of Limehouse, in the docks of Deptford, fitting-out basins to accommodate naval and merchant shipping lined both banks of the river to the east. Here, a man-of-war, HMS *Guardian,* had just been taken out of reserve to be fitted as store ship to the New South Wales colony.

Dotted around the waters of Deptford and Woolwich were the prison hulks, worn-out shells of naval ships no longer fit to go to sea. The hulks had been a stopgap solution to overcrowding in the prisons when transportation to America was suspended, it was thought, temporarily. As pressure on land prisons had never eased, they had never been scrapped. By the time the *Lady Julian* convicts were rowed past, some had been there for over a decade with hundreds of male convicts living in irons aboard each one. They slept in fetters, meagerly fed, continually prey to fever and kept at heavy labor from dawn to dusk in the government dockyards. When the air was still and the weather warm, the smell of them could pollute the river from bank to bank. Hulk after hulk, festooned with bedding, clothes, weed and rotting rigging, lined the river like a floating shantytown. As the lighters rowed through and among them at dawn, the chain gangs were being loaded into similar boats to be rowed ashore and start the day's labor, catcalling their sisters in irons as they went.

From now on, a couple of lighters would draw up to the *Lady Julian* each day bearing cold, damp women to be hauled aboard. Eighteen women were brought down from Warwick, ten came down the Thames from Maidstone, three from Nottingham, three from Reading, ones and twos from all over the country: pig thief Sarah Gregory and her baby daughter from Hertford, a 68-year-old shoplifter and an 18-year-old milkmaid from Northumberland, a maidservant and a mugger from Chelmsford, a housebreaker from New Sarum reprieved from death. It was John Nicol who received them, helped them over the side, stowed their chests and boxes below and took them down to their new quarters. His uppermost emotion was chivalrous sympathy. Most, he wrote, were "harmless, unfortunate creatures, the victims of the basest seduction."

In April, a lighter bearing a single occupant made its way toward the *Lady Julian*. Four women should have been in it: Elizabeth Barnsley, Ann Wheeler, Sarah Roberts and Alice Haynes. Ann Wheeler was too sick with gaol fever to be taken from the Newgate Infirmary. Alice Haynes had been kept back at the last minute while a petition for her release was considered. Sarah Roberts had been "detained upon a representation from Mr Akerman[9] that she was big with child, and near the time of her delivery, so that she could not be removed to the Vessel in the River without considerable danger and hardship." Elizabeth Barnsley, neither sick, pregnant, nor suitable material for clemency, was alone in the lighter when she allowed herself to be handed up by John Nicol and introduced to Agent Edgar. It did not take anyone long to realize the grande dame of the *Lady Julian* had arrived.

Elizabeth Barnsley soon made her mark on life aboard. It was her boast that her family had been highwaymen for over a hundred years. Highwaymen were the glory boys of eighteenth-century crime, dashing figures on black stallions with lace about the cuffs and a winning way with the ladies. Certainly Elizabeth's brother, who often visited

---

[9] The governor of Newgate Gaol.

Alice Haynes
Free Pardon.

George R

Whereas Alice Haynes was at the Sessions
holden at the Old Bailey in December 1787, tried &
convicted of stealing a Card of black Lace, and was
sentenced to be Transported for seven Years for the
same, And whereas some favourable Circumstances have
been humbly represented unto Us in her behalf inducing
Us to extend Our Grace and Mercy unto her and to grant
her Our free Pardon for her said Crime. Our Will
and Pleasure therefore is, that You cause her the said
Alice Haynes to be forthwith discharged out of
Custody and that She be inserted for her said Crime
in Our first and next general Pardon that shall come
out for the poor Convicts in Newgate, without any
condition whatsoever. And for so doing this
shall be your Warrant. Given at Our Court
at St James's the 8th day of June 1789, In the
Twenty Ninth Year of Our Reign.

To Our Trusty & Welbeloved
James Adair Esq. Recorder
of Our City of London, The
Sheriffs of Our said City
and County of Middlesex,
and all others whom it
may concern

By His Majesty's Command.

W W Grenville

A free pardon for Alice Haynes, shoplifter, granted shortly before she was due to board the *Lady Julian*. (Public Record Office, HO13/7) her on board the *Lady Julian* in the Thames, made an impression on John Nicol. Even thirty years later, he remembered with uncharacteristic awe that he was "well-dressed and genteel in his appearance as any gentleman"—and sufficiently devil-may-care that he did not mind his sister's advertising his profession. Elizabeth certainly had cash of her own, and fine clothes in trunks in the hold. Within hours of her arrival on ship, she had requested Agent Edgar's permission to exchange her vulgar convict's uniform of brown serge for something better fitting in which to receive her friends and family. He refused, but promised she could wear her finery once they had put to sea.

Mrs. Barnsley was not the only woman receiving visitors aboard the *Lady Julian* at Galleons Reach. During the spring months, the decks of the ship were scenes of constant activity. There were parents who had been present in the courtroom, had visited in prison and were now desperately petitioning the authorities to have their daughters pardoned, pleading youth and ignorance and pledging themselves as security against the girls' release. There were families from outside London who had undertaken a long and expensive coach journey to bid farewell to a daughter or a sister whom they doubted they would see again. There were friends and relations bringing letters to an officer of the marines currently in Sydney Cove by someone who had known someone who had once met someone else who knew him, in the hope they could win their wife or mother more food, less hard labor, a better hut. There were parents who had pawned their last possessions to provide their daughters with a few guineas which might buy them an earlier release or an easier life in the colony. There were journalists and illustrators searching for stories and touching pictures. And, until the day before the *Lady Julian* set sail, there were relations, advocates and well-wishers working against the clock and the odds to secure a pardon or a reduction of the sentence, concocting letter after letter to persons of influence with whom they had even the vaguest connection who might be persuaded to help, hoping desperately as departure day crept up that someone would relent and save them.

It is likely that Sir Joseph Banks paid a visit aboard. When he was not at Revesby Hall, Lincolnshire, he spent much of his time at his London house at 34 Soho Square, from where he kept a finger in several expeditionary pies. In August 1788, just before he had intervened in the affairs of Mary Rose, he had been setting up an expedition to penetrate the interior of Africa through Sierra Leone. It was to be led by his friend Mr. Lucas, another gentleman passenger of Captain Cook on those early, formative voyages in the 1770s. In April 1789, Sir Joseph's interest switched to Sydney Cove and he was called on to advise on the fitting of the *Guardian*.

Lord Sydney's office had given some thought to Governor Phillip's requests for food, more skilled labor and women. HMS *Guardian,* a sleek frigate of 900 tons refitted as store ship, would make a swift passage and could carry supplies for many months to Sydney Cove. Twenty-five male convicts with some skill in horticulture and agriculture were being selected from the Portsmouth hulks, promised special privileges in the colony and prepared for embarkation on the *Guardian.* A handful of nonconvict superintendents on a salary of £40 per annum were also to sail. These were the men intended to supervise the public works on which the convict gangs were engaged in Sydney Cove. They were an eccentric and heterogeneous bunch. Two of them had been handpicked by Sir Joseph Banks from among the royal gardeners at Kew. Another was a widowed Hessian soldier, Philip Shaffer, one of the mercenaries brought in by George III from his ancestral German territories to fight the American colonists. He spoke little or no English and relied for translation on his 10-year-old daughter, Elizabeth. There was a flax dresser called Andrew Hume who, it was supposed, would whip the Norfolk Island hemp industry into profitable shape; a farmer named Thomas Clarke; Philip Devine, already superintendent of convicts on the Woolwich hulks; James Reid, "formerly an American planter" and presumably kicked out of a previous colony for his loyalty to the British flag; and John Barlow, ex-army officer and surveyor who had been "employed as an engineer in Jamaica." There was also a middle-class black sheep who seems to have been quietly advised it would be a good idea if he left the country for a time, John Thomas Doidge.

Yet another of Cook's old officers was given command of the man-of-war. Edward Riou had been 13 years old when he sailed on the captain's final voyage as midshipman, serving under both Lieutenant Edgar on the *Discovery* and Lieutenant Bligh on the *Resolution*. He was now 26, a rising naval star whose personal acquaintanceship with the guru of the antipodes made him a natural for the commission. The *Guardian* was to carry plants to start up the colony's plantations and Sir Joseph, at Riou's diplomatic invitation, personally supervised the construction of a special plant cabin on her quarterdeck. During the first week of June, he visited the ship with a piece of chalk in his hand to draw up lines across the timbers for the shipwrights to work to, large enough to accommodate ninety-three pots of fruit, herbs and vegetables from Kew for the colonists to use "in food or physic." His protegée Mary Rose was on board the *Lady Julian* at Galleons Reach, a quarter mile away.

The other compassionate gentleman with a penchant for protegées and an interest in Botany Bay had not forgotten the women he had supported in Newgate. At least four of the women on the *Lady Julian* were still receiving their "pension" from Lord George Gordon. John Nicol went to Newgate once a week on their behalf and "got their allowance from his own hand." During one of these visits, he found "decent-looking" people waiting for him in the gaol guardhouse. They had come to the capital to seek news of their lost daughter and had tracked her as far as Newgate Gaol.

Sarah Dorset, 19 years old, had been arrested at a chophouse in the City of London nearly eighteen months before. She had run away from her family home with a man but "had not been with the villain who ruined her above six weeks" before he abandoned her and "she was forced by want upon the streets." Taken up after an inept attempt to steal a cloak, she was sentenced to seven years' transportation. When her parents arrived at Newgate, the gaoler recognized Sarah Dorset's name and told them to wait for John Nicol on his weekly visit to Lord George Gordon. "The mother implored me to tell her, if such a one was on board" and it was Nicol's unpleasant task to break the news to Sarah's parents that although the girl was alive and well, she was bound for Sydney Cove. "The father's heart seemed too full to allow him to speak," he wrote, "but the mother, with streaming eye, blessed God they had found their poor, lost child, undone as she was."

John had them rowed on board the *Lady Julian*. He put them in his own berth and went to find Sarah Dorset so the family could be reunited away from the curious or derisive stares of others. When Sarah, disbelieving, saw her parents, she fainted and then "in the most heart-rending accents, implored their pardon. . . . She . . . had not been from her father's house above two years . . . so short had been her course of folly and sin." Sarah Dorset held out no hope for a pardon, with or without her parents' help. She had already petitioned Lord Sydney from her cell. To Sydney's request for a summary of her case, the sentencing judge replied dourly that she "appears to me a very proper subject for the Colony at Botany Bay." There was nothing further she could do. The day John Nicol rowed her parents aboard in April 1789 was the last time she saw them.

Sarah Dorset was not the only convict on board whose petition had been turned down. The character references which accompanied a petition from Catherine Wilmot of Chelmsford were from the keeper of a livery stable who had known her for two years as "quiet and Industrious" and who believed she "got her living by selling hardware and going to Fairs"; and from a victualler, who had known her eighteen months as a woman who "travels and sells hardware in a basket." They were not inspiring. A marginally more encouraging one came from fellow parishioners, who reported she "always behaves herself as becometh" and noted she had four children, "disconsolate, scattered at present and in real distress." The recorder of London was not convinced: "I see no reason to change my opinion, nor to think that her children will be prejudiced by not being brought up under such a Parent."

Thirty years later, only those women whose characters or history were most remarkable remained in John Nicol's mind. He remembered one young girl because all on board believed her to be the illegitimate daughter of Prime Minister Pitt. "She herself never contradicted it," he wrote. "She bore a most striking likeness to him in every feature and could scarce be known from him as to looks." Maddeningly, he did not name names. The prime minister had a 14-year-old cousin, Thomas, who ran away from school in January 1789 and begged to go to sea. His father agreed and a midshipman's commission was arranged for him on the *Guardian.* He would sail to New South Wales alongside the ship which carried a girl commonly believed to be his cousin's by-blow. One can only speculate on what links, if any, bound them.

To most contemporaries participating in or discussing the great adventure of the convicts for Sydney Cove, their fate was deemed a terrible one. This, certainly, was how much of the establishment wished it to be considered, for of what use was a penal settlement which was not a terrifying deterrent to crime? However, there were women on the *Lady Julian* who regarded their fate more as an escape from intolerable conditions in their country of birth than as a punishment. "Numbers of them would not take their liberty as a boon. . . . We have good victuals and a warm bed," they told John Nicol.

> We are not ill-treated, or at the mercy of every drunken ruffian, as we were before. When we rose in the morning we knew not where we would lay our heads in the evening, or if we would break our fast in the course of the day. Banishment is a blessing to us. Have we not been banished for a long time and yet in our native land? . . . We dared not go to our relations whom we had disgraced. Other people would shut their doors in our faces. We were as if a plague were upon us, hated and shunned.

Many years passed before Nicol wrote his memoirs and some of what he wrote must be held suspect. However, clearly many women had good reason to feel relief at being in any place of safety where they no longer had to struggle every day to feed and defend themselves. Those who had been beaten into wretchedness by several years of poverty and ill treatment may well have felt this way.

But if some were relieved to be leaving behind a life of wretchedness, thinking any future, even penal servitude on the other side of the world, must be better than what they had recently gone through, others were still struggling to avoid what fate and His Majesty's judges had decreed.

6

CAPITAL CONVICTS CONDEMNED

There were other ways to clear the gaols of convicted felons than to transport them. Not all those convicted of a capital offense found their judges and prosecutors would help them escape the gallows. Among those on the Newgate Capital Convicts Condemned list were Catherine Heyland, 34, and Christian Murphy, 19, convicted separately that they "one piece of false, feigned and counterfeit money and coin, to the likeness of one shilling, falsely and deceitfully, feloniously and traitorously, did forge, counterfeit and coin."

The Westminster Forum debating society had recently discussed the following motion: "Is not that Law cruel and unjust which inflicts the punishment of Burning alive on a Woman for the same Offence which subjects a Man only to the usual forms of execution?" Its timing was apt. Two people had just been surprised in a Westminster garret by Peace Officer Treadway and two colleagues, acting on information that "bit-culls"[10] were at work. They found the keyhole stopped, put their ears to the door, listened and burst in.

"The prisoner James," claimed Treadway in the Old Bailey, "was rubbing something in his fingers." Seized by Officer Meecham,

---

[10] Coiners.

William James alias Levi put his fingers to his mouth. Meecham immediately squeezed him by the jaw but he had swallowed the evidence and only black foam squirted down the officer's sleeve. In the window, there was a saucer of wet sand and a heap of old sixpences, two finished counterfeit sixpences and a pipkin. With them was a file, some "scowering paper," a piece of cork, some "black stuff" and a pair of pliers. By the fire, the officers found a crucible and "over the garret window, outside, between the cieling [*sic*] and the roof," an iron flask. On the mantelpiece there was a phial of acquafortis, a vessel to carry the metal to the mold, brass scales and white arsenic. It was a coiners' kit.

John Nicholls, monier of the mint, was called on in court to identify a good and a bad sixpence. The equipment was unfamiliar to the jury, if not to the more experienced judge and an expert witness was asked to explain its use. The flask, he told them, was the mold used to take an imprint of the good coin in coarse, wet sand, first one side and then the other. After this, the pores of the coarse sand were filled with finer sand, "otherwise what is cast would come out in little spotty holes" and it was smoked over a fire until dry. When set, the casts were filled with brass or tin which had been melted in the crucible and screwed together. The molten metal was refined to resemble copper or silver—copper by mixing it with white arsenic, which turned it one shade whiter "to what we call East Indian copper, or tutteneg"; and silver by adding acquafortis, which, mixed into any compound containing a trace of silver, "brings the silver to the surface and throws it white." Once the false coin had set, it was smoothed with the file, brown paper and cork. As the expert witness testified, William James and Catherine Heyland had "the complete apparatus for coining."

There could be no doubt what had been going on in the Westminster garret, nor that the coiners would be sentenced to death. For William James, the only thing that mattered during the hearing was that the judge and jury should be convinced the guilt was his alone and Catherine merely a bystander or, at worst, an unwilling accom-

The chapel in Newgate Gaol where couples would call across to each other during services. (Rowlandson and Pugin, Stapleton Collection, UK/Bridgeman Art Library)

plice. Throughout the trial, he interrupted judge, prosecutor and witnesses to challenge their evidence on Catherine's involvement. The court did not believe him.

Catherine and William were not the only coining couple to be tried during the April 1788 sessions. Jeremiah Grace and Margaret Sullivan were also found guilty of treason. William, Jeremiah and Margaret had no hope of mercy but Catherine had found a sponsor in Mr. Bloxham, sheriff of the City of London. He believed her innocent—or, at least, not so guilty that she deserved the sentence due to be pronounced. As sheriff, Mr. Bloxham was called on to participate in the ceremonies which attended executions at the Old Bailey. He had seen countless hangings and, in June 1786, had seen the coiner Phebe Harris tied to a stake and burned to death outside Newgate Gaol. It was not a sight easily forgotten.

On Monday 23 June, all four convicted coiners returned to the courtroom after a month in the cells to be told the date of their execution. William James alias Levi and Jeremiah Grace would be hanged on Wednesday outside Newgate Gaol. Catherine's execution was to be stayed by a month but Margaret Sullivan was to be burned at the stake. She had two days in which to prepare herself. The next day saw the first of the *Times'* attacks on the barbarity of Sullivan's sentence, demanding "must not mankind laugh at our long speeches against African slavery . . . when . . . we roast a fellow creature alive, for putting a pennyworth of quicksilver into a halfpennyworth of brass?"

Margaret Sullivan spent Tuesday night in prayer with a Catholic priest. She refused the gift of strawberries sent her by Mrs. Bloxham. Early Wednesday morning, the prisoners in Newgate heard the first sounds of a crowd congregating in St. Paul's Churchyard and the inns of the Old Bailey. At six, St. Sepulchre's bell began to toll and Sheriff Bloxham's men dragged out the apparatus of execution: a covered-in walkway from the Debtors' Gate and steps to a portable scaffold which towered above the crowd. People struggled for the best view. Young men climbed onto the balconies of the houses opposite the prison. The King's Head did roaring business. Miniature gallows were on sale as souvenirs at the Magpie and Stump.

At seven, William James and Jeremiah Grace were led to the scaffold, hooded, with their hands tied behind their backs. The noose went around their necks and there was a roar of "Hats off!" from the back of the crowd. The chaplain made his pious and inaudible speech. Just before eight, Catherine Heyland, inside the prison, heard the noise of the crowd as the platform dropped and William kicked at the end of his rope. Fifteen minutes passed and Margaret Sullivan, clad in penitential white, emerged with the priest. She was taken to the stake, made to stand on a stool and faggots were placed around her. With ceremony and deliberation, the sheriff's men appeared with flaming torches and the body of Margaret Sullivan, guilty of treason, was ritually turned to ash before the crowd in the street and the dignitaries of the City, Sheriff Bloxham among them, on the viewing platform erected for the occasion.

London was shocked. It had been two years since the last woman was burned at the stake and the sickening smell of human meat floated down Newgate Street to the City and down the Strand to the Thames. Margaret Sullivan's execution was seen as savage, senseless, utterly out of step with enlightened thinking and abhorrent in its application to women only. "It has been the boast of the country, that there was no barbarity annexed to our punishment of criminals," wrote the *Times*. "Is the burning of a woman no torture? Shame on such barbarity. The very savages in the wildest parts of the world pay respect to their females, whilst Great Britain selects their tender bodies as the only objects fit for excruciating torture."

For Catherine Heyland, it was the start of a month of terror. Now began the cat-and-mouse game of respites. She was due to burn in four weeks' time, on 21 July. Parliament was in recess and the men who could save her, the secretaries of state and those who had access to them, were in the country for the summer. Three and a half weeks passed without word from them.

By the last of the evening light on Sunday 20 July, men were at work outside the prison walls. A stake was secured and faggots placed around its base. Inside, Catherine was with the chaplain. Gifts were sent her by well-wishers, notes brought in from the outside world. Sheriff Bloxham was not there. He was desperate that a woman he believed innocent should not die in so dreadful a way. While Catherine prayed, the sheriff galloped toward the country house where the secretary of state was spending the weekend. He arrived at three in the morning, demanded to be taken to His Lordship's bedroom and within an hour was galloping back to London with the paper in his hand. Already the crowds were gathering in St. Sepulchre's yard. Two hours before the torches were due to light the faggots, Catherine Heyland was allowed a further four days of life. On Monday, the secretary of state returned to London, importuned by Sheriff Bloxham before he could draw breath. On 24 July, when orders had already been given to erect the stake once more, Catherine was finally reprieved from her dreadful penalty "during His Majesty's pleasure."

By March 1789, Catherine Heyland had been on the Capital

Convicts Condemned list for almost a year, one of 25 women under sentence of death (there were 74 on the equivalent list for men) waiting for the date of their execution to be announced or a pardon to be granted. Six days after 108 women left Newgate for the *Lady Julian,* the ghastly performance of the stake and the faggots was repeated, this time for 19-year-old Christian Murphy. Again, the male accomplice was hanged first and again Catherine Heyland heard the crowd enjoying a spectacle in which one day it could be her turn to star.

The following month, however, an event occurred whose impact was felt throughout Britain but had a particular effect on Catherine Heyland, Nelly Kerwin and twenty other women on the Capital Convicts Condemned list. It led to a sensational trial in the Old Bailey. In April, King George III officially regained his wits and a national day of thanksgiving was celebrated. There were fireworks, floats, lights, street parties and traffic jams around St. James and St. Paul's, and singing, bells and volleys of gunfire across the river. In Lincolnshire, Dr. Willis was guest of honor at receptions and balls where "his adulation is indescribable."

In London, some of the Newgate convicts condemned to die were to be pardoned as part of the general thanksgiving and, at the Old Bailey sessions of April, this caused a fight almost literally to the death. During the five-day sessions, some of the disorderly women in the dock became such a cause célèbre in London society that Mrs. Fitzherbert and the Duchess of Cumberland graced the public galleries of Court Number One during the closing stages of their trial.

The usual thieves and muggers appeared in the usual succession of brief hearings and swift judgments from 20 to 23 April. On 24 April, the female Capital Convicts Condemned were brought up from their cell, "put to the Bar and informed that his Majesty's pardon was granted to them on the following conditions, viz:

Catherine Heyland, Eleanor Kirwin alias Karavan, Sarah Cowden, Sarah Storer, Martha Cutler and nine others: transportation for the term of their natural lives.

A courtroom in the Old Bailey Sessions House: judge to the left, defendant to the right, jury between them and public galleries behind. (Guidhall Library, Corporation of London)

Catherine Hounsam and seven others: transportation for seven years.

"Do you accept the terms of the pardon?" asked the recorder.

"Yes," said Catherine Heyland and fifteen other women.

"No," said the remaining six, and the fight began.

"I will die by the laws of my own country before ever I will go abroad for my life," said Sarah Cowden. "I am innocent and so is Sarah Storer."

"Before I will go abroad for my natural life, I will sooner die," and "I will not accept it, I am innocent," said Martha Cutler and Sarah Storer.

The other three women who refused, Nelly Kerwin, mugger Sarah Mills and maidservant Jane Tyler, were professional criminals. But Martha Cutler, Sarah Cowden, Sarah Storer or all three of them may genuinely have been innocent of the assault on the king's highway for which they had been sentenced to hang. Their vehement assertion of innocence certainly suggests righteous anger.

The crime of which they stood accused went thus: Henry Solomon, resident of Whitechapel, knew the three women and their unidentified male accomplice by sight. They called him by name, he said, as he passed the entrance to Gun Alley on his way to the barber so he turned up the court toward them. At the far end, Storer knocked Solomon's hat off his head and slipped inside an open door. Three or four others surrounded him, taunting and jeering, daring him to get his hat back and finally shoving him in after her. Once inside, he said, "All three of them together threw me down on the bed." Storer rifled his pockets and passed fourteen guineas and ten shillings to Cutler, who disappeared. The other two then kicked him out, threw his hat after him, and told him he might go about his business. A passing couple had heard the scuffling and looked through the window. They were on the point of calling the watch when Solomon staggered out and it was principally on their evidence that the three women were convicted.

In the dock, all three had excuses which rang tired and unconvincing. Cowden was only visiting, not there at the time of the offense; Storer had heard Solomon come in and "says he, I have been robbed and the first I meet, I will make suffer for it"; Cutler claimed Solomon was taking his revenge for some unspecified wrong. There were defenses heard day in, day out and the judge was unimpressed. Odds on, they were guilty—but what causes a qualm about the verdict was the passion with which they were still fighting back fourteen months later.

The recorder, taken aback by this stony-faced rejection of His Majesty's graciousness, warned the other women at the bar that "if you do not accept of the King's pardon now, it will be too late hereafter; you may depend upon it, that every woman who now refuses to accept the King's pardon, will be ordered for immediate execution." But the others, too, did not hesitate in their rejection of the terms offered. "I will go to my former sentence," said Sarah Mills. "I had rather die than go out of my country to be devoured by Savages."

Jane Tyler, too, preferred to "die first, I think I have suffered hard enough to be in gaol three years for what I have done."

Clever Nelly Kerwin was more circumspect in her approach, but of the same mind: "I hope this honourable Court, nor any of the Gentlemen in company, will not object to what I shall say. . . . I do not intend to object to my sentence but I am not in a situation to go abroad; if I was, I would go . . . I have two small children . . . I have no objection to confinement for life . . . I cannot live long . . ."

The government, however, was determined to clear the cells as they had not been cleared in the haphazard run-up to the departure of the First Fleet, when several convicts—including Nelly Kerwin—had escaped boarding through one device or another and had clogged up the cells ever since. This could not be allowed to happen again. The insistence of the six on "going to their former sentence" was not due only to the terror of exile among savages. It was also a calculated gamble, and this was why the recorder was insisting so brutally on the inevitability of immediate execution.

Nelly Kerwin had been in Newgate since July 1786 and should already have been executed or transported with the first convicts to Botany Bay. In October 1786, a "panel of matrons" had confirmed her to be pregnant, her baby due in June 1787. In mid-April, she miscarried and when her cellmates went on board the Botany Bay ships, Nelly was in the Newgate Infirmary, her execution "staid until His Majesty's pleasure should be known." His Majesty's pleasure could not be known until the next Old Bailey sessions—by which time the Botany Bay fleet had left the country. Two years later, Nelly was gambling that ill health, small children and three years in gaol would win her an unconditional pardon.

The court of April 1789 would not allow such cases to remain in gaols where space was so desperate that every extra body counted. They had to die, or go. So on 24 April, the six recalcitrant women were taken back to the cells to think about it overnight. On 25 April, they were back at the bar to be asked again if they would accept the terms of their pardons. The recorder once more made the government's intentions brutally clear:

> Your not being inclined to accept that pardon arises from a hope that you shall not be sent off so soon as the other Prisoners . . . this sort of conduct will be considered as an aggravation of your offences and if you have any hopes that your sentence will be altered, you had much better accept of the King's pardon now, and try what interest you have to get that sentence mitigated but if you go from the Bar now, you will remain under sentence of death and you may depend upon it that you will suffer death with the first culprits, at the next execution.

Twelve hours of contemplation had not altered the women's resolve. All six refused, the recorder lost his temper and there was uproar in the courtroom.

"Let these women be confined in separate cells and fed on bread and water!" he shouted. They could think it over, in solitary confinement and on a punishment diet, until the June sessions came around.

Successive departure dates for the Second Fleet to New South Wales had come and gone; transportation lists had to be finalized and the women embarked. Pardons, petitions, pleas of sickness and pregnancy, movements on board ship and off again became too much for prison clerks to keep up with. Records fell into disarray. Women released or too ill to travel were not canceled from the Transportation Register. Women who arrived at the last minute were never added. Lord Sydney agreed to a petition from Surgeon Simpson of Newgate that ten women for whom "a further continuation of . . . confinement will be dangerous to their lives" be released back onto the streets. Not all their names were removed from the transportation list. Sarah Roberts was brought to bed of a male child in Newgate Infirmary, where she would remain until she was pardoned in October. Her name, too, remained on the list, as did Ann Aborough's, who was already on board the *Lady Julian* when her petition was forwarded to Lord Sydney.

Ann Aborough's mother had been working with determination. First, she had gone to Lord Loughborough to plead her daughter's case. Next, she acquired a "certificate" from the "churchwardens and other respectable inhabitants" of her parish to back up the petition sent, with Lord Loughborough's recommendation, to Lord Sydney. This stated that Ann was the only child of respectable parents, who had been twenty years in the parish and were "willing to take her home and provide for her." "Under these very favourable circumstances," wrote Sydney, "I cannot but feel myself impelled to recommend her to His Majesty's Royal Mercy as an Object of Free Pardon." Two weeks before the *Lady Julian* sailed, the pardon was issued. Ann's name was never removed from the list of those transported.

At the end of the month, the six women who had refused His Majesty's mercy were brought back to the bar in the Old Bailey. Clearly, a starvation diet had had some effect. There were listless replies to the recorder's question from Jane Tyler: "Yes, I will"; and Martha Cutler: "Why, I must." But then the recorder came to Sarah Cowden, 21, headstrong and convinced of her own and her friend's innocence.

"I am willing to accept of whatever sentence the King passes upon me but Sarah Storer is innocent . . . I will accept it if that woman's sentence is mitigated."

"You have nothing to do with the case of any other person but yourself."

"I will accept of my sentence willingly, if this woman's sentence is mitigated."

There was another burst of temper from the recorder: "Remove all the women from the court but Sarah Cowden!"

When Sarah was alone facing the bench, he let rip.

"You will attend to this. The government of this country will not suffer the mercy of the King to be trifled with . . . if you refuse . . .

you must prepare to die the day following, you shall be executed the day following."

"I hope I shall have more mercy shewn me than ever I had at this bar," replied Sarah bitterly.

"If you are sufficiently prepared to die on Thursday next, the Court will give orders accordingly."

"That I am."

"Let her stand committed to the cells and let the sheriffs prepare for an execution on Thursday morning. Take her away."

Sarah Cowden was led back into the prison to uproar from the public gallery and pleas from both Counsel Garrow and Mr. Villette, the ordinary,[11] to be allowed to reason with her. Reluctantly, and still simmering, the recorder dismissed the men into the cells. In the meantime, Sarah Storer, object of Sarah Cowden's solicitude, faced a furious recorder and a public gallery on the edge of its seat.

"If at any future period the King would incline to grant you any further remission of your sentence, your submission to his will, will be an additional motive," the recorder told her and finally she accepted, but left the room wailing, "But not for my life, I never will, I never will."

It was now that Garrow reappeared to beg the recorder to allow Sarah Cowden back to the bar to accept her pardon. Possibly the news that Sarah Storer had accepted transportation for life had been brought to her cell and she no longer had reason to sacrifice herself. Possibly the recorder's argument that mitigation of a sentence was always a possibility, providing one was still alive, had been put to her more urgently and forcibly by Garrow. Possibly the ordinary had told her horrific tales of hangings gone wrong. However they did it, Garrow and Villette had managed in a bare quarter of an hour to turn her from passionate defiance to listless acceptance.

Mr. Garrow now raced back into the courtroom as Sarah Storer

---

[11] The prison chaplain.

was being led away. The dignity of the recorder's office, however, had been offended.

"I do not think the King's mercy should go a-begging. . . . I can show no indulgence to those who treat the mercy of the King with contempt."

"I only ask the Court, to consider the order not to be irrevocable."

"As to me, it is irrevocable. I shall order the execution."

Ignoring Mr. Garrow standing before him, the recorder donned the customary black square and read out the death sentence on ten men who had come before him during the sessions. As he came to an end, Mr. Garrow tried once more, begging his indulgence on behalf of "a very miserable wretch who deserves now, having seen the folly of her behaviour, humbly to intreat, that she may be permitted to accept that pardon of His Majesty's."

His plea was finally accepted and Sarah Cowden, too, was removed to the transportation cells.

It was not until two weeks later, in mid-June, that the secretary of state got around to reading the petitions for clemency on behalf of Charlotte Marsh, on board the *Lady Julian,* and not until 30 June, when the *Lady Julian* was on the point of leaving, that he decided she had acted under the evil influence of her mother, now dead of gaol fever, and that, as her husband was prepared to offer securities for her for two years, he could take her home.

Abandoning all hope of legitimate release, several reckless souls attempted escape while the *Lady Julian* lay in the river. Only one attempt was successful. It must have taken nerve to wait for the night immediately before departure and to keep the secret hidden that long, but it paid off. The night before sailing there was the traditional party: heavy drinking among the crew, barrels of gin rowed out to the ship from the inns along the riverbanks and the sailors and their girl-friends carousing below deck from an early hour of the evening. The watch, posted on the quarterdeck and resentful he had drawn the short straw and could not join the frolics below, was an easy target. The women offered him gin, flirted, offered him more gin and slipped over the side into a waiting boat. Their loss was not discovered until the morning and then it was too late for them to be rounded up and brought back on board.

As the records were hopelessly out of date, the exact number of women who sailed from London on the *Lady Julian* is unknown. John Nicol remembered there having been 245; the Transportation Register only listed 172, as none of the women from outside London had been entered on it. Sarah Whitelam, Mary Rose and the other Lincolnshire women are listed as sailing aboard the *Neptune* (which left four months later) when in fact they sailed aboard the *Lady Julian*. Ann Wheeler, Elizabeth Barnsley's fever-struck partner, is listed as sailing on the *Lady Julian* when she sailed aboard the *Neptune*. Ann Clapton, Charlotte Marsh, Alice Haynes and Sarah Roberts were all listed; the first was dead, the second two pardoned, the last nearing her confinement in Newgate Infirmary. One consequence of this muddle is that the identities of three of the four women who escaped over the side are not known.

The one escapee whose identity is known was 24-year-old shoplifter Mary Talbot, who fled the ship with her baby William. She was later retaken and received a death sentence, reprieved to transportation for the term of her natural life in December 1790. She left for New South Wales aboard the transport *Mary Ann* in 1791 and died on arrival in the colony. Whoever the other three were, the *Lady Julian* left without them.

7

LEAVING LONDON

*I*n the first week of July 1789, the *Lady Julian* left her mooring at Galleons Reach and sailed down the Thames with the tide, out to the coasts of Kent. She was making for Portsmouth and would anchor on the Mother Bank outside Portsmouth Harbour. Like the Thames at Woolwich, Portsmouth was crowded with prison hulks. The *Ceres* and *Dunkirk* hulks had once been ships of the line, engaged in battle with the Americans. They had fallen on hard times and were now home to 600 male felons, among them a handful intimately connected to women aboard the *Lady Julian*. Thomas Higgins, partner or accomplice of London receiver Grace Maddox; and George Simpson, brother, cousin or husband to Charlotte Simpson alias Hall, were held on the *Ceres,* along with William Pimlott, partner to Sarah Carter, with whom he had been convicted of stealing six cloth coats, a pair of sugar tongs and forty-seven shillings in cash two years previously. Thomas Gregory of Hertfordshire had both his wife Sarah and his infant daughter Elizabeth aboard the *Lady Julian*. William Bramsden, husband of Swallow Street shoplifter Sarah Young, went aboard the *Ceres* six weeks after Sarah was sentenced to death for stealing 9 yards of muslin. On 25 August, a petition arrived on Secretary of State Nepean's desk from Bramsden, begging to be sent out on the first ship to Sydney Cove to rejoin his beloved 18-year-old wife.

Thomas Barnsley, also aboard the *Ceres,* had been waiting for his sentence of transportation to be executed since 1785. In 1786, he had gone aboard the hulks, first in the River Thames, then in Portsmouth, and Elizabeth and their small children had moved from Reading to London to be near him. Two petitions had already been addressed to the magistrates from the *Ceres,* probably delivered by Elizabeth. Thomas, like his wife, was full of self-confidence and imagination. His petitions (or hers on his behalf) portrayed him as an honest man, educated, a musician by profession, reduced to penury by circumstance and forced to steal to keep his wife and children from the greatest distress. He strongly protested the way in which men of breeding like himself were "herded like animals" with men of the lower class. The Barnsleys did not lack contacts, or persistence—Thomas had managed to avoid sailing with the First Fleet and Elizabeth had got his petitions signed by an alderman and two City merchants. The magistrates did not budge. Stealing an entire trunk of tea off the back of a coach to Bristol did not conform to their idea of a man who turned to crime to feed his starving babies. The Barnsley marriage was a union of two clever and resourceful personalities. Despite a separation of four years and an end to Elizabeth's visits to the *Ceres* when she went into Newgate in February 1788, the bond between the two had survived. Their children, however, would be left behind: children over the age of 6 were not allowed to accompany their mothers. Nelly Kerwin's children were ashore somewhere in Portsmouth, boarded out since she entered Newgate. They, too, would stay in England when their mother sailed.

Lieutenant Edgar had allowed visits on board at Galleons Reach and was to countenance, possibly encourage, visits on board at every other port of call on the voyage out. The sympathy John Nicol noted in him for the women in his care would have inclined him toward permitting a last meeting with their men or, at the least, the opportunity to send them a message. On the other hand, he had just lost four over the stern in the Thames and it might have seemed a better idea to keep the women in strict isolation until out of British waters and away from dangerous contacts. Nor did it depend solely on Lieutenant Edgar whether the women of the *Lady Julian* and the men on the hulks were allowed to make contact. It also depended on the superintendents of the hulks and these were not men noted for their compassion. At the least, written messages of farewell were probably rowed from one ship to another. Mrs. Barnsley and Nelly Kerwin certainly had enough money to bribe someone to run errands, with or without Edgar's permission.

The *Lady Julian*'s stay in Portsmouth was brief. Back at the start of the year, it had been optimistically planned that she would be only one of a fleet of transports to Sydney Cove which would gather here and sail in convoy, guarded by HMS *Guardian* and a corps of marines. Confusion, countermanded orders, a change in agent from William Richards to the slavers Camden, Calvert & King, and a change in secretary of state when Sydney handed over to Evan Nepean had all delayed departures. The *Guardian* had sailed from the Thames to Portsmouth a few days before the *Lady Julian* but, because of further delays taking on stores and a full complement of seamen, she did not sail with her from there. The other three transport ships which would sail that year, the *Neptune, Scarborough* and *Surprize,* had only just been commissioned. The *Lady Julian* sailed late in the season and alone.

Just before she left, a harbor official's boat drew up alongside with a document for Agent Edgar. It contained orders for the last-minute release of one of the women aboard. A petition lodged in May on behalf of Susannah Bray alias Gay, a 22-year-old shoplifter from London, was being considered. Pending a decision, she must leave the ship and return to London. Susannah's chest came up from the hold; she made brief farewells and left. The *Lady Julian* sailed from Portsmouth minus one, piloted around the shoals of the Isle of Wight before heading down the Channel. One more woman was to leave the ship in British waters.

"The poor young Scottish girl I have never yet got out of mind," wrote John Nicol thirty years later:

She was young and beautiful, even in the convict dress, but pale as death and her eyes red with weeping. She never spoke to any of the other women or came on deck. She was constantly sitting in the same corner from morning to night . . . my heart bled for her—she was a countrywoman in misfortune. I offered her consolation but she heeded me not, or only answered with sighs and tears. If I spoke of Scotland she would wring her hands and sob, until I thought her heart would burst. . . . I lent her my Bible to comfort her but she read it not; she laid it on her lap after kissing it and only bedewed it with her tears. At length she sunk into her grave of no disease but a broken heart.

Because the embarkation records do not list women from provincial gaols and records drawn up in Sydney list only those who disembarked, the "poor young Scottish girl" cannot be identified. However, she was dead before the ship left Britain, of malnutrition, exhaustion, lingering gaol fever and lack of the will to live, buried in the English Channel in a rough coffin made for her by the ship's carpenter. Someone, perhaps Captain Aitken, said prayers and the convicts bowed their heads. Then the sailors went back to their tasks, the ship turned west and they picked up way once more.

By the last week of July, the *Lady Julian* was one of a throng of vessels in Plymouth Sound. This was one of the busiest ports in the country, full of working craft: East Indiamen, private merchantmen, pilot boats, delivery boats, the fishing fleet, His Majesty's men-of-war. The shores were occupied by yards, workshops and market gardens whose produce supplied ships of a dozen nationalities. Along the fringe of the Mount Edgecumbe estate, a battery of guns pointed seaward toward the French. In July, the icy cold, indigo blue water was scarcely visible among the mass of shipping crammed into the bay. This was the last provisioning stop before the Canaries, for those sail-

ing south for Africa or the Indies; or the Azores, for those sailing west
for America or Newfoundland.

The first task of a ship's company newly arrived in port was to
water the ship. Arrangements for watering varied in sophistication and
cost from harbor to harbor and country to country. In Plymouth,
water was collected from Drake's Leet, the conduit built for Sir Francis, scourge of the Spanish in another century's wars, which brought
sweet water from Dartmoor down to the Sound to be casked for shipping. Rowing casks ashore, filling them, getting them back on board
and stowing them safely was a full day's work or more for the men.

Meanwhile, Lieutenant Edgar was pacing the government abat-
toirs in Stonehouse Creek for beef, pricing up meat on the hoof at
cattle markets on Plymouth Hoe and visiting agents for the Tamar
Valley market gardeners to negotiate the price of greens. Most supplies and materials for the voyage had been commissioned directly by
the Admiralty, whether collected in London or Plymouth, but fresh
food had to be marketed at each port against a cash advance signed
for in London. There seems not to have been a purser on the *Lady
Julian* and his usual bookkeeping duties were part of Lieutenant
Edgar's brief, probably with help from John Nicol. Nicol, as cooper,
was responsible for ensuring food was properly preserved; Edgar was
ultimately responsible to the government for ensuring that the ship's
supplies remained within budget. The work of going ashore, placing
orders and handing over cash was done by Edgar and whichever of
the officers or tradesmen he trusted most. Nicol would have been one
of them. His honesty and experience had been vouched for by his
previous captain and he had an interest in ensuring that all goods
coming on board were properly casked—if they were not, he would
get the blame when the food went rotten. So the ship remained at
anchor and Nicol rowed Lieutenant Edgar across to the Hoe each day
with a pencil behind his ear and a scrap of paper for sums. They came
back each day with orders placed and some smelly delicacy in the
pocket of John's breeches, for Sarah Whitelam was now three months
pregnant.

The quantity of shipping in port, and the relative clumsiness of a large vessel under sail, meant sailing across the Sound to pick up supplies was impracticable. Either the ship maneuvered herself alongside the government stores in Stonehouse Creek and took everything aboard there or, more likely, Edgar employed delivery boats. While he and Nicol were placing orders for live meat ashore, the carpenter and his mate had been building cattle pens on the foredeck and poultry cages behind the wheel. Livestock had probably not been taken on in London for the short trip along the south coast, but for a voyage to Canary, thence Cape Town, it was time to get the cows aboard. The animals were penned into delivery boats—a small herd of cows, some goats, poultry, a few hogs and a flock of sheep—and brought across the Sound. The delivery boats came alongside, the smaller animals were passed up, then the cattle were forced into a canvas sling and hoisted on board, where a rope was slung around their necks and they were hauled forward. Seamen sweated and the deck steamed with fresh manure.

When the *Lady Julian* arrived in Sydney Cove a year later, there were eighteen women aboard her who had been delivered from West Country gaols in cities closer to Plymouth than London. Conceivably, these eighteen women from Exeter, Bristol, Gloucester and Taunton boarded at Plymouth, and Lieutenant Edgar knew nothing of them until he arrived in the Sound and found orders had been issued over his head for their delivery. It was not uncommon for the Admiralty to make such arrangements without the knowledge of captains and agents, relying on their ingenuity to accommodate extra cargo foisted on them. The shipwrights of Plymouth Sound were used to making and mending to deal with last-minute changes to an Admiralty commission.

Once again, John Nicol set up his blacksmith's anvil on board to knock the irons from the new arrivals: a predictable, forlorn group of thieves and clumsy burglars. As in the Thames, relatives and sweethearts came aboard to take their leave of daughters, sisters, wives, mothers, possibly grandmothers, as one of the Taunton women was

63 years old. They passed over a few coins and pledged faith above the banging of the hammers and the shouts of deliverymen shoving them out of the way. Below, chests and boxes were pushed forward to make room for those of the arrivals and the old girls squeezed up in the sleeping shelves to make room for the new. There were now somewhere between 225 and 240 women on board. Roughly 200 women and 5 infants were sleeping in the orlop. The rest of the women were sleeping, periodically or permanently, with the officers and crew.

The sailors' "right" to a female mate was a piece of sexual piracy deeply enshrined in Honest Jack the Seaman's idea of his rights. These relationships were not just a bit of roughhouse below deck to which the officers turned a blind eye; they were fully authorized, and equipped. Every seaman and officer on the *Lady Julian* was entitled "by law," as the *Times* reported in August, to oblige the woman of his choice to serve him as "mate" for the duration of the voyage. The paper published a coy commentary that month: "a ship is now laying [in Plymouth] which has 260[12] females on board, the youngest 11, the oldest 68 . . . the crew of the ship consists of 30 and 5 or 6 officers, each of whom is allowed to select a mate for the voyage. Government has ordered them baby cloaths for 60—supposing the salubrity of the sea-air may, during the long voyage, produce babies to every honest woman."

It was not only the forecastle which took advantage of what was on offer on the orlop. The custom of selecting a mate was also observed by the officers. One of the girls who came out of Exeter Gaol and probably boarded at Plymouth was 18-year-old Ann Mash, in prison since March 1788 for stealing wheat. Her stint on the sleeping shelves of the orlop was brief, for she had caught the eye of Surgeon Alley and was soon spirited away to his cubbyhole at the far end of the sick berth. Where the surgeon led, the men followed. "As soon as they were at sea," John Nicol remembered cheerfully, "every man

---

[12] The *Times* had yet another total number of women on board.

on board took a wife from among the convicts, they nothing loath." The "nothing loath" sits ill on the sensibilities of modern readers. One can only speculate on the attitude of the women toward the men on board—indeed, toward men as a species—and whether they believed it possible to have a relationship with any man which was not principally characterized by coercion. There are no records written by convict women to shed light on this. Sarah Whitelam may have felt affection for her man—although even this is not certain— but whether this affection had developed by the time she was taken "as wife" is unguessable.

However, there were some reasons for the women not just to accept, but to compete for, the position of sailor's mistress. Most important, there was protection. Every woman on board had by now lived some part of her life competing for the necessaries of existence, literally fighting for her share of a plate of pork or a glass of gin. Most on board had come from extreme hardship and were, necessarily, selfish and cunning. Many were unaccustomed to the security of being regularly fed and clothed at someone else's expense. Some must have regarded the sailors coldly as a source of extra food, extra drink, extra privileges and some safety from the stealing, cheating and bullying going on at the bottom of the ship. Every woman who had spent time in gaol had been warped by a system in which you bribed the gaoler or starved; bribed the bullies or were mugged; and bribed the trusty or were raped. Many must automatically have seen sleeping with a sailor as a way of bribing him to look out for "his" woman at the expense of the others.

The Royal Navy, and Commodore Phillip, persisted in their efforts to enforce decency far longer than later transportation ships, whose captains, officers, crew and passengers accepted cohabitation as normal and inevitable. The First Fleet had been run as a military operation and its officers' and administrators' decision to keep the women apart from the male convicts and sailors went against the merchant-shipping traditions of the slave and convict trade. Riots had occurred whenever the First Fleet ships put into port and the men got drunk and attempted to raid the women's quarters. One of the First Fleet lieutenants, Ralph Clark, wrote despairingly of the difficulties he had experienced trying to prevent fraternization. On his ship, the seamen "brock thru the Bulk head and had connection with . . . those damn whores" before they had even got to Lands End. Nor was this a one-way sport. "The desire of the women to be with the men was so uncontrollable," another officer wrote, "that neither shame . . . nor the fear of punishment could deter them from making their way through the bulkheads to the apartments assigned the seamen." Sailors and male convicts risked heavy punishment if the women escaped their quarters by night and crept into the men's to visit someone who had caught their eye on deck. This did not stop it from happening. Ralph Clark's men "brock thru" once again just south of Cabo Verde. The men were flogged and the women put in irons, although, had it been Clark's decision, "I should have flogged the whores as well." Brutal though the *Lady Julian*'s rough and ready cohabitation sounds, it was not an unreasonable way to guard against the consequences of sexual frustration among young single men and women living in close proximity.

The sailors were also of a class and sort which was familiar to the women on board coming, as they did, from areas where seamen just like these lived, partied, drank and formed their friendships and romantic partnerships. Seamen, dockworkers and ships' coopers were the natural partners of women from Limehouse and Shoreditch. In contrast to the folklore which has grown up around the transportation of convicts to New South Wales, the voyage of the *Lady Julian* was a humane one and, for women coming from the brutalities of gaol, preceded by the brutalities of the streets, and heading for hard labor in Sydney Cove, it was an interlude of tranquillity and care. Cohabitation and easy communication between the women and the sailors were among the reasons the women of the *Lady Julian* enjoyed different treatment from that on some other convict ships.

More questions arise than can be answered about the nature of the relationships which developed aboard the *Lady Julian*. These were

not aspects of the voyage which appeared in letters sent home or journals kept at sea. We cannot know, for example, whether money or
other inducements changed hands, nor whether refusal was an option
for women or coercion an option for men; nor can we know whether
some seamen maintained more than one "wife" at once. Possible
answers can only be arrived at by inference and deduction. Some
sailors may have remained faithful to the first mates they chose from
among the women, others not. Probably there was a short period of
chopping and changing before thirty or so women settled into cou-
pledom and the rest remained cloistered on the orlop. Too much
license would cause fights, among the women as much as the men,
and the formation of stable couples on board would reduce the spread
of disease. If seamen and convicts were allowed uncontrolled access to
each other, the pox would go around both forecastle and orlop like a
bushfire. Eighteenth-century ships were chronically and routinely
undermanned; if even one man from a watch was out of action in the
sick berth, his watch mates were put under a severe strain.

A muster would have been drawn up for the *Lady Julian* with
details of every man taken on. It no longer exists, or has not been
found, so we only know the names of those seamen mentioned in
other records, principally the baptisms in Sydney Cove of babies conceived during the voyage out. Not all the women sleeping in the forecastle gave birth, however, and the names of sailors who did not
father a baby are lost. We only know for certain the names of seven
women taken "as wife" by this early stage of the voyage.

If the girls we know about were a typical sample of wifehood
before the mast, they seem to have been chosen on the basis of youth.
Youth meant not only prettiness, but a lower risk of disease. Sarah
Whitelam and Sarah Dorset, in the bunks of John Nicol and Edward
Powell, respectively, were both 19 or 20. Margaret Wood, a professional burglar from London, was also 19. She had been sentenced to
death at the age of 17, spent two years in gaol, was respited in April
and now shared a hammock with Edward Burgis. The other "wives"
were even younger. Two Warwickshire girls, Mary Warren and Mary

Barlow, were 18 when they became pregnant to Sam Braiden and Edward Scott. Ann Bryant, from Maidstone, was just 16 when she was convicted in April 1789, went aboard the *Lady Julian* immediately after her trial and was taken as partner by seaman William Hughes. She seems to have been taken under the wing of the gentle Ratcliff prostitute Sophia Sarah Ann Brown, at 27 years of age almost old enough by eighteenth-century standards to be her mother. The youngest "wife" was Jane Forbes, 12 when she was tried for picking pockets and convicted of stealing eight shillings and 14 when seaman William Carlo took her into his hammock. It sounds like cradle snatching and perhaps it was. However, we do not know anything of Carlo other than that he was old enough to go to sea and father a child. He may have been the same age as Jane Forbes—plenty of seamen were.

It may be that we only know about the younger "wives" because they did not have the older women's knowledge of contraception and swiftly became pregnant. A sailor's woman might be checked over for him by the surgeon to make sure she was clean of the pox but when it came to contraception, it was unlikely anything except a few words of advice was on offer. The days of mass handouts of condoms to men in the service were far in the future. Pregnancy was, of course, a woman's problem, as was any other unfortunate consequence of sexual intercourse. Condoms existed but were more to guard men against venereal disease than women against conception. Known as "English overcoats," they were generally designed for gentlemen of means and were sufficiently expensive to put them beyond the means of any but the most obsessively hygienic seaman. They were made of animal membrane and available in three sizes from London dealers such as Mrs. Phillips who, in 1776, "hath lately had several orders for France, Spain, Portugal, Italy, and other foreign places" and invited "captains of ships, and gentlemen going abroad" to procure "any quantity of the best goods on the shortest notice." Clearly England was leading the way in many fields of maritime exploration at the end of the eighteenth century.

There was naturally a body of knowledge among the women about how to prevent pregnancy and the advice of the orlop hold was more useful to the teenagers in the forecastle than any dispensed by Surgeon Alley. It was already known to physicians that sperm had some role in conception, hence the need for something to block its entry into the cervix. Nobody in Europe, physician or layman, would know about the fertilization of eggs from the ovaries for another fifty years. However, if the women on the sleeping shelves of the *Lady Julian*'s orlop deck did not know the exact sequence of the events inside them, or its terminology, surely after years of cohabitation or life on the streets they knew their way around the menstrual cycle well enough to realize some moments were more risky than others.

The most common method of prevention was simple douching after sex, with water and vinegar, alcohol, salt, soda or some other disinfecting and scouring substance. Some women used a syringe for this; some crouched over a pot of boiling liquid and fumigated themselves on its steam; others soaked a sponge with the mixture and inserted it like a tampon to absorb the semen. Rudimentary caps were also used. These ranged from half a squeezed lemon to beeswax, melted and carefully shaped to fit. These items may not have been available on board ship but the seamen who had sailed in the South Seas might have known of the technique used by islanders. They inserted seaweed into the vagina as a barrier. They may even have known of the custom of the Marquesas Islands, where group sex was common—one woman, several men—and etiquette was that the last man in sucked his own and everyone else's semen from the womb. About twelve women became pregnant on board the *Lady Julian*. Far more than this had sex during the voyage and, given that most of the women were of an age to be fertile, it seems some method of prevention was being used. Seawater and vinegar douches were routine, if ineffective; the low rate of pregnancy can more probably be attributed to the common practices of withdrawal, anal sex and abstinence at risky moments.

As the tide turned and Plymouth Sound began gradually to drain on 29 July 1789, the *Lady Julian* sailed out under topsails. She bulged with temporary excrescences: cattle pens, poultry boxes, shacks erected in the waist for storage and accommodation. The guns of the Grand Battery on Lord Mount Edgecumbe's estate slid slowly past to port, and the sound of workmen's hammers from the landing place below echoed across. Their Majesties were expected daily to visit the Mount Edgecumbes and there was much to do. The entire landing place was to be covered in soft red baize to welcome the royal feet as they stepped from the barge. A triumphal arch had still to be constructed for them to walk under and a posse of twenty-four small flower girls, in white with blue sashes, had yet to be taught to curtsey. This was the women's last clear view of England. Fewer than thirty would ever return.

That same week, the first refugees from the revolutionary mob on the other side of the Channel began to arrive from France. Among them was Lord Mazarin, who fell to his knees on the beaches of Kent and declared, "God bless this land of liberty!"

8

BECOMING IN TURNS OUTRAGEOUS

A couple of hours out from Plymouth Sound, the *Lady Julian*
cleared Penlee Point and headed west toward the open waters of the
Atlantic. Keeping a good offing from the rocks of the Cornish coast,
the easterlies took her round Ushant, from where a course was laid for
the northwesternmost corner of Spain. When the Spanish coast was
sighted, she would head off due south for the Canary Islands.

The first few days out were busy ones for Nicol, responsible to
Lieutenant Edgar for the storage and distribution of provisions. His
stores were probably kept forward of the women's quarters on the
orlop—a labyrinth of chests, trunks, barrels of biscuit, gunpowder,
sacks of flour, oats, malt and, stacked against the bulkhead dividing
the stores from the convicts' sleeping shelves, scores of wooden boxes
containing bottles of liquor. For most of the two days it took to leave
the Cornish coast behind, John Nicol was busy below deck, checking
his casks.

For the first several hours of activity, all women were confined to
the orlop, well out of the seamen's way. Leaving and entering port are
the busiest times for a crew: between these two moments of frenetic
activity, as long as nothing untoward happens, life on board a well-
run ship sailing at the right season is uneventful—trimming the sails,

cleaning, disinfecting, cooking, mending sails and nets. But the first moments of a ship's voyage, from when she leaves port until her course and sails are set, are terrifying to the uninitiated. The noise can induce panic in those who cannot attribute each sound to an ordered activity. Sails flap deafeningly until the wind begins to fill them, ropes crack, urgent commands are shouted incomprehensibly, men run from one side of the ship to the other. When the sails were set and the ship was in good order, her motion settled and crashes and shouts on deck became fewer. The orlop hatches were removed and there would have been calls for the women to come on deck. Some would already have been suffering their first bout of seasickness and hung over the side to vomit into the salty water or gaze at the Cornish headlands. Then they left Cornwall behind; from now on, it was parts beyond the seas.

By the time the *Lady Julian* left Plymouth Sound, she had become familiar to most women on board. For many, she had been home for several months. They knew their way from the orlop to the 'tween deck to the forecastle. They were familiar with the galley and knew where the tradesmen and officers messed and slept. They had watched work being done to the hull and masts; they had seen vast areas of canvas laid out on the dockside and later knotted to the masts and spars; they had seen cables and shrouds attached and tested as the ship was rigged in Deptford. They were familiar with the feel of timbers beneath bare feet and the smell of her bilge. They knew what was meant by aft and forrard and leeward and below, which was the mizzen and which the main, which was a halyard and which a sheet. But a sailing ship at sea is a different animal from a sailing ship in port—a foreign land, with laws and language incomprehensible to strangers.

The small world of the *Lady Julian* now ran on three 8-hour watches, its work dictated by shifts in the direction and force of wind and current which could occur at any hour in the 24-hour cycle. Constant prediction and detection of these changes was the task of the officers commanding the watches. At every hour of the watch, a senior officer was looking upward at the sails, or forward to the fore-castle, commands were passing from mate to midshipman, midship-man to bosun, bosun's pipe to barefoot seamen streaming upward and outward to trim the sails. It was the number and position of sails up, far more than the rudder, which kept the ship on course. Upward of twenty separate sails could be set and then adjusted, according to the direction and strength of the winds, and the choreography of the men among the masts was crucial to the ship's speed and the ease of her movement. One member of the team aloft stood lookout at the masthead. Another two manned the wheel below while a gang of oth-ers padded ceaselessly about the ship checking, splicing, coiling, patching, mending, greasing, painting—the whole unending business of "making shipshape."

The sailors themselves were different at sea. The women had known ordinary men, with ordinary skills. They suddenly became creatures of prehensile ability who would swarm 50 feet above deck up a rope and spend hours aloft protected only by a sense of balance. The young gentlemen and ship's boys were no longer spotty lads who blushed at the convicts' jibes. The carpenter, whom the women had seen in the Thames engaged in tasks not so different from those of any onshore chippy, revealed his own arcane knowledge of the ship's body. He was her physician: it was his task to know where she was scarred and how well she had healed, where her weak points were and how much she could bear, the age and seasoning of her skins, the warps and wrinkles in her timbers and the level of water which washed around her belly. The most impressive transformation was that of Lieutenant Edgar from a kindly old sot with a flask in his garter to ship's navigator. It was he who would draw the *Lady Julian* by an invisible thread of calculations and sights through months of empty horizons into the mouth of a river he had never seen 13,000 miles away.

The *Lady Julian* herself was a different creature at sea. The parts of the ship moved differently, each in relation to the other. The behav-ior of walls and floors changed; even the separate timbers moved in a different way. Everyone had to learn how to stay in time with the heave of the deck away from and toward her and to flex the knee to lengthen and shorten a leg whose support was never constant. Everyone now learned how to approach the ladders from orlop to 'tween deck and from 'tween deck through the hatch by catching a movement which helped her up and waiting through the next, which could send her sprawling back. The women discovered handholds they had never noticed to keep themselves upright when the deck tilted. They found where to get shelter from spray or sun, where to stand for air and light, where and when to vomit.

For many on board, the first experience of being at sea was this: vomiting copiously over the side of the sleeping shelf, or the deck if they could reach it. Little could be done to alleviate seasickness; many officers were also suffering during those first days at sea. Years in the service were no guarantee against vulnerability—Nelson was a famous vomiter. His solution was to forsake the bunks with which officers' accommodation was equipped and sleep in a hammock. This remained stable while the ship moved around it, whereas a bunk bucked and plunged with the ship. The hammock protected most ordinary seamen against seasickness. There was more vomiting over the side of bunks aft of the mast than there was over the side of hammocks before it—and there was most of all in the sleeping shelves at the bottom of the ship.

The movement of the ship may have made the women queasy but in other ways conditions were pleasanter on the open sea than they had been in Plymouth Sound. The seawater through which they were moving was clean, whereas in the Sound (and even more so in the River Thames) they had sat in water soiled by their own refuse each day until the tides cleansed their berth. In the heat of July, Plymouth Sound had smelled like one vast privy. As they sailed toward Spain, they left their effluent in their wake and the air was clean—or cleanish. One stench provoker they had not left behind was the ballast.

Ships of the vintage of the *Lady Julian* were ballasted with a noxious mix of sand and gravel. Boards partitioned the hull like the sections of a quilt and an even quantity of ballast was loaded into each section. It went in loose, not casked, making it tricky to remove and replace and impossible to clean. It then rattled and swished about the bilge for years, growing steadily more foul as it absorbed the waste of years of life on board. Dead rats, dead cats, compost from mounds of vegetable peelings, feces, urine, rotting fabric and decomposing sick all lay below the boards. The smell of an old bilge was notorious: on one of the First Fleet transports, bilge gas seeping out not only blackened the wooden wall panels of the cabins on the lowest deck but tarnished the officers' gilt buttons. Even with the bilges shut, the stink of the ballast pervaded the ship, strongest at the lowest level where the women slept. The only place where the air was completely free of the smell was the windward quarter of the quarterdeck, and this small space, by unwritten law, was sacred to the captain.

Apart from its uncleanable bilge, the ship was as clean as salt water, gunpowder, holystones,[13] whitewash, vinegar and dozens of women on hands and knees scrubbing the decks could make it. It was believed that foulness trapped in the air contributed to or caused typhus and scurvy, the two diseases most common to crowded prisons and ships, and that sweet-smelling and free-flowing air would keep these at bay. "I would recommend," wrote a respected physician and writer on the prevention of scurvy, "putting a red-hot loggerhead[14] in a bucket of tar, which should be moved about, so that all the ship may be filled with this wholesome antiseptic vapour." Whenever conditions allowed it at sea or in port, the air between decks was rigorously "cleansed" with this and other methods. Braziers burned aromatic herbs, when available, or the men boiled up cauldrons of pitch below deck. Another method of dispersing foul air was to explode small quantities of gunpowder between decks. Its acrid smoke was, like the vapor of tar, believed to dispel any "myasma" from polluted breath or perspiration.

---

[13] Soft sandstone used to scour decks.
[14] A poker heated and inserted into a bucket of pitch to melt it.

During the daytime, toilet arrangements at sea were clean and effi-
cient. The "heads" was an open platform with holes cut in it, lashed
to the aftmost section of the bowsprit. This was the lavatory, through
which sailors and women urinated or defecated directly into the sea
below, rinsing off with a bucket of salt water. It was cleaner and easier
than today's method of the pump toilet. The women of the *Lady
Julian* also enjoyed the advantage of not wearing any knickers. They
just hitched a petticoat, squatted, rinsed and staggered back to their
seat in the forecastle.

By night, when 200 women were shut into the orlop hold, it was
all rather less hygienic. The orlop was equipped with "easing-chairs,"
or commodes. The most prized berths were furthest from these and
closest to the hatches, which gave some ventilation. The majority of
women had now been living together in an all-female environment
for months, even years, and their menstrual cycles would have started
to synchronize. One week each month, the distinctive odor of menstrual blood was added to the smell of the easing-chairs. Wads of
folded fabric were used as sanitary napkins, pinned to the bottom of
the stays or held up by a piece of cord around the waist. They
absorbed not only blood but salt water from spray, and chafed the
thighs and groin. If there was a rush of blood too great to be
absorbed, it ran into the women's clothes and remained there until
next laundry day. The passage from Plymouth Sound to Santa Cruz
de Tenerife in the Canary Islands was roughly the length of one menstrual cycle. With fresh water a precious commodity at sea, the
women had a choice of boiling their pads in salt water with the other
laundry, which would render them irritating in the extreme to the
flesh, or packing them away for washing when they got to Santa Cruz
and more fresh water was available. If they chose the second course,
the smell of 200 dirty sanitary napkins stuffed under mattresses in the
orlop hold must have almost beaten the ballast.

Despite the smell of old sand, urine and menstrual blood, the
orlop deck of the *Lady Julian* was a cleaner and more comfortable
place to sleep than many women had endured before coming on

board. There were cockroaches, lice, fleas and rats—but what tenement, let alone gaol cell, did not have these? What the tenements and gaol cells had lacked was the discipline and rigorous hygiene enforced by good officers at sea. This ensured that their quarters were clean and their bedding dry, as long as weather conditions permitted. The cleaning and airing of clothes and hammocks which protected long-haul seamen against rheumatism and fever was imposed from the top, notoriously to grumbles from the seamen themselves. Orders were bellowed down the waist for the hammocks to be brought out and aired, the men complained they had been out and aired yesterday and were bellowed at to get them out and aired again. Extreme captains lined up both men and officers and inspected their linen. Edgar's old brother officer William Bligh, who took paternalism a little far but was nevertheless a sound Cook-trained officer, wrote testily that "simply to give [the seamen] orders that they are to keep themselves clean and dry as circumstances will allow, is of little avail, they must be watched like Children." The women in the orlop hold were to be treated with the same benign strictness. Edgar and Surgeon Alley were responsible for seeing that at least twice a week the bottom boards of their sleeping shelves were brought on deck and scrubbed with salt water, that the sides of the orlop hold were scraped and the floorboards swept. As a direct result, they lived in greater comfort during the first stage of their voyage to Sydney Cove than in the gaols and tenements they had just left behind.

The endless cleaning, scrubbing, scenting and airing served the second purpose of keeping the women occupied. The *Lady Julian* was now a ship at sea but she was also a gaol and, just as the ship ran to unwritten laws on deck, so did the gaol below. The majority of the women were faceless and harmless—a docile mass which curled into the sleeping shelves at the bottom of the ship by night and sat in groups about the deck by day—but some were troublemakers. Fighting among women convicts was as vicious and frequent as among men. "If there was ever a hell afloat, it must have been in the shape of a female convict ship—quarrelling, fighting, thieving, destroying in private each other's property from a mere spirit of devilishness," reported the surgeon of a later ship. Scarcely an officer sailed on a female transport but did not somewhere report in exasperation, like Lieutenant Clark, that "the damned whores the moment they got below fel a fighting amongst one another."

The codes of Newgate were alive and well on the bottom deck after lights-out. "Among such a Number that has been Convicted for Different Depredations on the public it is hardly to be thought when reduced to the lowest Ebb of poverty but they will Rob one another," wrote a shocked middle-class observer, but this is exactly what convicts on all transports did. Each woman kept very few personal possessions in her shelf, as all trunks had been stowed away when they first went on board. But those few personal effects they had—a blanket, a drinking cup, a spoon, trinkets, a few coins, a bottle of liquor— were as unsafe from each other on the *Lady Julian* as they had been in the lodging houses of St. Giles or the cells of Newgate. As in any concentration of people in a confined space, convicts in the orlop hold quickly developed their own rules and hierarchies. Gangs formed. Those who had committed vicious assaults in Seven Dials or Cable Street for trinkets worth pence were not going to stop committing them on board ship. Some became bullies and others became victims.

More fortunate women had been taken away from this situation and into the relative safety of the men's accommodation. It is possible that those women taken as wife by the officers took advantage of their position to demand services or gifts from the women they had left beneath them on the orlop, given the strict notions of hierarchy in the eighteenth-century mind, and the compulsion never to pass up an opportunity to acquire the property of others which dominated many of these particular eighteenth-century citizens. Officers' mates may have exempted themselves from cooking and cleaning tasks, requiring other women to perform these for them; they may have gone as far as demanding presents, or at least letting it be known that presents would be acceptable, to win an officer's favor or protection.

Down on the orlop, it was not theft alone which beset the weaker convicts, but the intimidation which led to it and covered it up. When the hatches were barred at dusk, the weaker were left at the mercy of the stronger below deck. A stolen item could not go far from its owner within the contained world of a ship at sea but a victim who complained to the officers placed herself at great personal risk by night. A diary written by a convict who sailed in 1798 recounts what an informer could expect from the gang leaders below deck. He nearly had his tongue cut off. In the end, his tormentors contented themselves with sticking needles through it and then beating him senseless.

After the initial shock of being at sea, those among the women who were habitually abusive or troublesome found their feet and reverted to their old habits. Once more, the seamen could expect a running commentary on their mothers, physiques and sexual activities from an irritating few who were always the last up the hatch in the morning, the last down at night, the laziest with mops and holystone, the first to get into a fight. This group was led by a woman John Nicol remembered as Nance Ferrel, who may have been the 34-year-old Ann Flavell from Gloucester, who appears in other documents but whose indictment and sentence have been lost; or the Bett Farrell who broke into a house in Smithfield to steal the washing. The men had found that the best method to deal with Nance and her friends when they were disobedient or abusive was simply to send them below, where the movement and lack of air would soon have them retching and begging to come back up and promising to be good. The crew was perplexed when Nance, then one after another of her little group, became "in turns outrageous, on purpose to be confined."

It was during a routine overhaul of the casks stored forward of the bulkhead which closed off the women's quarters that Nicol discovered two of his casks had been broken into. One entire hogshead of bottles of port had been drunk, and the empty bottles neatly replaced. Another had been started, with the empty bottles concealed at the back and full ones brought forward. Exploring further, he found a box of candles gone and a hole in the bulkhead. The ladies had been holding drinking parties. Nicol placed everything neatly back in its place so as to alert no one and climbed the ladders to consult with Edgar. The lieutenant had a punishment up his sleeve. Nicol went off giggling to prepare a barrel and Edgar gave the order that next time Nance and the girls swore at the men, they were to be ignored. Shortly afterward, Nance herself appeared with a few followers. Choosing her man, she fired off a list of casual curses and waited. The sailor blinked and went about his tasks. The women moved on, Nance shifted up a gear in language and imagination, and insulted the next man in line. He, too, continued coiling his rope. The women then turned to the petty officers, who smiled and passed on. Steaming past the midshipmen, Nance tore through the ranks until she had climbed the ladder to the quarterdeck—a piece of impudence for which a seaman would have been flogged—and was insulting Captain Aitken himself.

Lieutenant Edgar now beckoned to John Nicol, lurking behind the wheel. Nance was seized and an empty wooden barrel with holes in the top and sides was forced over her head. For the seamen and officers, it was a great joke. They came running to mock. So did the women, although not too obviously as they did not want to find her standing over their beds with a darning needle during the night. At first, Nance made the best of it. She strutted up and down the quarterdeck, playing to her audience below, pretending not to care; she danced a little minuet back and forth, feet and head moving like a turtle's; she cracked some jokes. But a wooden barrel is heavy and its whole weight rested on her shoulders and she could not sit: if she rested the barrel on the floor, her legs were forced into a painful crouch. Eventually, she begged to be released, promising good behavior, and the jacket was removed.

Nance's good behavior did not last long. "There was no taming her by gentle means," Nicol wrote. Within a week, she was cursing as roundly as before. This time, the officers were not as lenient. "We were forced to tie her up like a man, and give her one dozen with the cat o'nine tails and assure her of a clawing every offence. This

alone reduced her to any kind of order." Brutality was never far
away.

The *Lady Julian* sailed on, her decks once more quiet, toward the
Canary archipelago. Two and a half weeks out from Plymouth Sound,
she passed Madeira and changed course a couple of degrees to head
due south for Tenerife. Sailing through the archipelago was a novel
experience for the women—their first taste of gales at sea. In fact, these
were short-lived gusts of gale force rather than the true gales they
would experience some months later in the Southern Ocean, but still
exhilarating. Around the string of African islands, the northeast trade
winds have the trick of dividing at the northern end, creating a huge
eddy around the island, and reuniting at the southern tip. The winds
suddenly accelerate to full gale force down the length of each coast
before fading away to almost nothing at the southern end. The seas
remain gentle. The *Lady Julian,* under full sail, forged along and
finally they sighted the low-lying coast of the island of Tenerife.

Santa Cruz de Tenerife is on the northern coast of the island, sheltered from the prevailing winds by a pronged headland. Well before
the first sails were reduced, the women were sent below. They
sweated in their sleeping shelves and listened to the noises on deck as
the *Lady Julian* approached land. An eleven-gun salute from the
Castillo de San Juan woke the babies. There was a terrific flap and
slither of canvas and a scream of hemp as the mainsails came down to
reduce the ship's speed through the water. Water breaking against the
hull gentled as she slid into more sheltered waters, then a sharp turn
through 90 degrees as the ship brought her bow up into the wind
threw them into a heap. Babies wailed over the echo of orders relayed
by speaking trumpet from quarterdeck to waist and lung power from
waist to forecastle. The massive anchor cable forward thundered out
and they floated slowly backward until a slight tug brought the ship
to rest when the anchor bit. She settled to a steady quiver against the
cable and there was silence, broken only by the slap of water against
her side and the pad of the seamen's feet on deck. When the hatches
were removed, the women came up the ladders for their first glimpse

of foreign parts. They saw a dirty beach, a castle in the far corner of the bay, a ring of guns and fortifications; low white houses shimmering in the August heat with ragged mountains rising behind and a snow-covered peak just visible in the distance, a stone pier with windmills to one side and a port full of slave ships.

9

SANTA CRUZ DE TENERIFE

*B*locks squealed and the captain's barge was lowered into the water. Captain Aitken and Lieutenant Edgar stuffed themselves into their best breeches, adjusted their tricorns and were rowed off to represent His Majesty to the Spanish governor and request permission to land. It was a formality which would become familiar to the women at later ports of call. The seamen set to work bringing up the empty water casks, shoving the women out of the way to roll them along the deck and lower them over the side into the longboats.

A river flowed down into Santa Cruz from the mountains of the hinterland and supplied both the town and visiting shipping. The water was conveyed along a gently sloping aqueduct to a pier in the bay, supported over the gullies in the hills by posts stout enough to hold it through the winter floods. When the captain and agent returned from visiting Governor Branquefort, the longboats rowed off with their first load of empty casks to be filled from the pier tanks. The water brought on board in Plymouth Sound three weeks ago was already brackish and the fresh water eagerly drunk; too eagerly, women rushed to the heads with "the flux"[15] as their

---

[15] Diarrhea.

systems readjusted. The seawater around the hull began to pollute
the air.

That day, or the next, there was an orgy of laundry on board. At
sea, dirty linen was washed in salt water, which turned it clammy and
stiff and caused rashes under the collar, in the armpits and, for the
officers, around the groin. Women and seamen were spared the rash
by the looseness of skirts and the baggy knee-length "trowsers" worn
before the mast. Officers' breeches fit snugly around the crotch and
underneath them, saltwater rash itched like poison ivy. Fires were lit
on deck, cauldrons of water boiled, heaps of dirty clothes dumped
next to them and parties of women rolled up their sleeves and set to
for the biggest laundry day since Plymouth.

With nothing in the way of detergent, the dirt was boiled and
then beaten out of the linen. Stripped to the minimum required by
decency, the women did the washing. The top deck trembled as rows
of them, up and down the waist of the ship, thwacked its timbers
with shirts, shifts, sheets, hammocks, trews[16] and a vast pile of sanitary napkins. Rivulets of filthy water trickled down the sides. By the
evening, the rails and rigging of the ship were festooned with drying
clothes and laundry had turned to horseplay. Faint female shrieks
floated across to other ships at anchor. Shadows were cast of capering
figures throwing water at each other and those crews in Santa Cruz
who had not heard the news that a ship full of English whores was in
port wondered what was going on.

Casks full, laundry done; now the provisioning rounds began and
Lieutenant Edgar went ashore to place his orders. His priorities were
greens and fresh meat. A well-established shambles on the waterfront
took care of ships' fresh and salt meat orders. Bulk fruit and vegetables were procured from the orchards and market gardens of Oratava,
a small town a few miles inland.

Officers applied to Captain Aitken for permission to sleep out of
the ship, taking up lodgings on dry land for the duration of their stay

---

[16] Sailor's trousers which came to mid-calf.

in Santa Cruz. Not all could go at once, clearly; those who slept out of the ship here would forgo the privilege in Cape Town and vice versa. Those women taken "as wife" by the officers perhaps came into one of the privileges which went with their status and followed them to their beds ashore as they had followed them into their berths afloat. Seamen were also allowed ashore in small groups, accompanied always by an officer. British seamen in the eighteenth century were known for causing trouble where late night bars served cheap liquor. Officers spoke gravely of "the Enormities which English seamen are too apt to commit in foreign Ports," and local authorities were anxious that each ship take responsibility for the behavior of her own men. In some ports, groups of ordinary seamen could not go ashore without an escort from the local militia, but the governor in Tenerife permitted them to be escorted by one of their own officers. The officers of the *Lady Julian* were aware of their responsibilities—not only would "Enormities" damage the name of the ship, her commanding officer and the British marine, but if one of the men in their party was arrested and incarcerated, the captain would face a fee of several dollars to get him out. One part of this would be recuperated from the man who had caused the trouble and another from the officer who had allowed him to do so.

Decisions as to which of the officers and which of the men could be allowed ashore at any time were taken by Captain Aitken, advised by the first mate, according to well-understood regulations and order of precedence. Lieutenant Edgar had the more difficult task of deciding which of the women could go ashore, with whom and when. It comes as something of a shock to realize from John Nicol's memoirs and journals left by later convicts that some prisoners spent their time in ports en route not fettered in the hold, as convict legend would have it, but strolling the streets and getting in some shopping. A society pickpocket who sailed in 1792, George Barrington, was treated by the officers almost as one of themselves, dining with them on board ship and accompanying them on day trips whenever they were in port. Women on the *Lady Julian* presumably did the same. A handful were of similar status to Barrington—literate, amusing, presentable.

Mrs. Barnsley was unquestionably the First Lady of the ship. It was Elizabeth Barnsley, highwayman's sister and shoplifter of distinction, who had requested Lieutenant Edgar's permission to wear her own fine clothes on the Thames. He had to refuse then, but as soon as the *Lady Julian* left Plymouth Sound, she reminded him of his promise to let her do so when they put to sea. Elizabeth Barnsley therefore lived in clothes acquired in Bond Street while her shipmates lived in brown serge. It is unlikely that she slept in the hold. Money would have found her a better bunk and a little privacy on the *Lady Julian* as it had done on the Master's Side of Newgate, perhaps in one of the huts built onto the waist of the ship. Surprisingly, she does not seem to have been unpopular—in fact, quite the opposite, as she had qualities which made her a leader among the convicts. She was 29 when the ship sailed—too old to be competing for the attention of the seamen (who were probably rather in awe of her anyway)—and thus steered clear of scraps over sailors' favors. She was intelligent and literate and this skill alone would have attracted admiration. She would have been able to express the other women's requests and complaints to the officers and be listened to. Last, she was generous with her money.

In Tenerife, Mrs. Barnsley decided she would treat her circle to a cask of Canary wine, which she would herself choose from one of the bodegas along the shore. Lieutenant Edgar was informed of her wishes. He had no reason to deny her and it would not have been shrewd to antagonize a clever woman with a following below deck. Elizabeth Barnsley was rowed off to be escorted through the wine cellars of Santa Cruz, probably by an officer. She was, after all, a lady. She was also a thief and a liar and an officer escort would prevent embarrassing incidents.

Weary Watkin Tench, lieutenant with the First Fleet, thought that "there is little to please a traveller in Tenerife." He damned the town with faint praise as "neither irregular in its plan, nor despicable in its style of building" and was displeased by the "importunity of the beggars and the immodesty of the lowest class of women." Santa Cruz certainly lacked the glamour of the South American cities and the prosperity of the Dutch ones and for men who had traveled the world, perhaps there was little here that was not bigger, brighter, higher or hotter somewhere else. But for the women, Tenerife represented all that was exotic. George Barrington would describe the governor's palace as having "the appearance more of an auberge than the palace of a Spanish grandee." Forecastle wives like Sarah Whitelam, Mary Warren and Ann Bryant, who had spent their lives in English market towns, did not know what a Spanish grandee's palace looked like, nor that the governor's palace fell short of it. If you were 19 and came from Lincolnshire, Tenerife was the height of exoticism. It was the women's first experience of being surrounded by the sound of a language not their own. They had never seen a peak the height of the Pico de Teide or lived in a climate in which snow covered a mountaintop while sultry heat hung over the beaches. They had never walked along streets overlooked by a painted Virgin, nor seen bougainvillea, palm trees, banana plants, grapes hanging from the vine and fresh dates, nor urchins with the brown skin of Spain instead of the pinched pallor of London. Women did not walk the streets in black drapes and a scarf over their head in provincial Lincolnshire; they did not cross themselves when they passed a church in Maidstone. The *Lady Julian* wives did not see the dull town which bored Lieutenant Tench. They saw dark skin, fruit, color and the insistent presence of an alien church in the nuns and friars who passed them on the streets, the statues in niches, the murals, the genuflections, the bells and the incense.

Not all had brought money with them from England to go shopping with Mrs. Barnsley but some on board were willing to earn it on the way out. By now, word had gone out around the town that 230 fallen females were aboard the squat little ship flying a Red Ensign in the harbor. When small groups of them appeared in the streets, accompanied by boisterous British seamen, some islanders would cross themselves and let the shutters down, others spat and muttered but the more charitable reacted with pity. Pity could mean cash. One of John Nicol's Santa Cruz anecdotes concerns a group of Jewish convicts led by a woman called Sarah Sabolah, probably an alias or family name of the Jewish thief Sarah Lyons, convicted the previous year of stuffing 7 yards of handkerchief silk up her skirt in a London drapery.

Sarah Sabolah's Santa Cruz exploit must have been carried out with the knowledge of the officers or she and her friends would never have got a lift to the beach or acquired their props, a couple of bolts of cloth and some pieces of wood. She and her group were dropped at one end of the quay, robed themselves in borrowed black and shook the froth from the crucifixes they had knocked together in the orlop hold. Then they assumed suitable expressions and processed solemnly from one end of the main drag to the other. Even among a people as accustomed to lavish displays of penitence and piety as the Canary Catholics, the trudging line of barefoot English convicts, bowed beneath their crosses, caused a stir. The *paseo* parted to let them through and the convicts accepted the coins and benedictions pressed on them. Sarah Sabolah must have been a woman of some cunning to have come up with the scheme in the first place and may have sewed her share into her seams for a rainy day. Others had probably drunk the profits away before they left Tenerife.

Scamming the burghers of Santa Cruz was not the easiest way to make money. "We allowed the people to come freely aboard; the seamen and captains of the visiting ships paid us many visits," John Nicol remembered. There was nothing unusual in the shipboard commerce of sex, but usually it was the prostitutes who were rowed out to the men, not the men who were rowed out to the prostitutes. A splendidly simple explanation was offered by a historian in 1990: "the women—mainly London prostitutes—turned the ship into a floating brothel," bringing to a resounding conclusion the tradition of blaming prostitution on the prostitutes. Where there is a prostitute, there is a pimp—and who played this role in Santa Cruz? Once again, the rules which governed life in Ratcliff and Newgate emerged aboard the *Lady Julian* and some of the "half the prize and half the profit" must have gone into the sailors' sea chests.

We enter the realm of pure hypothesis when imagining negotiations between seaman and seaman's "wife." Who knows what deals were struck by a sailor who saw his pretty hammock mate and her little friends in the orlop not only as recreation but also potential cash cows? A bottle of wine, a length of embroidered ribbon, a trinket, a quarter dollar? Whatever the deal he made, it seems to have been tolerated at the top. Lieutenant Edgar had a better idea than most of what awaited the women. He knew that any money made turning tricks in Santa Cruz would serve them well in Sydney Cove—allowing prostitution was an act of pity as much as of negligence. So the seamen from the other ships in port and thrill seekers from the shore rowed across to the ship full of whores and, throughout the *Lady Julian*'s stay in Santa Cruz, some of the shelves in her hold, the hammocks in her forecastle and the huts on her deck were turned over to commerce.

It must have been the seamen who advertised the ship's wares and made the assignations, making sure the promised party of half a dozen pox-free girls was waiting when the group of neighboring seamen rowed over; perhaps collecting the money and dividing it among the girls when they rowed off again. However, the business community on board did not consist solely of men. It was by agreement and negotiation, not by male coercion, that some women sold sex in Santa Cruz. The girls most in demand were not necessarily those best able to defend their own interests. In the network of request and negotiation which sprang up in Tenerife, female pimps must also have played their part. Theirs could have been a protective role—an advisory service by the more to the less experienced on how to make the most of the situation. But there was probably as much pressure exerted and as many deals struck in the orlop as in the forecastle. There was one bawd down on the shelves with no fewer than three of her former girls on board: Elizabeth Sully had apparently run Poll Randall, Mary Butler and Mary Bateman in Cable Street. She and other canny women would have been making their own deals with the forecastle in Santa Cruz.

The quarterdeck, too, was implicated in these transactions. Lieutenant Edgar and Captain Aitken clearly countenanced the sale of sex on board. Officers used prostitutes no less than seamen and plenty of officers came on board in Santa Cruz. When the officers of the *Lady Julian* passed discreet orders for the entertainment of visitors, the likeliest go-between from captain's cabin to orlop deck was his steward, John Nicol. It would have been John who reported back the orlop's estimate of cost and conducted negotiations between the two until agreement was reached. A forecast of the entertainment value of the women chosen would determine whether they were invited to join the officers for dinner first in the captain's cabin or if the officer simply received his female visitor in some secluded spot. Aitken and Edgar presumably did not receive the sort of cash for services that the men in the forecastle and the pimps in the orlop would have wanted but no visiting officer would turn up without a box of fine cigars or a particularly good bottle of port for the captain's table.

The officers participated in the Santa Cruz pimping for reasons of prudence as well as interest, as much to keep charge of the situation as to profit by it. The only way a woman could escape the *Lady Julian* was to sell herself to a seaman from another ship in return for being smuggled away. Two women off the First Fleet had already escaped Sydney Cove on the French ships of exploration which had nosed in a few days after the British arrived. The men with them had been turned down. Four women had already escaped in the Thames and Edgar could not afford the embarrassment of losing any more in Tenerife.

The most faithful of the convicts' customers, in John Nicol's memory, were the crews of two slavers on their way to or from The Gambia. The men on board could have been British, Spanish, American, Portuguese, French, Danish or Dutch, for all these nationalities were eager carriers of slaves from the African coast. Most visitors to Santa Cruz were interested in the produce brought down to the wharfside markets to supply shipping: blankets, oil, corn, vino seco, fruit, vegetables, "milch goats," pumpkins, onions, figs in season, grapes. An encounter with "the abandoned dock women of Tenerife" was also considered an essential diversion for the younger visitor, but the real money made from ships passing through the bay came from slaving. The silver dollars of the slavers who bought in stores at Santa Cruz on their way from the Americas to the African coast were the engine of the Canary economy.

Canary slave profits did not come only from spin-offs of the trade, however: a slave market was held every Sunday outside the Castillo de San Juan and officers ashore probably stopped by to watch. Slavery had been outlawed in Britain by a high court judgment of 1772, by which any Negro bought as a slave elsewhere became a free person from the moment of setting foot in England. (The judgment did not extend to preventing British merchants from participating in the overseas slave trade.) Most of the city women on board the *Lady Julian* had already seen black skin before they were confronted with the chained Negroes on sale in Santa Cruz. London shoplifter Elizabeth Smith alias Cave had committed her crime with a Negro accomplice, named in the court records only as "Thomas, a Black Man." A colony of Negroes manumitted under the 1772 judgment lived around the docks of most sea cities, along with Chinese seamen looking for a berth to Canton, lascars looking for a berth to Calcutta and other floating foreigners.

A humanitarian, usually Christian, objection was beginning to be heard to the participation of British merchants in the overseas slave trade. Much of the public comment hostile to transportation of convicts was couched in terms borrowed from criticism of slavery. Until France became the home of people power later that year, it was Britain which was considered, and considered itself, the champion of sturdy egalitarianism. Its citizens were notorious for the defense of their liberties, particularly in contrast to the serfs across the Channel. These liberties belonged only to male British citizens, of course; despite the constant John Bull rhetoric about liberty, Britain was the country where "a married woman was the nearest approximation in free society to a slave" and the rights of an unmarried one little better. Romantic convict history, the stuff of ballad and campfire verse, would draw on a supposed fellow feeling among the downtrodden—

convicts, slaves, Aborigines. This is "the flimsiest sentiment," to borrow a robust phrase from Robert Hughes. It is profoundly unlikely that any woman in Santa Cruz drew analogies between the situation of the African slaves on sale and her own situation on board the *Lady Julian*. Political comment was alien to the lives of these women. Fear of the savage was not. They did not see brothers and sisters in suffering among the merchandise blinking in its fetters outside the Castillo de San Juan. They saw "savages," "blacks," "Africans," seminaked creatures with sores around their mouths, frightened and incomprehensible, ripe with an alien sweat. The men who traded them and took some of their profits aboard the *Lady Julian* were probably no more odious to the convicts than were the seamen in the forecastle of their own ship.

In the second week of September, watered, provisioned and cashed up, the *Lady Julian* left Santa Cruz and headed for the Dutch settlement of Cape Town at the southern tip of Africa. This was another well-worn international trade route. Cape Town was the principal stopover before and after the Dutch Spice Islands and the British trading networks on the coasts of India. It was intended to be a ten- to twelve-week, 6,000-mile passage before the Trades with a brief watering stop at Cabo Verde. They would not arrive for five and a half months.

The first brake on the voyage were the slave ships they had picked up in Santa Cruz. When the British ship set sail, the two crews of slavers decided to travel south in convoy "for the sake," said John Nicol, "of the ladies." The route to São Tiago, Cabo Verde, took them west-southwest about 400 miles off the west African coast. For three days, the Peak of Tenerife was clearly visible behind them, its summit still snowcapped. Daily, it seems, cheerful slavers rowed across for rest and recreation with the connivance of Captain Aitken and Agent Edgar, driven by compassion or profit. A week out, the man at the masthead spotted the islands of São Nicolau and Boa Vista on the starboard beam. The following day, the little convoy made São Tiago. Canvas flapped, hemp howled, the anchor bit the sand eight fathoms below. The women emerged into a fierce heat.

They had left the rule of the Spaniards behind. Porto Praia was a far smaller harbor than Santa Cruz, and the town far poorer, its inhabitants more peasants than merchants. The Kingdom of Portugal was in charge here and the islands were "exceedingly oppressed by the Portuguese soldiery, who exact an exorbitant toll from the country-men who bring their commodities to market." A Portuguese cartel controlled both price and supply of provisions to visiting ships. Who-ever was selling, the *Lady Julian* had to buy for the voyage to Cape Town. Nicol had been made cautious by previous Cabo Verde expe-rience: "The Portuguese here are great rogues . . . I bought 2 fat sheep from one of them. The bargain was made and I was going to lead away my purchase, when he gave a whistle and my sheep scampered off to the fields." New purchases were haltered as soon as dollars changed hands, reluctant bullocks tied to the painter of a cutter and swum out to the ship, bellowing. The decks of the *Lady Julian* once more steamed with dung. Watering arrangements were more primi-tive in Porto Praia than in Santa Cruz. The closest well was about 1,200 yards up the beach, down which a rolling way for casks had been constructed. At the bottom end, the casks had to be roped together and floated out to the ship.

Among the convicts, the poorer women who had not had the means to treat themselves to Canary wine in Santa Cruz found they could do business in Cabo Verde. The islanders willingly swapped food and wine for their clothes and trinkets. Bargains were struck on the beach at Porto Praia, where "the Air is remarkable Hot and to Europeing very unwholesome," which would be bitterly regretted further south. They stayed only one day here, possibly to avoid the mooring fee exacted by the Portuguese "Captain-Moor." His shoddy palace stood some way out of town and it generally took more than twenty-four hours, especially in the heat of summer, for a slovenly guard to amble over and collect the $4 fee. Porto Praia was the *Lady Julian*'s last, brief stop in the Northern Hemisphere.

The sea route from Canary to Cape Town bulges far out into the Atlantic Ocean, following the currents which swirl in an inverted "S" between Canary and the Cape—clockwise to the north of the equator, anticlockwise to the south. Ships heading for the Cape sailed along the northern currents from the African islands as far as the coast of Brazil with a following wind, then turned and headed southeast with the wind on the port beam. The right season for this passage was autumn, when the seas were still kind and the trade winds were steady. If the Trades blew well and constantly, it was a swift and pleasant voyage. The area of risk straddled the Equatorial Line, a 200-mile stretch of fitful ocean known as the Doldrums, and it was here that the *Lady Julian* would sail into serious trouble a few weeks later.

For the first week out from Cabo Verde, the sailing was easy. With the trade winds blowing a consistent Force 4–5 from the northeast, there was a minimum of work to be done trimming the sails and the sailors aloft took advantage of the good weather to put in a few days on maintenance, checking the hemp ropes for chafe. Ship's companies often spent good weather days preceding a rougher passage later on a long voyage cutting out and sewing a complete new set of sails. The *Lady Julian* would need one leaving Cape Town for the gales of the Southern Ocean. Skilled women may have helped the men on deck with this, or they may have been kept to picking oakum, the traditional prison task of untwisting condemned rope into lumps of hairy fluff which was part of the mixture stuffed between the boards of a ship. These were pleasant days, with all the women and most of the men on deck, whittling, mending, knotting, painting, greasing the blocks and making all the small pieces of equipment which were necessary for the ship and kept them from being idle. With a deck full of women to be talked to, keeping the men busy was important for discipline.

Enough unpleasant tasks needed to be done that the men were in little danger of going soft. Pumping was one. If Lieutenant Edgar followed the same rules of shipboard health as Captain Bligh in equatorial temperatures, the first mate had the men pumping water from one side of the ship to another for a sweaty hour or two each day to cool the air below deck. When pumping was finished, there was the utterly foul task of slushing down the mast. Some unfortunate was given a pot of old dripping from the galley and sent to the masthead, from where he worked his way down rubbing in the fat with his hands as he went. It preserved the wood and helped the tackle run up and down the mast more easily; it was also a usefully nasty task to hand out to a lazy seaman. His colleagues meanwhile sat under the awnings which kept the fierce afternoon heat off the decks, their backs against sun-warmed blocks, spinning yarn or manufacturing rope bands and points, explaining their Tahitian tattoos and their American scars to the little groups of women around them.

It was equally unwise to leave the women idle with lovelorn slavers on either bow who might, with initiative and provision of a small boat after dark, offer a getaway to a choice of continents. The women on female transports were kept as strictly to a daily routine as was practicable in the changing weather conditions through which they passed between London and Sydney Cove. At five o'clock, convict cooks were on deck to prepare breakfast. At sunrise, the hatches were opened and tubs of salt water placed next to them. As women emerged from the orlop, they pegged their bedding out to air on the yards and rigging, were given a bucket of water from the bathing tubs to wash, then formed messes for breakfast. During the day, they were kept in work parties for as long as the agent could find work to keep them busy.

On all transport ships, "trustys" from among the convicts were made mess captains for each group of six or eight convicts. Female "trustys" were known as "matrons." It was they who collected the rations for their mess from the cook or John Nicol, supervised the airing of linen and the cleaning of crockery after meals, kept order as best they could in their mess and relayed any petitions or complaints to the agent. John Nicol does not mention who was given this responsibility on the *Lady Julian* but it was presumably the older women who had some clout below deck. Elizabeth Barnsley and Nelly Kerwin were probably too grand for the job. Humbler but

motherly women in their thirties and forties like Mary Anstey, Warwickshire shoplifter; coiner Catherine Heyland; Mrs. Elizabeth Dell,
the 46-year-old mother from Reading sailing to be reunited with her
convict son; Susannah Hunt and Mrs. Ann Peter Rock, all of whom
went on to lead deeply respectable lives in the colony (bar a little
bigamy), were probably those chosen by Edgar for this task.

Agent Edgar had some information on the previous lives of most
women coming on board, particularly those out of Newgate, whose
records were more easily available. He knew which women had
worked in kitchens, which on farms, which had nursing or child-care
skills, who could read, write, add up figures and weigh rations. Elizabeth Parry, taken on as cow keeper in Islington and Mary Rose,
farmer's daughter from Lincolnshire, would have milked the cows in
the bow. Sarah Acton had stolen ten sucking pigs and kept them
under the bed in her Smithgate lodgings; Sarah Gregory, from Hertfordshire, had stolen "one live pig, one spade sow pig, and two bar-
row pigs." These two, with Sarah's little daughter, might now have
been tending the hogs. If stealing sheep on Dartmoor indicates some
knowledge of husbandry, Susannah Mortimore now slung her baby
on her back and set about tending the sheep and milking the goats.
Women like Sarah Whitelam, from country gaols which released
their prisoners during the summer months to help on local farms,
were now cleaning out the poultry, collecting eggs and sluicing away
the night's dung with buckets of seawater. Catherine Hounsam,
kitchen maid in Grosvenor Square, might have been peeling vegetables with some of the other ex-maidservants—Mary Hook, Rachel
Turner, Mary Cowcher alias Christmas, Ann Kemp, Martha Daniels,
Mary Lewis—there were dozens of them. Forger Nelly Kerwin perhaps helped Lieutenant Edgar keep his ledgers up to date, under strict
supervision, or took dictation for Captain Aitken's dispatches. Nurse-
maid Ann Howard may have helped Surgeon Alley bandaging cuts
and applying leeches in the sick berth. Those who had no particular
skills or were under punishment made up the day's cleaning party,
swabbing and disinfecting below deck, holystoning above.

Cleaning, laundry, food preparation, tending the animals, water throwing, hair pulling, horseplay and drinking did not mop up all the female energy on board. The twenty best needlewomen had already been commandeered by Captain Aitken, who had spotted a business opportunity waiting in Sydney Cove and invested in a quantity of linen. With no raw material or equipment for weaving in the colony, no soap for laundering, no thread but gut and no needles, the captain had reckoned that clean linen shirts would be as much in demand as sex and liquor. Free labor from the convict women was available. Lieutenant Clark had the women of the First Fleet ship *Friendship* run him up trousers, gloves, nightcaps, even a new frockcoat on the voyage out—whores they might be, but handy ones with a needle. Part of the storage space in the orlop hold of the *Lady Julian* had been quietly set aside for the captain's own little business venture. His bolts of linen were now brought up and his private labor force issued with needles and thread.

There was heavy shipping in these waters for they were following the trunk of the sea route south from Europe. This would soon divide: traders would go east toward the Cape and the Spice Islands beyond and whalers would go west toward South Georgia and the Falklands. The *Lady Julian*'s course was also taking her across the southern axis of the golden triangle which connected Europe, North America and the western coast of Africa. Southbound ships brought cheap cloth and arms from Europe to Africa. Westbound ships crammed their holds with slaves for North America and the Caribbean and those sailing east from the New World took raw American materials back to Europe. The peeling forts and seedy boulevards 400 miles to the west produced the human oil to service a vast trading and production machine—spices for the Dutch in Batavia, sugar for the British in the Caribbean, cotton for the Americans in the Deep South. It has been estimated that about six million Negroes had been sold out of western Africa as slaves already that century. Some of them had replaced the convict labor from Britain which American ex-colonists no longer wanted.

About 100 miles out from Porto Praia, the slave ships finally peeled off west toward the cluster of European settlements around the mouth of the River Gambia, "to pick up their cargo of human misery." The phrase was Nicol's—he had seen slaves at work in the sugar plantations of Granada, where the women would sell themselves for "a bellyful of victuals," and had no illusions about the life which awaited the slavers' cargo.

Two hundred British convicts had landed on this coast back in 1782, part of an intended First Fleet to Africa. All but fifty had perished. These were not pleasant thoughts: how many aboard reflected that a similar fate might have overtaken the colony they were sailing toward? The *Prince of Wales* had brought back news that the Sydney colonists were alive and managing, but that ship had left New South Wales in July 1788, over a year ago. One year was more than enough time for a thousand people, alone in an unknown land, to be wiped out by famine, drought, disease or hostility from islanders. News had not yet got back to Britain, but a third colonial experiment on the African coast, 600 miles further south, had just gone disastrously wrong.

When the British-German army which had fought the American colonists came back to Europe in 1783, disorderly women and crippled veterans were only two of the groups of urban poor who began to colonize the streets. Many of the colonial loyalists who had fought with the British forces either went to Nova Scotia, still safely British, or came back to Europe with the defeated army. The former American planter James Smith was probably among them; he was now aboard HMS *Guardian* as superintendent for the unborn plantations of Sydney Cove. Negroes from the American colonies, often brought back by masters who were then forced to free them under British law, joined a black population in Britain already estimated at about 14,000. They drifted to the cities, where they joined the destitute and unemployed already there. Finding a colonial home for black loyalists and freed slaves was a project which ran parallel to finding one for convicted felons in the 1780s.

The same year that the eleven ships of the First Fleet to Botany Bay left England, two ships were leaving for the proposed settlement of Freetown, Sierra Leone. Squeezed among the "Poor Blacks" returning to what was imagined to be their homeland was a bunch of "Whites . . . chiefly men and women of an abandoned character." As with the New South Wales expedition, no advance party had been sent to prepare the ground. The "Poor Blacks" and "abandoned Whites" sweated on board while the captain went ashore and negotiated the purchase of 20 square miles around the Sierra Leone River from King Jimi, the local chief.

About the time the *Lady Julian* sailed past Sierra Leone in 1789, a rumor was going around the camp in Sydney Cove among "some of the most ignorant" that "they are to be left by the troops and the shipping to perish by themselves." The "most ignorant" had a better grip on the recent history of penal colonies than the officer who reported the rumor. What the Sydney convicts feared was exactly what had happened in the African settlement three years earlier. The ship to Sierra Leone had dropped her 411 passengers and sailed back to England leaving London skinners, second-generation slaves, housebreakers and disorderly girls to fend for themselves on 20 square miles of malarial African coastline. Eighteen months later, 130 were alive. The inland blacks had consistently raided and stolen from the land they had sold the English captain, and Freetown had degenerated into an African Lord of the Flies. Just after the *Lady Julian* left the River Thames in 1789, a British man-of-war cruising the African coast set fire to a town just down the coast from Freetown, also ruled by King Jimi. The attack had nothing to do with the Freetown colonists but King Jimi decided to take his revenge there. His envoys gave Freetown three days' notice to evacuate before the camp was sacked. Its inhabitants dispersed in panic onto the islands, crazed with fear and fever, where they were waiting for rescue as the *Lady Julian* was heading off into the Atlantic.

Those on board fortunately knew nothing of the fate of the Sierra Leone settlers. The *Lady Julian* had now turned her back on the African coast and was heading more west than south. The fauna of the sea was changing as she went. There were sharks, pilot whales, sperm whales and bottlenose dolphins around her and the ship's diet changed accordingly. With a tidy ship and little work aloft while the winds held, the seamen turned to fishing. Each mess had its own area and its own collection of lines and the ship dragged fish gut over her sides from bow to stern. Whenever the silver wriggle was sighted, news went around the deck and men rushed to untie and recast their lines in the most promising area. When the women realized that by maritime custom whoever caught the fish also ate it, they started catching their own. The seamen's women were luckier—they got a share of whatever their men caught. The rest of the convicts set themselves to learning the skills of sea fishing, stealing equipment from wherever they could find it.

Mostly they caught bonitos, glorious large fish which thrashed about the deck until someone knocked their heads against a block and they died, their flesh turning an astonishing range of colors as the breath left. What they could not catch were the numerous dolphins and porpoises which played around the ship, because for this they needed a harpoon. Harpooning was technically the prerogative of the first mate aboard a merchantman. On the *Lady Julian,* it was the bosun who excelled with a pair of grains.[17] He stood on the quarterdeck with his harpoon, braced for the throw, watched by women and crew waiting for the shout from the lighter below which meant there was porpoise for supper.

As they neared South America, the waters were still thick with slavers and merchantmen, mainly the Portuguese compradores who plowed between the continents, picking up slaves collected for them by the coastal chiefs in Africa and selling them on to plantation agents in Brazil. The lookout frequently sighted a friendly flag on the horizon, signals went up, the two ships veered toward each other and hove to. Captain Aitken passed the order for his barque to be made ready, put on his best hat and was rowed halfway toward the fellow

---

[17] A type of harpoon.

captain rowing toward him. They would sit there, gently riding the waves while the seamen backed their oars, swapping news of who had been seen, in what latitude, of the weather immediately south and north, of seafaring gossip and warnings of increased harbor fees and changes in the personnel commanding foreign ports. If it turned out either ship was going on to an appropriate harbor, correspondence and messages were rowed over to be carried by the other.

Captain Aitken comes across as rather a lonely man. He figures hardly at all in John Nicol's account, although as officers' servant Nicol had daily contact with him, far more than the average seaman before the mast. Aitken did not seem to attract the same affection as Lieutenant Edgar. A captain dined both junior and senior officers at least once weekly but these were rather awkward occasions, with the young gentlemen in too much awe of the boss to crack the jokes they would have made in their own mess and the captain unable to unbend for fear of losing authority. The only real conversations he could have, perhaps, were with the captains of visiting ships.

One day, the *Lady Julian* sighted a south whaler sailing up from the Falklands. Signals were passed, perhaps the ships hove to and the captains met, then parted to continue their separate journeys. A week or so later, the whaler sighted another British flag, this time on an imposing man-of-war—a fifth-rate armed frigate, twice as large as the *Lady Julian*—and hove to once again at 2° 14' north.

The man-of-war was HMS *Guardian*. She had still been in Portsmouth Harbour when the *Lady Julian* sailed for Plymouth Sound in mid-July and had not left Spithead until the second week of September, far later than the Admiralty had intended. The *Guardian*'s commanding officer, Lieutenant Riou, had been instructed to reach the colony as swiftly as possible. He had stopped briefly at Tenerife to take on wine, bypassed Cabo Verde and made it to just north of the equator in a little over three weeks. Lieutenant Riou now learned from the whaling captain that the far slower *Lady Julian* was plowing south a few days ahead of him.

10

CROSSING THE LINE

$\mathcal{I}$t is about two weeks' sailing in good winds from Cabo Verde to the Equatorial Line, the zero degrees and lifeless air which held a curious, semimythical place in the lore of the sea. The ceremonies of "Crossing the Line" were a high moment in a voyage but could easily degenerate into grotesque and violent horseplay. The men who took control, and directed the humiliations inflicted on the young and the unpopular, were ordinary sailors. The officers took a back seat, although first mates, and even captains, were ready to step in if order was threatened or practical jokes became too dangerous. This was an uneasy occasion on a ship whose crew was not happy or which carried some seaman, officer or passenger to whom too many people had taken a dislike. Men had been keelhauled[18] on the equator, or dragged behind their ship for a mile at the end of the rope, not as punishment from the senior officers but as licensed high jinks among their mess mates. On a transport ship which sailed in 1792, the cook was suspected of keeping back a part of the company's rations to sell later for private profit. He was nearly killed when his ship crossed the

---

[18] Dragged on a rope beneath the keel, from one side of the ship to the other. Occasionally, men did not survive the punishment.

Line. The seamen tied his hands, fastened him to a block and tackle, ran him 50 feet up to the main yardarm, let go the rope and cheered as he hurtled 50 feet back down into the sea—once, twice and a third time, until the first mate stepped in and the man was released to retch and gasp on the deck. There could be a curious connivance between quarterdeck and forecastle when a captain was "obliged" by the master of ceremonies to surrender his protection of a hated purser or an unpopular junior officer and hand him over to the mob in the bow.

Not all ceremonies were so rough. Giggling seamen aboard the *Lady Julian* now gathered in the forecastle, excluding the women, for these were masculine mysteries and half the fun would be making the ladies jump and squeal. A request emerged from the huddle and was carried to the bosun. The bosun fetched his grains, received permission from Captain Aitken to mount the quarterdeck and struck heroically until a fat porpoise was speared. Further errands were run to the galley for a large knife, and to John Nicol for a piece of iron hoop.

Seamen disappearing into the forecastle looked sly and refused to say what was going on. The tropical dusk came suddenly and the women were sent below to interpret the noises filtering down the hatches and from behind the forecastle bulkhead. A dim rumble and a splash overhead were empty casks being rolled to the forecastle and filled with seawater. A creak of wood and another splash were seamen raising the boards and taking water from the bilges. More splashing as this went into the cask; faint guffaws. Depending on who was to end up in which barrel and the forecastle's opinion of his personality, the seamen were spitting, urinating or defecating into the casks.

The sound of preparations continued for some hours and then there was a patter of feet across the deck. Officers' voices bellowed and the women were thrown against a beam as the ship made a lurching quarter circle turn into the wind, came to a halt and settled to a new motion with her sails loose. There were shouts down the orlop hatches to come on deck. The night was now truly dark and the gleam of stars and yellow lanterns on the sea disorienting after the black of the hold. They waited in groups, uneasy; then a gong boomed and a group of manic figures heaved itself over the bow and onto the foredeck. King Neptune and his Nereids had arrived and the party could begin.

The lanterns behind the party of capering drunks which had vaulted up from the gratings cast inhuman shadows. King Neptune was wrapped in the skin of a porpoise, its snout towering above his head to twice the height of a man. His followers had tattooed their faces with red dye and wore trailing wigs of seaweed. They advanced toward the quarterdeck through the throng, causing pandemonium as they went. Women screamed and knocked each other over trying to escape the thrusts of Neptune's pitchfork and the lunges of his drunken attendants. When the royal party stood facing the row of officers drawn up on the quarterdeck, Neptune's great book was produced and handed to the king by an acolyte. Neptune hammed it up, squinted and licked his fingers to turn the pages in a parody of his literate superiors, checking his list to see whether there was any officer on board who had not yet crossed the Equatorial Line. Virgin officers were forfeit a double liquor ration; virgin seamen had to undergo initiation rites.

With everyone's attention on the quarterdeck, a commotion among one tangled group of women went unnoticed. One among them must have fallen down and been kicked in the stomach during the scrum which had followed Neptune's entrance over the bow. So had others—but this woman was pregnant. As Neptune demanded Captain Aitken's rum, the injured woman was being carried into the forecastle or down the ladders into the sick berth by her friends. They got her into a hammock or bunk, curled onto one side to fight the pain in her belly. To women experienced in childbirth, it was obvious what was happening. Someone went for Surgeon Alley; someone else may have pushed through the crowded deck to find the father. Shouts and screams came down the hatch and a roar of approval as Captain Aitken passed over his bottles of flip[19] as payment for crossing Nep-

---

[19] Rum and sugar.

tune's frontier. The lantern swayed as hundreds of feet rushed to the
foredeck to see the virgin mariners shaved by Neptune's barber.

Those seamen (and any officers Captain Aitken had chosen to
relinquish) who had never before crossed the equator were having
their hands tied behind their backs and being seated on the planks
over the barrels. The Nereids soaped their faces with a mixture of tar,
dripping,[20] crud from between the boards and dung. Neptune's barber brandished the blunt iron hoop which served him as razor and
went to work. The victims struggled, overbalanced and disappeared
into the bilge water. Sailors climbed onto the rails; women pushed for
a view. The boys in the barrels splashed about, unable to get a purchase with their feet against the slime of the bottom, swallowing great
gulps of filth. Eventually they were hauled out and when they had
their breath back, it was round two: they were hurled over the rail to
be washed clean at the end of a rope.

If Surgeon Alley had been found and came to attend the woman
below, he could do little to stem the miscarriage. He probably let
blood from her arm with leeches or an incision, this being a general-
purpose first step for an overheated or malfunctioning body. It did
not work. In any case, the older women knew better what to do for a
woman losing her baby than a naval surgeon. The matrons and mothers were alerted, probably Elizabeth Barnsley, a mother of two or
three infants and a known midwife; perhaps Nelly Kerwin, another
mother who had herself suffered a miscarriage at seven months in
April 1787; perhaps Susannah Hunt, the 40-year-old teacher from
Ipswich. More lanterns were brought and hung from the beams. Hot
water came. Younger friends and men were told to go. When it was
clear they could not save the baby, their main task was to ensure that
all the dead child's appendages left the mother's womb. Infusions
were needed; ashore, they would have been hartshorn or camomile.
On board, it was China tea, probably with opium drops. Eventually
the fetus was heaved from the mother's body into the basin held

---

[20] Grease left over from cooking fatty meats.

beneath her by her midwives and her belly massaged to expel the afterbirth. When the last clot of blood had hemorrhaged from her, she was given laudanum to numb the pain and send her to sleep. The party still raged on deck.

It was time for the boys to "confess their amours" to the king and, said John Nicol, the number confessed was "astonishing." When the last salty anecdotes had been obtained, the music began, and the dancing. Finally, in the forecastle for those who got that far, and on deck for those who did not make it, bleary copulation among the empty bottles—until officers' voices and officers' boots forced them up, halyards squealed and they turned south. It was while their hangovers were still fresh, and the initiates still picking lumps of tar from their hair, that the ship struck the Doldrums.

About 100 miles to either side of the equator, winds die and currents slap against each other. It was, and is, a notoriously likely spot for a vessel under sail to be becalmed. Lucky ships sailed these 200 miles in three days or less with the Trades behind them. The less lucky took weeks. When the *Lady Julian* turned at the end of Neptune's party to fill her sails and sail south, her crew found that yesterday's white crests were now a lifeless, oily sea and the fresh winds which had blown her along since Cabo Verde had died. Sails hung like empty sacks and the ship floundered, wayless. The motion was unpleasant. A ship which cannot make way is a graceless beast and her shuddering under the aimless slap of cross-current waves induces more nausea than the rhythmic plunge of passage. The idle days of the Trades were on hold until the crew could get the ship through the Doldrums and pick them up again on the other side.

When wind is scarce, there is more work for the men among the sails—and for the officers commanding their adjustments—than when it is blowing strongly. Sailing through the Doldrums meant trimming sails every few minutes to catch the latest cat's-paw of wind, each blowing in a different direction from the last. The men at the sheets came off each watch tired and demoralized by the log readings—a mile an hour, even less. Lieutenant Clark, suffering in the same spot two years previously, recorded fretfully one evening that they had "gone 10 miles back again from where we was yesterday."

On and below deck, the women suffered too. Heat was intense; humidity intolerable. The hot air had previously been made bearable by the breeze created by the ship's way through the water but now the air was stifling, heavy. Sir Joseph Banks had been caught in the Doldrums in October many years before. "The nearer we approached to the calms," he wrote, "still damper everything grew. This was perceivable to the human body and very much so, but more remarkably upon all kinds of furniture: everything made of iron rusted so fast that the knives in people's pockets became almost useless and the razors in cases not free. All kinds of leather became mouldy. Portfolios and trunks covered with black leather were almost white . . . mould adhered to almost anything."

Any movement among the bodies packed into the orlop by night, lying under awnings on deck by day, caused a debilitating sweat. They dehydrated, just as the rationing of water began. On the First Fleet, the ration was cut here to three pints per day per person, which, the surgeon said, was "a quantity scarcely sufficient to supply that waste of animal spirits the body must necessarily undergo, in the torrid zone, from a constant and violent perspiration, and a diet consisting of salt provisions." The *Lady Julian* convicts did not reach the dangerous levels of dehydration that those on worse run transports suffered. A convict on a 1798 gaol ship wrote of the effects of the regime commonly imposed on transport and slave ships, of convicts' being confined for up to twenty-three hours per day below deck. Corruption and intimidation on his ship were such that the convicts responsible for distributing water to their messes hoarded and sold it instead. Casked water fetched two shillings a pint; rainwater from the tropical showers which leaked down the hatches was sold for ninepence a quart. Aboard the *Lady Julian*, women were allowed free access to the deck during the day and had a more conscientious agent and surgeon to watch for abuses.

The stench which plagued the ship in harbor caught up with her again. Becalmed, a pool of effluent from the heads and the galley spread around her. This became home to a long green train of plant life which trapped sewage and scraps of food in its fronds. Men lowered lighters to hack away what they could of it, but could not reach it all. Thunderous tropical showers briefly cleaned the deck but the relief they brought steamed away in minutes.

There were various theories about how to make way when becalmed. Some seamen thought watering the sails to make the canvas heavy would allow them to hold more wind. Others held that knocking a wedge into the foot of the masts to stop them moving in their shoes had a better effect. But the only proven way to get a ship through windless waters—and away from its own cesspool—was to tow it. Thus watch after watch, the small boats went down and the men towed the ship across a glassy sea. The Doldrums meant exhausting work for the men and unending nights of discomfort. It was in the Doldrums that Surgeon Alley diagnosed his first case of scurvy and the *Lady Julian* sprang her first serious leak.

Surgeon Alley had been in the service since 1783 and had seen plenty of cases of the sailors' diseases: scurvy, the pox and rheumatism. He was also familiar with the less serious but equally common *mals de mer*: nausea and the constipation caused by a salt diet and lack of fresh greens. It was the job of the surgeon on a transport ship to visit the convicts on the orlop hold when they were seasick, to ensure good hygiene in their sleeping areas and to supervise their exercise and diet. So far, there had been routine treatment of minor injuries, attempts to allay seasickness, checks for pox and any sign of lingering gaol fever which would require quarantine. In mid-October, Surgeon Alley became a very busy man.

"The Scurvy," wrote Lieutenant Edgar's old colleague William Bligh, "is realy a disgrace to a ship where it is at all comon, provided they have it in their power to be supplied with Dryed Malt, Sour Krout and Portable Soup." That his cargo should get scurvy was a particular embarrassment to Edgar, pupil of Captain Cook. During all three of Cook's voyages of discovery, the captain and his surgeons had been charged to perform and record dietary and other experiments on the seamen to test theories about the prevention and cure of the scurvy. During his first and second voyages, which had both lasted three years, he attained astonishing success in keeping his men free of scurvy: not one died of the disease on either voyage. However, too many different vegetables, essences, preserves and dried foods were experimented with to draw firm conclusions as to which had been responsible for keeping the disease at bay. Among them were pickled cabbage, mustard, vinegar, essence of malt, citrus juice, powdered offal, sugar, molasses, carrot marmalade and soda water. Captain Cook had insisted that every man take his ration of these, whether he liked it or not—and frequently he did not—and that they be varied whenever possible by fresh fruit and greens locally available wherever they put in.

Cook knew that somewhere in this cocktail lay part of the secret to keeping a crew healthy but himself believed that diet was not the most important factor in beating the scurvy. In his opinion, it was living conditions that were the key to a healthy ship. With "plenty of fresh water and a close attention to cleanliness," he concluded, "a ship's company will be seldom afflicted with scurvy, though they should not be provided with any of the antiscorbutics before mentioned." The system of three watches, not two, he believed essential; also the purification of air below deck. For Captain Cook, keeping the men clean, dry and living in sweet-smelling air was more important than feeding them lime juice.

We can presume that Lieutenant Edgar adopted many of the revered captain's methods of keeping a crew happy and healthy—as did Captain Bligh, although with disastrous results. We do not know Surgeon Alley's thoughts on the scurvy; there were so many different theories on its treatment flying around in the 1770s and 1780s, he may have had different ideas from the lieutenant. It is probable that a variety of cures were attempted on the women of the *Lady Julian*, in the hope that one of them would work.

The two most famous writers on the scurvy, Dr. Mead and Dr.

Lind, believed the disease was caused by the trapping beneath the skin of foul matter which then burst out as the black pustules which disfigured the bodies of sufferers. This waste matter, they thought, would normally have been expelled as feces or sweat but, as these natural cleansing mechanisms were clogged by a damp climate, inactivity or an unhappy state of mind, expulsion had to be induced artificially. Retention of waste could be reduced by bleeding, by eating raw onions to induce sweat, by purging with a saltwater laxative or by eating fruit, whose acid Dr. Lind thought would help break down the trapped matter and allow it to disperse. Some doctors believed other types of acid, particularly "elixir vitriol" (a dilution of sulphuric acid) and hydrochloric acid, added to the seawater purge were just as helpful in clearing waste from the bowels.

Cabbage was provided by the Admiralty as standard fare, preserved between layers of salt. This was now soused in vinegar and served as sauerkraut. It was not an attractive meal. Captain Cook had found his seamen would not eat it until he had it served to the officers with orders to express delight, noting wryly "the moment they see their superiors set a value upon it, it becomes the finest stuff in the world." "Portable soup" was drunk. This was a broth made from boiling up cakes of powdered cattle offal taken on board in the Thames, usually served as a sort of crude minestrone, with dried peas or any available fresh vegetables boiled up in it. Anything up to 4 pints of sweet-wort—"without doubt one of the best anti-scorbutic medicines yet found out"—was served to the sick each day when water supplies allowed. This was an infusion made by pouring boiling water over dried powdered barley, leaving it in vast tubs in the galley for four or five hours to steep and then straining it to get rid of bits of husk. There were probably also rations of "rob of lemon" and "rob of orange"—reductions of citrus juice—or wine and vinegar, also believed to have antiscorbutic properties, before noon dinner each day.

Despite all the various cures being practiced in the sick berth as the *Lady Julian* floundered in the Doldrums, a severe outbreak of scurvy had taken hold of convicts and crew. Fresh greens from Cabo Verde were running out and the ship still rolled in its own waste. One metabolism after another succumbed to a deficiency in vitamin C: "the smallest appearance on the flesh in a day or two spread broader than your hand and soon made its way to the very bone." Livid blotches erupted over the bodies of frightened women. Crops of pimples exploded around their mouths, their teeth loosened and their gums turned to fungus.

Temperatures by night were now so high that sleep was impossible. Below deck, melting tar dripped from the seams above the women's sleeping shelves and burned their faces and forearms. Even on deck, the heat was uncomfortable. Pitch bubbled between planks. The seamen's feet could withstand anything and the officers had their boots; the women wrapped scraps of tarpaulin around their feet to protect them from burning boards. Even the seamen, whose backs were tanned to leather, wore shirts if their work took them into direct sun in these waters. The glare off the sea was intolerable. The women's appetite left them; the deck was strewn with knots of fainting convicts.

Incessant rains fall across the equator at this season, with frequent violent thunderstorms. The *Lady Julian* should have left England in May like Arthur Phillip's fleet, but she had been delayed waiting for the assembly of a fleet which in the end was commissioned too late to join her. She began to suffer the consequences in the Doldrums. As Surgeon Alley worked in the sickroom, the carpenter, carpenter's mate and any other man skilled with tools were working to plug the leaks which calms, rains and the depredations of sea life feeding off her hull had caused.

Many running repairs could be made to a ship while she was under canvas but a leak far below the waterline was inaccessible. The men pumped as well as they could in the heat below deck. Boats went over the side to scrape off plants and animals and expose any leaks above the waterline. Fires were lit on an already unbearably hot deck, cauldrons of pitch boiled up and lowered to the men in the boats to caulk those leaks they could get at. If the ship sprang a bad leak below the waterline, they stopped it by fothering her, passing an old sail covered with oakum and dung beneath the keel from one side of the ship to the other to create a waterproof second skin over her hull.

By October, sixty women were on the sick list; the galley was low on fresh water and fresh greens; the ship was leaking badly. Although other ships had sailed thousands of miles before reaching a harbor where they could be beached, no captain would do this unnecessarily. Even when the winds picked up again south of the Doldrums, there was at least a 2,000-mile passage to be worked to Cape Town—a good three weeks' sailing, in sweltering temperatures. Lieutenant Edgar, Surgeon Alley, Captain Aitken and the first mate began emergency consultations in the chart room. Not only might the extra miles to the African cape prove fatal for some of the women in the sick berth, but the Dutch authorities would not even let them into the harbor if they suspected disease on board. The obvious place to make for was the sprawling, decadent city of Rio de Janeiro, where the First Fleet had put in two years previously. Instead of making another ocean crossing back toward the tip of southern Africa, they would hug the Brazilian coast, put into the Portuguese port to recover, and make the ocean passage from further south when numbers on the sick list had fallen and the worst leaks had been tackled. Captain Aitken's planned voyage to Cape Town would have to be interrupted.

News that the ship would be back in port earlier than expected must have come as a relief to everyone aboard: the scurvy sufferers, the heat stricken and most of all those women now in the last months of their pregnancies. From one hour to the next in mid-October, the winds freshened and the *Lady Julian* picked up speed on a broad reach southeast. Her motion was easy, her decks level. A couple of days later, the masthead sighted the white blur of Recife spreading up a hill, and the men aloft hauled the sails in to allow the ship to reach gently away from the coasts on the currents which now swirled her counterclockwise back out into the Atlantic. It would be only ten days' sailing with good winds on the beam to take them to the Tropic of Capricorn, where they would tack and head inland for the harbor of São Sebastião, the port of Rio de Janeiro. They were ten days of anticipation. The stifling, airless weather of the equator was gradually replaced by fresher breezes. The crew no longer spent the wearying hours aloft that had been necessary in the Doldrums.

For the women due shortly to give birth, these were weeks of apprehension. They were all first-time mothers, the eldest 19 or 20 and the youngest 14 or 15. They were nervous about the physical ordeal of childbirth and because no one could tell them exactly what conditions they could expect for their confinement. At least they now knew the name of the continent off which their babies would be born—but that was the extent of their knowledge of this Portuguese Catholic port for which they were heading. So far they had been in the care of Surgeon Alley (himself an expectant father by 18-year-old Ann Mash), their more experienced fellow convicts and their seamen partners. Sarah Whitelam was now seven and a half months pregnant, scarcely able to waddle up the ladder from John Nicol's mess to her seat beneath an awning on the deck.

John Nicol records not a word about the progress of her pregnancy. His attitude may have been colored by the fact that his own mother had died giving birth to a younger brother when he himself was still an infant. Death in childbirth was far commoner then than now—just another hazard of being born a daughter of Eve—but the circumstances of his mother's death may have left some scars on John. When it was obvious Sarah would have to give birth on board ship, or at best in a foreign port, one can only speculate on his thoughts on her chances and on the part he had played in getting her into this situation. Mary Rose had refused to have anything to do with the seamen and it was she who was looking after Sarah until dusk each day, when Sarah went back to John's mess and Mary returned to her shelf in the orlop.

John Nicol's work kept him away from Sarah during much of the day but his duties did not include standing watches. He could spend his evenings and nights in her company, except when shouted for to attend an officer. He was the most constant and entertaining of sailor lovers—a rough Othello to his temporary Desdemona. Sarah had little knowledge of the world. She had certainly never left England and it is unlikely she had ever left her county of birth before she was shackled to the coach which took her south to London. It was from John Nicol that she gained her knowledge of how the world fitted together, whence came the tea she had served her mistress in the parlor, the tobacco her master had smoked after dinner, the cotton shift she wore beneath her brown serge skirt.

It was John who explained to Sarah, Mary Rose and their group of friends sheltering from the sun beneath the awnings why it was that the American colonists had rebelled and what had happened over there in the New World during the wars. He told them about the great lakes dividing the rebel Americans from the loyal Canadians and the vast rivers up which the fur trappers disappeared for months on end each winter. He recounted his adventures fighting off American privateers in the Caribbean, cutlass in his hand and prize money in his mind, and the glory of overpowering an American vessel off Saint Kitts and sailing her into harbor. He told them of the miseries he had seen among the slaves there. He remembered how British seamen would intervene to save slaves from brutal punishments in the West Indies and how gentle South Sea Islanders would do the same thing for British seamen caught breaking ship in Tahiti. He described the horrors of being icelocked in Newfoundland and surrounded by hostile Indians. He told them of eating turtle off Cape Horn, snakes in French Canada and coconuts in Granada and emphasized the invariable superiority of the British seaman over seamen of any other race. What neither he, nor any other man on board, could tell the women about was New South Wales, for none of them had ever been there.

In the privacy of his mess, perhaps, he told Sarah Whitelam about his childhood in Scotland and the death of his mother; of the loneliness of his father bringing up five boys by himself; of the death of two of the brothers in childhood and the disappearance of the other two—the youngest to America, from where nobody had since had news of him, and the eldest as a lieutenant in the West Indies, where he died of his wounds fighting the French. He told her about his plans to settle down, how he had nearly done so before this voyage but had been tempted back to sea by the prospect of seeing New South Wales. He promised he would not desert her but would return to the colony to marry her and take her back to Scotland as soon as her sentence expired.

In his memoirs, John Nicol says that, had there been a clergyman on board the *Lady Julian*, he would have married Sarah Whitelam. We do not know why he did not get Captain Aitken to perform the marriage service instead: either John did not ask or Captain Aitken refused. There would be good reason for Captain Aitken to turn down a request, if one were made. He could not afford to lose his steward and cooper on the return voyage, which would happen if Nicol stayed in New South Wales with his young wife. Jobbing seamen looking for their next berth did not yet hang around the new port of Sydney Cove as they did in better established harbors and Nicol could not be replaced. Apart from this, Captain Aitken was probably not entirely clear on the legal implications of such a union. Was a seaman, or any other man for that matter, allowed to marry a woman in bondage to the British government? Sarah was government property and Captain Aitken could no more transfer her to the private ownership of a husband than he could transfer the rest of the stores aboard the *Lady Julian* to whatever merchant made him an offer for them.

Marriage might have been out of the question but sex was not. Pregnancy, of course, was the natural result of the cohabitation on board ship encouraged by the officers and participated in by the surgeon. Commissions would be appointed at the start of the next century to investigate allegations of mistreatment of convicts on the New South Wales passage. A clear gap would open between the men of practical views, such as Governor Phillip, with his suggestion of a whores' ghetto in Sydney Cove, and Lieutenant Edgar, with his easy acceptance of shipboard concubinage; and reformers who complained of moral pollution engendered by situations such as that developing aboard the *Lady Julian*. The practical men who ran the transportation ships and organized the Sydney Cove chain gangs thought moral pollution an acceptable price to pay for good order (especially if they only half believed in this concept anyway). To their minds, the bleeding hearts in the English shires did not understand conditions on the ground.

A modern view may incline more toward that of the bleeding hearts than the practical men—less because of the moral pollution of unlicensed sex than because of the degradation the system forced on many females. But modern critics are as far removed in time from the world of seamen, convicts and marines in the 1790s as contemporary critics were in class and circumstances. It could be that the practical men knew best.

Attempts at mutiny were not uncommon. Keeping the crew happy was one important safeguard against such attempts but did not guarantee complete protection. Attempted mutiny could be provoked by a desire to get at the cargo, short rations, an overferocious discipline or the ambition to get to the New World, where honey flowed and all men were rich. Within a decade, another transport ship carrying female felons would leave London to make the passage across the Atlantic Ocean and on to New South Wales. She never made it past the coast of South America. The *Lady Shore* was a far less happy ship than the *Lady Julian*. When she reached the waters through which the *Lady Julian* was now passing peacefully, her crew mutinied and put the officers over the side in a small boat. The men then took the ship into Montevideo but their plan backfired: they discovered they were at war with Spain when the Spaniards seized their ship as a prize and distributed the convict women as maidservants among the Spanish ladies of that city.

One woman on board the *Lady Julian* had already had firsthand experience of mutiny on another transport ship. Mary Kymes alias Potten was now aged 29. Her known criminal record began in 1783 when she committed a felony in Bristol for which she was sentenced to be transported to America on the *Mercury*. One day out from Portsmouth Harbour, the crew of the *Mercury* mutinied and the convicts escaped along the Devonshire coast. Over the next few years, most of them were taken up again as they returned to unsuccessful crime, and many of Mary's *Mercury* shipmates were now in Sydney Cove. Mary had also reoffended, been sentenced to death and conditionally pardoned in thanksgiving for George III's recovery from insanity. Six years after mutiny had saved her from America, she was on her way to New South Wales.

Another transport ship leaving England in 1792 would experience the threat of mutiny in Santa Cruz de Tenerife. A plan was made in the orlop and forecastle to rush the quarterdeck, seize the arms chest and make for America, "where," the ringleaders promised the other convicts, "Congress would give every man a tract of land for free." Most of the orlop hold remained unconvinced, and when the leaders made a break for the arms chest, few followed. The "Americans" were summarily hanged from the yardarm. And it was not only on transport ships that seamen could make trouble: as the *Lady Julian* neared Rio de Janeiro, Captain Bligh was recovering in Dutch Batavia after forty-one days in a small boat following mutiny on board the *Bounty*.

The creation of mutually beneficial relationships between males and females, and between officers and men, was prudent management. These were not the only relationships which had developed aboard the *Lady Julian*. By now, the connections which bound together this little township bouncing sturdily on toward Rio de Janeiro were many and complex. There were the clientage systems, run by the matrons or orlop gang leaders who would convey requests and complaints to the officers and who had some power to grant or withhold favors. There were simple friendships, some of which had begun in the streets or gaols of Britain, some of which were initiated on board ship. There were relationships between the generations. With the youngest female on board aged 11 and the oldest 68, the convicts easily spanned three generations. Although a handful of women had been allowed to bring their babies with them, many on board had had to leave older children behind. Elizabeth Barnsley had left at least two, as had Nelly Kerwin; Catherine Wilmot had left four. They were the natural candidates to take the younger teenagers and children under their wing. The crimes committed by the 13- and 14-year-olds on board disguise their ages: assault by Poll Randall and Mary Butler, prostitution by Mary Bateman and Jane Forbes and what narrowly escaped being manslaughter by 11-year-old Mary Wade and her 14-year-old friend Jane Whiting. Old enough to commit violent crime, they were also young enough to miss mothers, grandmothers and older sisters and seek out replacements among the women around them.

It was not only on the orlop hold that grieving mothers and lonely children formed relationships. There were seamen on board young enough to be the sons of some of the *Lady Julian* convicts. The most junior officers, midshipmen—known as "the young gentlemen"—were commonly sent to sea at the age of 12 or 13, often in ships commanded by relatives. Lieutenant Riou of the *Guardian* had entered the navy at the age of 12, Lieutenant Edgar at the age of 10. During the early years of a midshipman's commission, the ship was school and its officers and crew were family. Ships' boys, his equivalent before the mast, were of a similar age. However manly a face a midshipman or ship's boy might assume on deck, a young boy away from home for the first time missed his mother and his sisters and surrogate mother-son and sister-brother relationships must have been among the curious mix which brewed in the *Lady Julian* as officers, crew and convicts spent one month after another in close proximity.

11

THE BIRTH OF JOHN NICOL JUNIOR

$\mathscr{H}$MS *Guardian* had been only a few days north of the *Lady Julian* where she wallowed in the Doldrums and had followed in the wake of the female transport toward Recife. But while the *Lady Julian* continued south, the *Guardian* swung back into the Atlantic and made directly for Cape Town. There was no scurvy aboard the man-of-war, which carried only twenty-five convicts and was making excellent time toward Sydney Cove. On 24 November, she arrived in Table Bay, Cape Town, expecting to see the *Lady Julian* at anchor there. There was no sign, or news, of her. "I conclude," wrote Lieutenant Riou in a letter to Sir Joseph Banks, "that she is gone to Rio."

Far more worrying than the nonappearance of the *Lady Julian* and his former sailing master, Lieutenant Edgar, was the news Riou now received from the Dutch colonial authorities about affairs in Sydney Cove. Riou already knew, from the dispatches brought back by returning ships, that Commodore Phillip's fleet had sailed from Cape Town for New South Wales in November 1787. He was now given information no one in Britain had yet received: in early 1789, Phillip's flagship, HMS *Sirius,* had reappeared in the Dutch harbor to buy emergency supplies for a starving colony. The colonists had almost run out of the dry goods supplied by the Admiralty 13,000 miles away in

London and had had little success growing crops. Already, the colony was in deep trouble. Captain John Hunter had loaded up the *Sirius* on Admiralty credit and headed back across the Southern Ocean to relieve the camp and garrison. When this news was passed to Lieutenant Riou, he decided no time could be wasted getting the last supplies aboard the *Guardian* for Sydney Cove, and leaving as soon as possible. Consequently, HMS *Guardian* only stayed two and a half weeks at the Cape, the time necessary to take on livestock for the settlement. She set off to the southwest on 11 December 1789.

Five days after her departure, a Dutch brig arrived from Batavia bearing an illustrious British passenger. He was Riou's other former sailing master, William Bligh, lately of HMS *Bounty*. Captain Bligh had last been in Cape Town in May of the previous year. Then, he had been the proud and undisputed captain of his ship, with a prestigious commission. He had mentioned the possibility of dropping in on "our friends in Botany Bay" en route for the South Sea Islands but nothing came of this idea. Instead, he sailed directly for Tahiti with a shipful of happy sailors looking forward to love in the surf. What happened on board his ship and the small boat in which he and a group of men loyal to him spent forty-one days at sea is another story. He was to return finally to England in January of the following year, thus missing both Lieutenant Riou and Lieutenant Edgar in Cape Town.

November and December 1789 were significant months all around for the future of the settlement at Sydney Cove. In the River Thames, the three transports of the Second Fleet which had originally been intended to sail in convoy with the *Lady Julian* were finally ready to leave, carrying 928 male and 78 female convicts. Ann Wheeler, partner of Elizabeth Barnsley, had recovered from gaol fever and boarded the *Neptune* on 10 November. The same ship would carry Lieutenant John Shapcote, the boundlessly corrupt agent who was the *Neptune*'s equivalent of kindly Lieutenant Edgar. A few weeks later, the hulks in Portsmouth disgorged over a hundred male convicts, including Elizabeth Barnsley's husband, Thomas. He, too, sailed aboard the *Neptune*; Sarah Gregory's husband, also Thomas, went aboard the *Surprize*. The experiences these convicts were to suffer on what became known as "coffin ships" were among the worst of any voyage during the decades in which felons were transported to New South Wales.

By the end of November 1789, connections between Britain and New South Wales were strung out across the globe. The *Neptune*, *Scarborough* and *Surprize* were heading south toward Canary. HMS *Guardian* had overtaken the *Lady Julian* in the Atlantic Ocean and was in Cape Town. Colonists in Sydney Cove, Rose Hill and Norfolk Island were planting their second round of crops. And on the first day of the month, the *Lady Julian* had finally tacked her way into the harbor of São Sebastião, Rio de Janeiro.

Brazil was the proudest overseas possession of the Kingdom of Portugal and Rio de Janeiro was its capital. Portuguese navigators had been the first of the European explorers to open up the trade routes with Africa, South America and the islands of the Indies but since their early days of glory they had withdrawn all over the globe before the newer powers on the imperial scene. First Spain, then the Netherlands, then upstart Britain and France ousted them from settlements in three continents. In Brazil, however, they had hung on doughtily, and Rio in 1789 was still sending back New World profits to her masters in Lisbon. The masthead on the *Lady Julian* sighted Cabo Frio on 31 October and turned to sail west by north along the Brazilian coast. She was in sight of Sugarloaf Mountain to the left of the harbor of São Sebastião by the following nightfall and anchored 2 miles out from the town. The next day, she moved over the bar at the harbor mouth, with forts on either side, and waited for the guard boats to nose out and ask her business. Turtles crowded around her hull. She did not have to ride the gentle waves of the middle harbor for long before the slave-rowed launches arrived carrying representatives of His Excellency the Viceroy of the Brazils, son of the King of Portugal, to inquire the ship's business. They were not the first on the scene: small boys in homemade boats had raced each other from the shore as soon as sail was sighted and their urchin oarsmen had already swarmed up the side of the ship. The biggest ones stood in the boats, slicing up fruit with machetes, the middle ones balanced on the side and passed up the wares and the little ones hung off the rails and shrouds holding up pineapples, hands of sweet bananas, oranges, lemons and limes, shouting each other down in shrill Portuguese and pushing each other in.

An abundance of tropical fruit was not the only surprise in these little boats for the women. The children who rowed them were of a range of colors and features they had never seen. The seamen had seen and maybe even sired children of mixed race on their travels, but they were unknown on the streets of Britain. In Rio, cheerful miscegenation had been the rule for generations, accepted at all levels of society and even by the Catholic church. It was a singular city. Unions with native women had characterized the early days of most European colonies but when these matured and colonists began to hanker after respectability, native wives would usually be replaced by European ones and relations between the races hardened to bigotry. This change of attitude did not occur, or occurred only at the highest social level, in Rio de Janeiro and the result was a population of exhilarating variety. Among the little boys dripping on the deck with their lemons, there were skins of every color, from ebony black to sallow Portuguese white, and noses, hair and eyes of every racial type. Convict infants in tattered serge and ship's boys in tattered broadcloth stared at lithe brown children with scraps of cotton around their loins.

Meanwhile, Captain Aitken and Lieutenant Edgar sweated in the tight breeches and frock coats required to uphold George III's dignity when his officers faced a foreigner and went ashore. Much ceremony was observed. Formalities could take two days or more to complete but British sailors were welcome in Rio de Janeiro, especially any British on their way to see Commodore Phillip in Sydney Cove. Arthur Phillip had at one time served in the Royal Portuguese Navy, when England was briefly at peace and commissions hard to come by, and he was esteemed by the Portuguese authorities. He and his senior officers had been offered every aid and courtesy when the First Fleet spent a fortnight in Rio two years previously and the viceregal court was anxious to hear whether his adventure in New South Wales had been successful. Although the name of Aitken did not invoke the same respect as the name of Phillip, the captain of the *Lady Julian* was assured of all assistance. This was just as well, for he not only had sixty in need of medical attention, but at least six about to give birth.

With the tide rising, the *Lady Julian* now made ready to enter the inner harbor of São Sebastião. Once again, the women went below to clear the deck for operations. Once again, an eleven-gun salute made the babies cry and the timbers shiver around their heads. The ship anchored either just inside the Ilha das Cobras or opposite the Benedictine friary and, back on deck, the women had their first close-up view of a Portuguese colonial capital. What they saw was an estuary dotted with lush little islands, a harbor encircled by fortifications, guard boats rowed by Negro slaves passing among the ships, and a hot, glittering city spread up the hill before them "surrounded by high mountains, of the most romantic form the imagination can fashion to itself any idea of." If they had thought Santa Cruz the last word in gaudy Catholicism, it had nothing on Rio de Janeiro. There were churches everywhere and almost nightly ceremonies to one saint or another. The harbor seemed continually full of the reflection of devotees' candles and the infuriating tinkle of convent bells. This exotic scene would become familiar to the women, for the *Lady Julian* was to remain in the harbor of São Sebastião for the next seven weeks.

From a long description of Rio de Janeiro in the journal of the surgeon general of the First Fleet, it sounds remarkably like that other Portuguese colonial capital, Panjim in Goa, which has changed less in two centuries than the Brazilian one. One wide avenue, known to the English as "Strait Street," swept from the viceroy's palace through the town to the Mosteiro de São Bento, the grand Benedictine convent at the other end, and was the city's main socializing and shopping street. It was crowded with sedan chairs carried by slaves; chaises pulled by mules "found to answer better than horses, being more indefatigable and surer-footed; consequently better calculated to ascend their steep hills and mountains"; the captain's guard on horseback and trotting slaves on errands. Sedan chairs were particularly awkward because the obese of Rio preferred to move crabwise—one sidestepping slave mounted the pavement, another stayed in the street, and the sedan chair lurched along between them. Smaller streets ran parallel to or bisected Strait Street, wide enough to allow two carriages just to pass each other, flanked by high pavements so narrow pedestrians had to walk in single file. Ground floors were shops; the upper floors, closed in by latticework balconies, were family residences. Female shadows behind the fretwork looked down. Every street was watched over by a Virgin in her niche. Churches were everywhere—falling down, going up, in the process of restoration—each with their own faithful congregation, their own patron saint and their own claim to miracles. The cathedral of São Sebastião in what is now Praça XV de Novembre was half finished (it is still not quite completed) with an arresting image of the patron saint of the city on its facade. Further up was Santa Cruz dos Militares; then the Igreja da Ordem Terceira do Monte do Carma, in the first stage of construction; the Igreja da Nossa Senhora de Candelaria; and finally the Benedictines. Visitors on the streets at dusk would frequently find themselves caught up in a public procession, led by some mendicant friar with a lantern in his hand, to raise funds for a church roof.

Several of the officers who had not had shore leave in Santa Cruz now left the ship to take up lodgings in the town, and when the usual tasks of watering and making shipshape were completed, groups of seamen were also allowed off the ship for rest and recreation. The Portuguese of Rio were stricter than the Spanish of Santa Cruz and the sailors of the *Lady Julian* were followed wherever they went by a mournful Portuguese officer trailing his sword along the cobbles. Private Easty of the First Fleet marines had gone ashore here two years earlier and wrote in his diary that the Brazilian Portuguese "are a very strickt Sort of People the Solders have the whole Command of the Place thay have a great many Troops to the amount 6 or 7 Thousand

The city of São Sebastião, Rio de Janeiro, in 1787, where John Nicol Junior was born two years later. (Mitchell Library, State Library of New South Wales, Australia)

men." Rio was a city dominated by the military and the strict rules which governed its honor. "Although the dreadful custom of private stabbing is at an end," polite male society in Rio de Janeiro still dressed for vendetta. Gentlemen bristled with frightful swords. Boys as young as 6 strapped them on before they left the house and wore them with hauteur.

The military had more reason to be "strickt" when the *Lady Julian* passed by in 1789 than they had when the First Fleet was there in 1787. This was a decade of revolution for more than one New World colony and Old World colonizer. North America had won her revolution against the taxes, trade restrictions and prohibitions on manufacture imposed from Europe. In Brazil, a group of creoles[21] had decided to do the same, inspired by Thomas Jefferson. The 1789 *Inconfidência Mineira*, or Miners' Conspiracy, united poets, priests,

---

[21] Term used by both Spanish and Portuguese to denote those of European blood but colonial birth, in this case Brazilian-born Portuguese.

landowners, merchants and army officers under the leadership of "Tiradentes," a part-time dentist and lieutenant in the Brazilian army by the name of Joaquim José da Silva Xavier. Before the conspirators had had time to act, their plans were betrayed. Lieutenant da Silva had been hanged and quartered in the square later named Plaça Tiradentes a few months before the arrival of the *Lady Julian*. His head had been impaled on a pole and his limbs sent to be exhibited in the mining towns which had supported him. It was a death ritual as terrifying as those in which Margaret Sullivan and Christian Murphy had died. The other leaders were sent into exile to the Portuguese equivalents of Sydney Cove in Angola and Mozambique. Rebellion had been crushed, but Rio de Janeiro was an uneasy city at the end of 1789 and the Portuguese officers who accompanied the men of the *Lady Julian* were on edge, mistrusting both the creoles they ruled and the army they served. Nor had the civilian population recovered from the brief thrill of insurrection earlier that year, or its brutal end. The British officers, cadging invitations to midnight receptions from contacts in the military or the colonial administration, probably heard more about this than the seamen. The attempted revolution in Brazil, like the successful one in North America, was an affair fomented in private salons, not public bars.

The Portuguese in Brazil would have been more reluctant to allow even well-behaved convicts ashore, especially in the tense conditions of 1789, than their compatriots at Cabo Verde or the Spanish at Tenerife. Edgar and Aitken themselves may have decided it was not safe. However, a privileged convict who sailed in 1792 went ashore here, to stock up on little necessaries and encash bills at British merchants' offices in the city, so it is possible Elizabeth Barnsley, Nelly Kerwin and the other moneyed convicts of the *Lady Julian* also did so, accompanied by both a British and a Portuguese officer for safety. Chief among visitors' purchases were the country's "excellent tobacco" and "aquadente [which] spirit, by proper management and being kept till it is of a proper age, becomes tolerable rum"; tolerable, and very, very cheap.

The female felons of Britain would have been conspicuous on the streets of Rio. Any Portuguese ladies of good family who left their house on foot did so under impenetrable mantillas. Those not swathed in black lace were "women of the port"[22] or slaves. Private Easty had made some study of these two years before: ". . . the natives of this place are of a Dark Complecton much Like the Gipsies of England Likewise Great meany of the Coast of Gueany neagoes . . . thay ware no aparell Exept a Clout Jest around ther Privits the negos weman ware a Short kind of bed gownd wich jest Cover their Brists and Shouders and a Short Peticoat wich Come About half way down their thies thay ware no kind of Shirts or Shifts So that thare Bellies is naked." Portuguese Brazil was the single biggest slave purchaser of the eighteenth century. The streets were full of city slaves and the markets sold goods produced by plantation slaves on latifundias which stretched from Pernambuco to São Paulo: coffee, sugar, tobacco, rice, cotton, indigo, pimento. For Surgeon Alley, or Mrs. Barnsley, or whoever was buying the supplies for the confinement of the mothers-to-be on the *Lady Julian*, the wares of the Rio druggists were of particular interest. There were many apothecaries' shops in the little streets behind the main boulevards and Surgeon General White had found their products excellent and fresh.

John Nicol remembered, "I here [in Rio] served out twenty suits of childbed linen," implying that twenty mothers gave birth, but this was in memoirs inaccurate in other details. A document much closer to the date of the babies' birth was a letter written by another father-to-be, Surgeon Alley, in which he gives a total of births and deaths as far as Cape Town, from where his letter was sent. This states that five had died and seven babies had been born. However, the tally of five seems only to take account of deaths among those who embarked in England, not stillborn Rio babies or infants who survived days.

It is improbable that every baby born between the River Thames and Sydney Cove survived. Infant mortality rates in conventional

---

[22] Prostitutes who serviced sailors.

hospitals were high. They may have been higher still on board the *Lady Julian*; on the other hand, sick berths on well-run ships with a competent surgeon could be safer than city hospitals and the women may have been in better hands in Rio than they would have been in Limehouse and Seven Dials. Robert Bland, the "Man-Midwife" in the Westminster General Dispensary, kept records of births there in the 1780s. He compiled a table of 1,897 babies delivered in one year and his figures were grim: 1 in 270 mothers died in childbirth, usually because of an "unnatural Labour" in which the baby presented in a difficult position. More frightening still, 1 in 241 babies born at Bland's hospital that year had been "deficient or monstrous." In these categories, he included babies with webbed fingers, hare lips, "dropsical heads" and distorted spines, one missing part of its palate and two missing "a considerable part of the cranium." Bland also delivered a pair of Siamese twins, described as "a baby with two Heads." Hazards did not end with confinement. Two of his new mothers had been "seized with mania but recovered in about three months." Many others had delivered a baby safely but died soon afterward. One in sixteen lost their children within two months and one in seven within two years. This was the lottery Sarah Whitelam, Ann Bryant, Jane Forbes, Mary Barlow, Elizabeth Griffin, Mary Warren, Margaret Wood, Ann Mash and Sarah Dorset would play in Rio de Janeiro or out on the ocean beyond if their babies did not come in time.

John Nicol's only comment on the circumstances in which his son was born was that "the ladies fitted up a kind of tent for themselves" on deck. It was late spring in Rio and temperatures were rising. By Christmas, they would be approaching the fierce heights which the *Lady Julian* had just escaped in the Doldrums and the hills enclosing the harbor would keep the heat in and the air out. Despite its richness and ornament this was, wrote a First Fleet officer, "an unhealthy spot, excluded from refreshing sea and land breezes." A tent would be needed.

In John Nicol's memory, it was Mrs. Barnsley who played the part of chief midwife and apparently played it so successfully that she continued to practice after arriving in Sydney Cove. Someone forceful must have taken charge to ensure the awning was rigged and moved through the hours of sun to keep the deck in shade; that toilet buckets were regularly emptied and cleaned; that flies and mosquitoes were fanned away; that the women beneath the awning had adequate bedding and clean linen, fresh greens to relieve constipation, herb teas against backache, barley water against cystitis and pillows on which to place swollen ankles; that sheepish seamen who did not feel like fetching more fresh water and fruit were reminded of their responsibilities.

Spring was becoming summer; the sun rose higher and temperatures with it; humidity thickened. Repairs continued to the hull, masts, spars, sails, yards and shrouds which had taken a battering in the tropical storms of the equator or fallen prey to the teredo beetle which fed off the ship's timbers. Soon, work could only be done in the first hours of the morning or after the sun began to lose its strength in the late afternoon. Between these hours, little stirred in the harbor or the city. The noonday light was so dazzling on the water it hurt the eyes. When the heat lessened at dusk, the streets filled with blacks and Indians. Female slaves appeared from the doors of the houses with bundles of laundry on their heads to be washed at the stone fountains which stood in every street. Friars, priests and sisters passed among them and the whole street-borne population dipped and rose as it passed the statues which drew automatic genuflection from free and bond alike. When dusk became night, the slaves stopped their chores and knelt in long rows down the street, chanting their vespers.

On board the *Lady Julian*, there was fitful silence during the hot midday, broken by the sighs and scratchings of a deckful of women curled beneath old sails brought up from the hold to be made into shelters. Occasionally, small children scrambled over the rail, lifted a canvas flap and peered in at the foreigners dozing underneath. The women whose babies were shortly due were allotted their own patch

of deck and their own awning. Each was attended by a best friend or
group of friends. It seems Sophia Sarah Ann Brown was with Ann
Bryant, Mary Rose with Sarah Whitelam, Mary Barlow and Mary
Warren perhaps with other girls of their age from Warwick, Margaret
Wood and little Jane Forbes with former cell mates or surrogate
mothers.

Sarah Whitelam was into the eighth month of her pregnancy.
Since leaving London, she had gained anywhere up to 30 pounds in
weight. Her belly was now fully extended and she had had to give up
her convict serge, with its seams designed for the chaste. She or Mary
Rose had probably sewn a drawstring cotton skirt of some type for
her pregnancy. She could no longer wear stays so her swollen breasts
were unsupported and movement was painful. It was difficult to find
a position in which to lie or sit which did not leave some part of her
body aching. She and the other heavily pregnant women moved from
their backs to their sides on mattresses on the deck, drawing up first
one leg then the other. They were sleepy from the heat and the weight
of their bodies, waking occasionally from a doze to put a cushion
between their knees, turn a pillow for coolness or answer some question from Mrs. Barnsley. Frequently, they would rise carefully, turning to one side, swinging the shoulders round, pushing themselves up
to kneel and then staggering up to go and use the bucket.

The fathers, indeed all the seamen and officers, except Surgeon
Alley and perhaps Lieutenant Edgar, probably steered well clear of the
maternity tent. Although male doctors had been progressively and
controversially taking over the profession of midwifery in England,
most men still considered childbirth to be strictly a female business.
The pregnant women had probably moved out of the seamen's quarters and into huts or tents on the deck as soon as the ship reached the
quiet waters of São Sebastião. The life of the ship moved around
them. The birth of half a dozen convict babies was, after all, of little
importance to most on board. The chores of cleanliness and food
preparation still went on; so did the continual small jobs required to
keep the ship neat and watertight. There were 220 women aboard not

giving birth and 25 men not about to become fathers who also had to be tended and kept occupied. The agent, cook and steward still had to go ashore and make their deals for fresh greens, meat, coffee, sugar and rum. The officers still wanted to make their day trips and shopping expeditions. Seedlings for the Sydney plantations still had to be tracked down, haggled over and brought on board. Someone still had to feed the chickens, muck out the hogs and water the plants.

The babies waiting to be born in Rio de Janeiro would be born into circumstances of great singularity, to a convict mother impregnated by—a seaman lover? an unwilling gaoler? a camp guard? John Nicol and his *Lady Julian* colleagues had had no part in the decisions by which these women were being sent into exile. They were the mercenaries of their trade, merchant seamen who signed on for the most advantageous terms on offer. If it was by their labor that the women were physically transferred from one country to another, they were only obeying orders; and if one took "as wife" a 14-year-old girl, he was only doing what someone else would have done if he had not. Is this how the pregnant women saw the fathers of their babies? Analogies with camp guards who condoned or at least did not condemn the practices in twentieth-century gaol camps are inappropriate. Any analogy which assumes a twentieth-century view of morality and personal choice in an eighteenth-century mind is unreliable. Whatever the relationship between their parents, the ship babies of Rio were born into limbo. Their mothers had been exiled from one state. They were on their way to another not quite two years old, whose identity was still in question: not yet a nation, not quite a colony, not quite a gaol. Even the name of the territory to which their mothers would take them was uncertain. Would they be English? British? New South Welsh? New Hollanders? Antipodeans? Fundamental questions hovered over the extended bellies on board the *Lady Julian* from which six lost little ship-born creoles would shortly emerge.

The maternity tent was not the only corner of activity. Under canvas to one side of the ship's waist, the nine-month cycle of reproduction was just about to end, but in huts, hammocks and berths elsewhere, it was just beginning. John Nicol remembers nothing of Sarah's labor but does remember that in Rio once again "the ladies had a constant run of visitors." Wheeling and dealing between forecastle, orlop, visiting seamen and curious inhabitants of the port got under way in Rio with the same dispatch and efficiency as in Santa Cruz de Tenerife, with the same tacit acceptance from the quarterdeck. The liquor-soaked sponge on a string and candle-wax caps came out from beneath the orlop hold mattresses to be dusted off and inserted.

The pregnant doze of half a dozen swollen women under their tatty sail was interrupted in late November or early December when Sarah Whitelam went into labor. She was a first-time mother, young and, as far as we know, reasonably healthy. The little maternity ward on one corner of the deck swung into action. "She has frequent warm and cold fits, with urgent desire to make water &co. and is exceedingly restless as every situation appears unsupportable and uncomfortable to her . . . ," wrote Dr. Bland of this stage of labor in his midwifery manuals. Contractions came every five minutes or so. Someone checked the dilation of the cervix and soon "the Shews," the membranes of the uterus, ruptured and her waters broke. Shortly afterward, her bowels emptied. Mary Rose and Elizabeth Barnsley mopped, cleaned, changed, reassured. At 8 to 10 centimeters dilation, Sarah was in transition from the first stage of labor to the second, her contractions sharp and irregular, her breathing harsh. She ran with sweat; she may have had the hiccups, belching fits or vomiting that commonly accompany this phase. Her midwives gave her infusions of camomile, hartshorn or whatever herbs Mrs. Barnsley had been able to find ashore.

It was not yet the custom to lie down to give birth, so Sarah probably walked around during much of her labor. The upright position encouraged the baby to press downward and outward. The shackles and buckles which held women in place during later labors had not yet been thought of and there were no forceps to require a woman to be on her back for access. Any support required came from a chair or, commonly, a birthing stool. This was a seat in the shape of a horse-shoe, with the gap to the front, low enough that a woman squatted rather than sat on it, wide enough to provide handgrips and support for her lower back. Whether the ladies of England had provided any of these along with their suits of childbed linen goes unrecorded. If they had not, it was well within the ability of John Nicol or the ship's carpenter to make some, perhaps on a request from Mrs. Barnsley conveyed through the surgeon, perhaps on an order from Mrs. Barnsley directly.

Squatting on a birthing stool, or kneeling on the deck, Sarah pushed and minutes, hours, a day, two days later, John Nicol Junior emerged, wrinkled and slimy, with a great gush of liquid behind him. Someone checked the baby to remove the cord from around his neck and any membrane from across his face, then turned him slightly downward so mucus drained from him. Someone else placed a basin beneath Sarah's buttocks in readiness for the placenta and another rush of blood to slip out. After some time had passed, they tied and cut the umbilical cord and placed the baby boy at Sarah's breast.

Perhaps activity stopped and the ship held its breath when one woman after another in the maternity tent went into labor and gave birth. Perhaps everything carried on as normal except in that one cor-ner where the violent business of bringing life into the world ground on and a group of frightened teenagers bled onto the deck. Some of the seamen may have been shaken, others may have shrugged their shoulders, reflected that having babies was what women had always done, always would, and thought no more about it. Not even John Nicol, whose tenderness for Sarah he would express so vividly at the end of his life, remembered anything about his son's birth.

"After four weeks," wrote Dr. Bland, Westminster midwife, new mothers "can go abroad and should . . . at first, take an airing in a car-riage for two or three days, then walk a little when the weather is favourable and defer going to church until they feel themselves in the natural state of good health." For the new mothers of the *Lady Julian*, the first months of motherhood took a different course. At the end of December, they left São Sebastião and headed for the city at the Cape of Good Hope from which the Portuguese had been ousted by the Dutch East India Company, who would themselves shortly be ousted by the British.

12

THE WRECK OF THE *GUARDIAN*

Lieutenant Riou on HMS *Guardian* had arrived at Cape Town, been given the news of Captain John Hunter's emergency provisioning trip from Sydney Cove earlier that year, loaded up with extra stores and set off for New South Wales while the *Lady Julian* was in Rio de Janeiro. The *Guardian* had left the Cape on 11 December and sailed more south than east, a course which took her dangerously close to the Antarctic regions Captain Cook had circumnavigated in his second voyage of exploration. Among Riou's many problems was conserving fresh water for the mares, stallions, ewes, rams, goats, rabbits, poultry and the pair of exotic Mauritius deer he had taken on at Cape Town. The *Guardian* masthead sighted icebergs three leagues off on 22 December. They were at 42° 15', unusually far north for ice. On Christmas Eve, at 43° 40' south, another huge ice mass was sighted and the decision taken to try and scoop some chips out of the sea in order to melt them for the cattle. Two boats were hoisted out to go ice gathering. The operation was dangerous as iceberg waters hold lethal traps. By the time the longboats had returned with their chunks, fog had closed in around the ship and visibility was down to three quarters of a mile. Extra lookouts were posted but, struggling to find a passage into safer waters, no one saw the ice-mountain on the ship's

Cape Town, South Africa, in 1787, painted by a First Fleet officer. (Mitchell Library, State Library of New South Wales, Australia)

starboard bow until it was too late and the ship was impaled. When she tore free, her rudder was left in the ice and water was streaming into her hull.

Guns, cargo and fodder were all thrown overboard and the ship was fothered with one, then two layers of canvas but the water inside her continued to rise. Forty-eight hours of frantic activity followed; men pumped for their lives but one by one gave up the fight and drank themselves into oblivion on stolen liquor. On Boxing Day, Lieutenant Riou permitted any who wished to abandon ship. The boats went out and most of the seamen went with them. All but fifteen of those in the boats would perish at sea in these lonely waters where few ships sailed. The fifteen survivors had the astonishing good luck to be picked up by a French merchantman blown off course from Mauritius, which brought them back into the Cape on 18 January.

Riou stayed with his ship and the sixty people for whom there was no room in the boats stayed with him. A temporary rudder was rigged. His log for 28 December reads: "Steering was my first object, fothering if it was only to keep her up a day or two, and by standing to the northward a chance of the *Lady Julian* passing or some other ship." When the fifteen surviving men and their French rescuers arrived in Cape Town three weeks later, it was assumed the *Guardian* had gone down, one more victim of the Southern Ocean. Dispatches were sent to the Admiralty, personal letters to Riou's mother with the news of her son's death, others to Prime Minister Pitt with news of his cousin's. In the Southern Ocean, the *Lady Julian* did not appear, for she was still on her way from Rio to the Cape, nor did any other ship, and hopes turned to finding some desert island instead. No island loomed; they were finally saved when whalers were spotted who led them into the Dutch harbor of False Bay on 21 February, "covered in dirt and rags and with long beards, looking like men from another world." Riou's was an outstanding achievement, the equivalent in seamanship and charisma of Captain Bligh's a few months earlier.

The officers of the *Lady Julian* knew nothing of the mutiny on the *Bounty* or the shipwreck of the *Guardian* when their lookout sighted land on 28 February. They had made what was, for the *Lady Julian*, a reasonably fast passage: fifty uneventful days' sailing east from Rio to the African Cape. Within a couple of hours of the lookout's call, the astonishing flat-topped mass of Table Mountain was visible to those on deck. A little later, they saw the Devil's Peak and the Lion's Head, then the creases and folds of the hills running down from the mountains and finally the churches and low houses of the town cradled in the amphitheater between mountains and sea. By evening, they were at anchor in Table Bay, about 1.5 miles southwest of Cape Town, the Tavern of the Seas.

The huge bay was full of shipping. Dutch merchantmen put in here between Antwerp and Batavia, Portuguese between Lisbon and Bengal, French between Madras, Mauritius and Bordeaux, British between Calcutta and London. There were also Americans, whalers or private merchants dealing with any colonist who did not mind breaking a European monopoly. The Americans even had their eyes on trade with and emigration to Botany Bay. They had contacted Phillip's officers through a third party to sound out British feeling on the matter when his fleet was there in 1787. The one ship the men of the *Lady Julian* had not expected to see in the bay was HMS *Guardian,* which had come in a few days before them.

When Dutch company officials came out to greet the *Lady Julian* at the mouth of the harbor, they brought with them news of the shocking recent events. The guest houses of the Cape currently hosted survivors from two British ships, one overtaken by mutineers in the South Pacific, the other holed by the ice in the Antarctic. Lieutenant Edgar and Captain Aitken hurried to complete the formalities at the house of Governor van Graaf and then to track down Lieutenant Riou at his lodgings. From him, they heard the dramatic story of the *Guardian*'s misadventure firsthand. Edgar also offered a slightly sheepish explanation of the *Lady Julian*'s exceptionally long voyage. "Constant calms about the Equator," he told his ex-junior; "the female convicts much afflicted with Scurvy; the transport was very leaky."

Agent Edgar next paid his compliments to John Fryer, master of the *Bounty*, who had remained in the Cape when Captain Bligh sailed for England in January. Master Fryer and those of the *Bounty*'s company who were fit were helping Riou with the salvage operation on the *Guardian*. Some could not; the surgeon's assistant from the *Bounty* was confined and it was feared he had lost his mind as a consequence of the thirst and fear of his forty-one days in a small boat at sea. The misadventure of the *Bounty* and the fate of her captain, a man personally known to both Riou and Edgar, was a tale of there-but-for-the-grace-of-God fascination for his brother officers but it was the wrecking of the *Guardian* which had more immediate effect on Edgar's plans. The colony at Sydney Cove had been in distress when Captain Hunter had left Cape Town a year ago. If harvests had continued poor and no stores had since been received, how much greater distress were the colonists in now? It was imperative that the *Lady Julian* should take on as many extra stores as she could find room for and leave for New South Wales as soon as possible.

There would be no leisurely seven-week stay at the Cape as there had been at Rio.

Lieutenant Riou had only been in the Dutch settlement for a week. Those stores which had not gone overboard to lighten the *Guardian* among the icebergs were still aboard the listing ship at her berth in the harbor while he sought warehouse space to rent in town. It was decided that whatever stores could be transshipped from the *Guardian* would be carried on to Sydney Cove aboard the *Lady Julian*. What would once again delay her were the leaks she had sprung during her passage from Rio. Before any new stores could be taken on, her holds would have to be emptied of any cargo already in them and her decks cleared for repairs.

Nobody had better recent experience of plugging leaks than Lieutenant Riou and the carpenter of the *Guardian*, whose services were now lent to Edgar. The *Lady Julian* was piloted up the harbor and brought in to be thoroughly overhauled before she took on the rough waters of the Southern Ocean between Africa and New South Wales. If she was careened,[23] which is likely given the state of her hull, work was in progress for at least three weeks. Careening required the ship be beached and as much of her cargo as possible be taken ashore. The women were about to land at their fourth foreign city and their third continent. Casks and barrels were hauled on deck, lowered over the side, rowed or rafted to land and rolled up the beach to safety. With up to a thousand casks in storage, this was a hot and tiring job.

The Cape Town authorities were famously nervous of unconventional cargoes. When Commodore Phillip's fleet had put in two years before en route to Botany Bay, they had posted extra sentries along the beach and doubled the guard in the city. If the women slept out of the beached ship, on their orlop mattresses or beneath shelters rigged from deck awnings, they, too, may have been guarded by Dutch militiamen on loan to the accident-prone English, or may sim-

---

[23] The operation of beaching a ship—or bringing her into very shallow water—and exposing one side of her hull to repair it.

ply have been on parole. Where, after all, could they escape to if they crept up the beach at midnight and made for the town? There were only mountains and deserts beyond.

The ship emptied, careening could start. All sails were unbent and rowed ashore. The topmasts were detached, lowered and stacked on the beach. Cables were attached to cleats on the seaward beam of the ship, rowed ashore and taken once around trees. Teams of men then hauled the ship onto one side, exposing the leaks on the other. Getting the ship into a position where these were accessible could easily take two or three days; then they had to repair her hull. Fortunately, they were not without friends in Cape Town. The rump of two other British crews could lend a brawny shoulder and heave on the ropes. The beach became temporary camp, workshop and forge as carpenters and blacksmiths set up their equipment. Sails and spare canvas were spread across the sand, examined for mildew and bleached bone dry in the sun. One fire boiled cauldrons of pitch for the men working on the hull, another cooked the food prepared by the cook, his mate and their team of convicts to feed the women on the sand, the working parties and the officers.

While the ship was careened under the supervision of the first mate, Lieutenant Edgar got on as fast as he was able with provisioning. What was left of the *Guardian*'s company, supplemented by any man from the *Bounty* not incapacitated by fever or madness, was stock taking aboard the wreck and rowing off whatever the *Lady Julian* could not take on to Sydney Cove to be stored in the warehouses Riou had rented in town. Among the stores the *Guardian* had been taking to Sydney Cove were plants, some British, some African. The plant house which Sir Joseph Banks had chalked out on her quarterdeck in Deptford was gone and the ninety-three pots he had placed inside it had been jettisoned in southern waters. These had to be replaced. On hand in Cape Town was the English botanist Francis Masson, also part of Sir Joseph Banks' international plant-gathering network. Like James Smith and George Austin, the two gardening superintendents selected by Sir Joseph for Sydney Cove, Francis Masson had been plucked from

Kew at his instigation. From Cape Town, he had been conducting botanical expeditions into the interior since 1772, sending whatever he could back to Kew and making pleas to be allowed to go home.

Much of the livestock which Riou had bought in Cape Town for the Sydney Cove farms had also been lost in the wreck. Some had gone overboard. Smaller animals had been trampled and crushed when the cattle panicked, or drowned when the water washed over the hutches. Riou had managed to save his flock of twenty-two sheep and two Cape stallions. It was decided these would be transshipped to the *Lady Julian*, along with 75 barrels of flour, 100 gallons of wine and some Admiralty dispatches for Commodore Phillip. Five of the seven superintendents had survived the *Guardian* wreck and Edgar inherited these as passengers. All twenty-five gardening convicts had remained on board the *Guardian* and helped bring her safely back to the Cape. Riou had promised these men, "so meritorious, before and after the disaster," that he would petition for their pardon in recognition of the part they had played. It was arranged that the twenty-five convicts would remain in Cape Town and sail on the *Neptune*, *Scarborough* or *Surprize*, expected within days.

When the *Lady Julian* was pronounced as fit as she could be made by the carpenters, she was righted, reloaded and returned to her berth in the harbor. Work for the carpenters did not stop, however, for now they had to devise new accommodation to house the six humans, two stallions and flock of sheep which would join the ship's company for the last leg of the voyage. At the end of March, John Thomas Doidge came aboard, as did flax dresser Andrew Hume, Philip Devine and Hessian ex-mercenary Philip Schaffer with his 10-year-old daughter Elizabeth, the first genuine "young lady" aboard. They were probably accommodated in huts put up in the waist of the ship. Miss Elizabeth may have shared a hut with her father or Mrs. Barnsley or some of the officers may have been turfed out of their mess to hand it over to her.

These discussions, works and removal of stores took the whole of March to accomplish. The officers meanwhile went into lodgings ashore. The house favored by Commodore Phillip and his officers in

1787 belonged to a Mrs. de Witt, whose husband seems also to have been one of the merchants involved in supplying foreign shipping. It was a happy arrangement for all. The seamen may also have gone ashore. Well-to-do and trusted convicts on later ships went with them and presumably the well-to-do and trusted of the *Lady Julian* had the same opportunities. If they did, it was with an officer clinging like weed to their sleeves. The Dutch were more chary than the Spanish or Portuguese of foreign ship's companies, and especially of these gangs of convicts the British had started sending south.

The landing place stood at the eastern end of the town. None of the foreshore, which is now office blocks, gardens and municipal statuary, had yet been reclaimed from the sea. The first building passed by the newly disembarked was the massive pentagonal Castle of Good Hope, which was also a store and quarters for bachelor officers of the Company. A newer fort defended the western part of the town. In a different way, Cape Town was as foreign as Rio and Santa Cruz—teutonic and Protestant rather than Latin and Catholic but equally strange to Londoners and Bristolians. After their weeks in Rio, the ladies had become accustomed to streets full of trotting slaves and bright light but in Cape Town there were new ethnic and penal variations. Each European colony had its own take on the status and treatment of slaves. Each preferred a different nationality in the house or the fields. There were Negroes and "half-castes" among the Cape Town slaves but also Malaysians, brought from Dutch possessions further east to work as soft-footed houseservants. Too soft-footed; according to urban myth in 1780s Cape Town, Malaysian slaves "frequently assassinate their masters and mistresses" and were required to carry a lantern after dark. Slaves of mixed race were admired and expensive; the Negroes of Mozambique and Madagascar were liked best, as they were "affectionate and faithful" and "Hottentots"[24] from the interior were almost impossible to get hold of. There was more of a desertion problem among the Cape Town slaves than among those

---

[24] Bushmen.

of Rio. A popular day trip for visiting seamen was an excursion into the tableland from where an apparently inaccessible ledge would be pointed out by a local guide as the home of gangs of runaway Negroes. At dusk, their fires could be seen far above and dark tales were told of depredations made by night on kitchen gardens.

Equally popular, but considerably more strenuous, was a trip to the top of Table Mountain. This could be a "sultry and fatiguing expedition," but the view from the top was universally held to be one of the world's finest. The extreme neatness and regularity of the town became apparent from the mountain and the exact 90-degree angles at which its streets intersected each other were pointed out to visitors. It is hard to find a contemporary journal which does not describe the Cape as clean, regular and well-ordered. There was no vulgar Catholic excess here, but pristine, flat-roofed white houses such as survive in Bo-Kaap, only two stories high as a precaution against the strong winds of the summer, and a few decently imposing buildings for official Company business. The governor's house was one of these and the Company gardens in which it stood, part functional, part ornamental, were superb (although Watkin Tench was predictably sniffy about the little zoo the gardens housed. "It is poorly furnished both with animals and birds: a tyger, a zebra, some fine ostriches, a cassowary and the lovely crown-fowl"). The Dutch churches were soberly Lutheran and Calvinist and the Dutch ladies walked barefaced and forthright. On the surface, this was a more orderly society than Rio but for all its calm and efficiency there were glimpses of a justice shocking in its severity. The execution place was very close to the spot where visiting ships watered, just above the fort. It contained not only a gibbet, but a pole for impalements, wheels and six crosses for breaking criminals. Body parts which survived the executions performed here were suspended at street corners around the town.

Centuries of European miners, planters and latifundistas had subdued vast tracts of the older colonies in South America but outside the Dutch enclaves on the African coast, the land and its people reverted abruptly to their natural state. Tales of cannibalism and black ritual emerged from the bush, some true, some less true but all passed on with relish. According to a 1798 convict, who was not allowed off ship during his weeks in Cape Town harbor, the savagery of the bush also enveloped the city: "Elephant. Rhincerosses. Some with one Horn others two, Lyons, Tygers, Wolves in aboundance that infest the towns. Hynas Jackalls Wild dogs. & Cats. Swines. Zabra. Otters. Baboons Monkeys of a Silver Colour. Camelleopards also the great-Horned Animal resembling the Horse Ox & the Antelope. there is Serpent Scorpions Lizards. Locusts. Mosquitos that are venomous."

Even more chilling than the wildlife were the natives. The true and terrifying story of the *Grosvenor* merchantman was back in the Cape Town news when the *Lady Julian* arrived in March 1790. The *Grosvenor* had gone aground on this coast eight years earlier and those of her crew and passengers who survived the wreck, including several ladies, had been "detained among the Caffres, the most savage set of brutes on earth." Company troops had made several attempts to find and rescue them but they were eventually presumed eaten or enslaved. Then fresh news was received from the interior. When Captain Bligh stopped at the Cape on his way to Tahiti, he received an update from the Company commander. "In his travels into the Caffre country, he had met with a native who described to him, that there was a white woman among his countrymen, who had a child, that she frequently embraced the child, and cried most violently." The commander gave this man letters in English, Dutch and French, instructing him to have the woman make some mark on one, to prove her existence, and bring it back. He never returned and the story subsided; but when the *Lady Julian* arrived the following year, another sighting had just been reported. Preparation of expeditions into the bush to track down the survivors of the *Grosvenor* was a hot topic during the weeks the *Lady Julian* spent at the Cape. It was little reassuring to those on board who feared savages awaited them along a coast further south.

During their month in Table Bay, the season changed. Late summer became autumn. Every ship entering the harbor now struck her

A romantic view of the wreck of the *Grosvenor* merchantman off South Africa in 1782. (Worlds Edge Picture Library)

yards and topmasts as a precaution against the violence of a southeast wind which could drive ships completely out of the bay. Delays in Britain and the weeks spent at Rio meant the *Lady Julian* would be crossing the Southern Ocean dangerously late in the season. The ideal time to make this passage was spring, when Commodore Phillip had taken his fleet east two years before. The *Lady Julian* had been in Table Bay less than two weeks when the first casualties were claimed by autumnal gales. On 12 March, eight seamen and the bosun of the *Guardian* came over the side with the news that a fishing vessel was in distress at the mouth of the harbor. A launch was immediately lowered and the eight *Guardian* men, with the bosun at the tiller, made for the spot where the vessel had been seen. They were just in time to hold her with a small anchor and cable taken from the *Lady Julian* and stop her short no more than three cable lengths from the surf where, "had she come ashore, she must have been dashed to pieces without a probability of saving the Lives of the Crew."

Cape Town was the place where reality bit, even for the most non-chalant. The Southern Ocean was a dangerous sea and the winds which had begun to howl through the rigging in the shelter of Table Bay warned of a rough passage. The *Guardian* had been wrecked in this ocean three months before and half her company drowned; the *Grosvenor* had been bashed against the African coast by frightful waves and the fate of her survivors brought a shudder. And if the *Lady Julian* survived the passage, realization now crept through the orlop that there was nothing left between them and Sydney Cove, no more delays, no foreign ports, no friendly slave ships. On 31 March, the *Lady Julian* left Table Bay with the "Cattle rather uneasy." She sailed into hazy weather and gales from the southeast.

13

CAPE TOWN TO SYDNEY COVE

*T*he day after the *Lady Julian* left the African cape, a reduced food allowance was announced in Sydney Cove: "to every person in the settlement without distinction: 4 pounds of flour, 2½ pounds of salt pork and 1½ pounds of rice, per week." It was the beginning of a disastrous month. The Cove had been empty of shipping for three weeks since the colony's two remaining ships, the *Supply* and the *Sirius,* sailed to Norfolk Island with 65 marines, 5 marine wives, 116 male and 67 female convicts and 27 of their infants. The advance party of 23 people who had sailed to Norfolk in February 1788 had sent back promising reports to Governor Phillip—so promising that he decided to relieve the public store in Sydney Cove by sending up as many mouths as he thought the island could feed.

The conclusions reached by Edgar, Aitken and Riou in Cape Town as to the colonists' dismal prospects were substantially correct. The mainland harvest of summer 1788–89 had been poor and a meager yield was further reduced when the stores in Sydney Cove were overrun by rats in February. The colony lived in hunger and civil unrest lurked beneath the food shortages. The same month the rats invaded, six marines were discovered stealing food from the public store. Governor Phillip imposed the maximum penalty *pour encour-*

ager les autres and they were hanged outside the store. Bad feeling already festered between the civil government and the marine corps, which considered its rights to include a privileged food ration, and its duties to exclude manual labor, horticulture and the supervision of convicts. A note of rage creeps into Phillip's otherwise sane and balanced dispatches when he mentions the marines. Now the food crisis sharpened the tension between these two crucial colonial elements. When hope faded of a store ship from England, two more emergency victualing expeditions were planned, the first to China, the second to Batavia. The *Sirius* was to drop off her passengers at Norfolk Island and sail on to China for food. The *Supply* would return to Sydney Cove with some of the marines due for relief from Norfolk duty, then turn and follow the *Sirius* north.

Events on Norfolk Island changed these plans. Norfolk was a fearsome place to make a landing. It took five days for the men and women on the two ships to get ashore, along a lifeline shuddering in the surf which broke over their heads. They could only go ashore at low tide, in small groups. The boats had to maneuver themselves sternfirst toward a rocky promontory which was cut off when the tide rose. On the sixth day, the ships attempted to turn away from the beach and sail for the safety of deeper waters but the *Sirius* was caught in currents and impaled on coral as the *Guardian* had been on ice, with her bilges bleeding into the sea. The *Supply* sailed south alone on 24 March, bearing dreadful news for the garrison in Sydney Cove and leaving over four hundred people marooned on Norfolk Island.

The *Supply* arrived between the Heads on 5 April. The news that the *Sirius* was lost shook the colony. There was now only one ship to connect Sydney Cove with the civilized world. Should anything happen to the *Supply*, sailing valiantly between the three settlements, or undertaking another dash to buy supplies from the Dutch, the colonists would be utterly isolated. Two years had already passed with no sign that anyone in London remembered the promises of further supplies "within the year." They had been thrown increasingly on

Norfolk Island, 1788: taking provisions off the wreck of the *Sirius*.
(Barnaby's Picture Library)

their own resources and, by a stroke of atrocious luck, had lost one of
the most important of these.

By May, work was almost at a standstill. The official hours for
convict labor were cut back to end at one o'clock. Men and women
on the rations issued by the public store in Sydney Cove could not be
expected to work longer hours. About 90 percent of their diet now
consisted of wriggling rice, infested with weevil. The peas were finished. The plots of land sown with lettuce and corn on Garden and
Clark Islands and dotted about the settlement under an increasingly
corrupt armed guard would not be ready to harvest for weeks and a
spate of desperate night thefts was reducing the already dismal acreage
of plants left to ripen. Despite the evacuation of 280 mouths to Norfolk Island, the townships of Sydney Cove and Rose Hill still struggled to feed themselves. Scurvy had taken the camp; Phillip himself
was suffering badly. Venereal disease had spread. Everyone was malnourished. For two weeks, the governor weighed the risk of losing the

colony's only remaining ship by sending it on another provisioning run against the risk of starvation before the promised ships from England came in. Perhaps his faith had been dented in two years of waiting for a signal from the men at the South Head that a Red Ensign was sailing in. On 18 April, the *Supply* left Sydney Cove for Batavia to buy food.

The same week that the *Supply* sailed from Sydney Cove, the *Neptune,* the *Surprize* and the *Scarborough* were leaving Cape Town. They had arrived in the African harbor within days of the *Lady Julian*'s departure, been greeted by Lieutenant Riou and learned of the disaster which had befallen the *Guardian.* Agent Shapcote of the *Neptune* was less accommodating than Agent Edgar when it came to carrying on stores saved from the wreck. Riou commented sourly that Shapcote did not want to lose the storage space he had allotted to the liquor and other items in short supply in Sydney Cove, which he would sell there on his own account. It took veiled threats before Shapcote agreed to take on beef and pork and, wrote Riou, "had not a misunderstanding existed between Lieutenant Shapcote and myself . . . I could have sent many articles which would not have taken up much stowage in the ships under his direction that would have been very acceptable to His Majesty's colony in New South Wales." They also took on the twenty-five gardening convicts. There was far more room for them in these ships than on the crowded little *Lady Julian*: forty-six convicts had already died on the *Neptune,* eight on the *Surprize* and fifteen on the *Scarborough.* More would be heaved over the side in the Southern Ocean.

There was now more shipping heading for New South Wales than at any time since December 1787. The *Lady Julian* was three weeks out from the Cape, nearing Kerguelen. The *Neptune, Surprize* and *Scarborough* were a couple of weeks behind her and catching up. A second store ship, the *Justinian,* of which Edgar knew nothing but which had left England after the three transports, had stopped at neither Rio nor Cape Town. She was now sailing a couple of degrees north on a course which would bring her to the heads of Port Jackson within a day of the *Lady Julian*. Despite delays in putting the intended convoy together in Britain, the leaky *Lady Julian*, with sickness and childbearing aboard, had taken so long to cross the world that by the time she got into the Southern Ocean, the rest of the fleet had almost caught up with her.

As these five ships sailed west, the *Supply* was sailing north between Norfolk Island and the coast of New South Wales on her way to buy flour in Batavia. On Norfolk Island, the population had suddenly increased from fifty to almost 500 when the *Supply* and *Sirius* offloaded passengers and then the company of the wrecked *Sirius* was also forced to stay behind. Among the newcomers was Major Ross of the marines, sent to relieve the previous lieutenant-governor of Norfolk Island. Ross immediately imposed martial law and introduced capital punishment for the theft of food but even this deterrent could not prevent thievery and starvation. The Norfolk Islanders were saved by the discovery of the muttonbird, a fat innocent creature which lived in great colonies of burrows on Mount Pitt, in the center of the island. Muttonbirds had never before been hunted and, when they flew back to their nesting sites at dusk each day, they had no collective memory of death to protect them from the cosh. The colonists drove paths through trees held together by thick strands of vine to get to Mount Pitt. They went out daily through April and May to wait for the birds which returned to their burrows at dusk, club them, grab them by the legs and bash their heads against stones, poke baited hooks down the burrows and raid their nests for eggs. The muttonbird kept the islanders going through the desperate winter of 1789, the howling southeasterlies of July and August, the "evils, three in number, viz Blights, Grubs and Paroquets" which destroyed their first crops. By August, French beans, lettuce, cabbage and potatoes were coming up to relieve the island's reliance on Mount Pitt. They were grown in small fenced plots tended by at least two people, one of whom picked off the grubs while the other scared away the parrots. More gardens were being cut from the woodland and the gardeners were learning how to harness the fertility of the soil. Homegrown salad stuff was gradually added to the settlers' diet, but not before the muttonbird had been hunted to extinction.

The *Lady Julian* was now sailing through seas "mountains high." During autumn and winter in the Southern Ocean, the wind averages a Force 5–6. Spray continually soaks the deck, the bowsprit goes under completely and temperatures drop to freezing. A full gale will blow once every two weeks on average and last anywhere between 8 and 48 hours. Elizabeth Schaffer, her father and the other superintendents, wrecked here four months ago in summer, were now returning in winter conditions toward the scene of their terror. Their experiences, the even more recent wreck of the fishing vessel of Cape Town and the fate of the *Grosvenor* were fresh in the mind, and the horror story traditionally told to the nervous in these waters now started its rounds. Over a century before, two Dutch merchantmen had put out from the Cape into angry seas and been taken by a storm. One survived and struggled back to the Cape; the other went down with all hands. When the surviving ship left the Cape a second time, the nervous crew saw the ghost of the *Flying Dutchman* bearing down on her out of the mist with dead men in the rigging, dead officers on her decks and a terrible silence among her sails. The story spread among sailors of all nationalities and thereafter one of the watch aboard any ship sailing at dusk south of the Cape would see a ghastly galleon "standing for [the onlookers] under a press of sail as though she would run them down."

When a gale rose, the sufferings were intense aboard the *Lady Julian*. She shipped water straight down the hawser holes and onto every deck. When waves driven by a screaming wind engulfed the top deck, a river of seawater crashed down the orlop hatches. Water entered a ropy old ship like the *Lady Julian* from all sides. It shot down the hatches, it hung in spray on the air, it crept in from beneath. Old tar leaked like the devil in heavy seas. It groaned at each forward plunge and more salt water worked its way in through stretching seams and shrinking timbers. Men at the pumps fought the water around the clock in rough water but sometimes the sea forced itself into the ship's belly faster than the men could force it out. The eeriest sound in a Southern Ocean gale is not the scream of wind or the groan of overstretched canvas but the rumble of the wave imprisoned in the ship herself, rolling like an underground stream around her bilge. It ebbs and flows from bow to stern, thunderous as it passes, then fading away, and returning.

On other transport ships, convicts were washed completely out of their beds on the orlop deck and onto the floor in these seas. Many of the women on board the better run *Lady Julian* who had not already done so would now have left the orlop and gone to sleep wherever they could find space on the 'tween deck above. Their time on the weather deck was curtailed, their bedding and clothes remained wet and they coughed on the spray which penetrated every level of the ship. Those who had bartered their clothes for wine in Cabo Verde shivered and begged the surgeon for extra blankets. When too much water was shipped, the galley stove could not be lit and no one got hot food. Extra rations of grog were ordered for the men brushing ice from the yards aloft and the women in miserable huddles below so the glow of alcohol could boost cold peas and biscuit made soggy from spray. The cold was intense. Sailing through in December 1787, Lieutenant Clark noted "what must it be in winter if it is now so cold in the middle of Summer" and never took off his greatcoat or wore less than two pairs of stockings. The men on watch during fierce weather worked in extreme cold. Seamen in the rigging could not wear gloves, for this would interfere with their work. They were continually subject to frostbite and friction from the ropes. Blood froze as it left the cuts on their hands, nails were torn out by the roots from frozen fingers and icicles hung from the rigging.

Fore and aft hatches were battened down all day and all night when the weather was wild. This lessened the water washing into the orlop and 'tween decks but did nothing for the air quality. Easing-chairs overflowed and it was a brave woman who would stagger up steps to empty her bucket into a Force 9 gale and a deck streaming with water. Two menstrual cycles, dreadful seasickness and few laundry days passed between the African Cape and New South Wales.

Somewhere between the Cape and Port Jackson, "man overboard"
was called on the *Lady Julian.* The carpenter was caught by a wave
and went over the side. Most likely he was trying to mend a spar or
yard brought down by the winds. He may, like the second mate of a
First Fleet transport who also went overboard here, have been trying
to urinate from the heads, or, like a rash convict, have been trying to
hang linen from the bowsprit. There was no chance he would be
picked up—the captain would not risk the ship's being overwhelmed
by waves over the beam and he was anyway lost from sight in seconds
in these wild waters. The ship's company was already one down with
a man left sick in Rio. Now they had to maintain her without the
help of the carpenter.

For Lieutenant Edgar, as navigator, this was the most challenging
leg of the voyage. There can have been no man on board the *Lady
Julian* who had already sailed this passage as the only possible second
timer would have been a returning First Fleet seaman. When Edgar
had sailed to New Zealand with Captain Cook in 1776, he had covered a large part of the route he was now navigating on the *Lady
Julian*: from the Cape to the waters south of Van Diemen's Land.[25]
There the routes to Sydney Cove and New Zealand would diverge,
the *Lady Julian* turning to the north where the *Discovery* had continued to the east. It was still thought that Van Diemen's Land was a
part of New South Wales. It was not until 1798 that a Lincolnshire
man, Matthew Flinders, would circumnavigate the island, to praise
from Sir Joseph Banks, always a fan of enterprising lads. The charts
Edgar was using on board the *Lady Julian* in 1790 were those drawn
from the surveys made by Captain Cook twenty years earlier, when
he mapped the coast of "New Holland" from the position of present-
day Melbourne east and north as far as the Torres Straits. Since Captain Cook had handed in his charts to the Admiralty, only eleven
British ships had used them. Those eleven were the First Fleet to New
South Wales. Nobody had had reason to sail the vast, bare, lonely

---

[25] Tasmania.

passage from Africa to New South Wales before the British set up their colony in Sydney Cove.

There was fresh blood on board the *Lady Julian* during this passage. The presence of Miss Elizabeth Schaffer, who had just survived the wreck of the *Guardian,* would have put several noses out of joint. She was only two years younger than the youngest of the Rio mothers but of a different class. Although not quite old enough for the attentions of any gallant officer—and anyway chaperoned by her father—some concession had to be made to convention in her presence. Activities behind doors and below hatches remained unchanged, but a little more discretion was practiced to shield her from the behavior which, after so many months in this little self-contained world, had become the norm.

Elizabeth Schaffer's periodic presence in the captain's cabin may have put a damper on the social schedule hitherto enjoyed but, given the conditions into which the ship was now sailing, this would anyway have been curtailed. The women were less visible than they had been in warmer waters. They came on deck in smaller groups and for shorter periods. Most of their meals were taken below. Nevertheless, in this two-month passage, Superintendent Devine discovered Margaret Smith and Superintendent Doidge discovered Charlotte Simpson alias Hall. If they did not consummate their relationships on board, they certainly did soon after, as both couples had babies a little more than nine months after arrival in Sydney Cove and remained together some years. Margaret Smith, a 23- or 24-year-old from Liverpool, does not seem to have had any existing connections in the colony. Twenty-one-year-old Charlotte Simpson alias Hall had committed her crime with the George Simpson taken from the *Ceres* hulk in Portsmouth and now a couple of weeks' sailing behind her on the *Surprize.* The order of Charlotte's surnames suggests they were not spouses or de facto partners. If they were, she had weighed up the benefits of maintaining an existing liaison with a convict against those of initiating one with a superintendent and chosen accordingly.

Six weeks out from Cape Town, the man at the masthead sighted

Tasman's Head, the southernmost point of Van Diemen's Land. According to Edgar's charts, they had another fourteen to eighteen days' sailing before they came to Port Jackson. They swept past the coast of Van Diemen's Land with a wind on their beam which pushed them in toward the shore with the ship at 45 degrees to the waves. Some of Cook's men had described a narrow escape from giants on this coastline fifteen years before. The men had gone ashore here on the never-ending search for fresh greens. A gong sounded in the woods while they were picking their wild celery and then they stumbled across steps cut over seven yards apart. They deduced from this that the natives of these parts were giants, and fled for their ship in Adventure Bay. It was a scary story and it added to the horrors of the hold on the *Lady Julian*. The coast of the unfriendly giants was behind them by nightfall. The following day, they veered northward, now sailing with the wind hard behind them, reduced canvas and a level deck.

Two weeks' sailing further north, the colony in Sydney Cove continued to stagger through its second winter, its colonists cold and apathetic. Scurvy and dysentery spread and, in May, smallpox was diagnosed. No one knew where it had come from. It entered the camp at the end of April and on 2 May the first victim died. Throughout the month, the sickness struck indiscriminately at convicts, marines and officers in the Sydney Cove camp. Several died, already weakened by malnutrition, but there were fewer victims within the camp than without. The worst affected were the Aborigines, who died in scores. Small boats put out daily from the cove to land on the beaches in the river, collect their bodies and take them over to the north shore for burial. The sight and smell was gruesome; dingoes invaded the beaches after dark and fed from the recent dead. It was the colony's lowest moment yet.

The day of 2 June 1789 was wild and stormy, with low cloud and a strong wind from the south. It was seventeen months since the arrival of Governor Phillip and his fleet and five since the passing of the year within which they had been assured of relief. The lookout on

A British view of Aboriginal women in Port Jackson, 1788. (William Bradley, Mitchell Library, State Library of New South Wales/Bridgeman Art Library)

the South Head had been manned since the earliest days by three marines. It was not an envied post. They were cut off from Sydney Cove by half a dozen headlands and it was rumored that their hut had been built in an Aboriginal graveyard whose ghosts were offended by the intrusion. The men maintained a fire outside their hut night and day for warmth; its flames also kept the ghosts away. The flagpost at the lookout could be seen from Dawes Point and every day a few marines and convicts would walk down there, more from habit than hope, to gaze south toward the Heads where no flag ever hung, until 2 June, when the signal went up that a sail had been sighted.

It was far too soon for the *Supply* to have returned from Batavia— unless she had been wounded on her voyage north and was stumbling back, like the *Guardian* to Cape Town, with holes in her hull and half her company lost. Up at the lookout, the men did not lift their eyes from where they had briefly seen a sail far out to sea. No ship reemerged from the spray. Night fell with no further sighting and the next day the colony gathered at Dawes Point. When the flag was finally run up again, there was pandemonium in the camp. People ran from Dawes Point through the huts shouting the news, burst into tears, embraced. Lieutenant Tench recalled the moment with uncharacteristic emotion in his journal:

> My next door neighbour, a brother-officer, was with me but we could not speak; we wrung each other by the hand, with eyes and heart overflowing. We raced for the harbour, begged to be among the governor's party, pushed through wind and rain and at last we read the word "London" on her stern.

It is seven miles from the Heads at the entrance to Port Jackson downriver to Sydney Cove and it took some hours for the first boats to appear bearing hysterical officers drenched with spray. They were in time to see the *Lady Julian* sail into peril. The Heads are about three quarters of a mile apart, a good enough gap in decent weather but not when both wind and tide carry a ship onto the North Head. The *Lady Julian* very nearly came to grief here. Caught by a strong southerly behind her and the last of the tide, she was blown perilously near the rocks of the North Head. Her crew, hauling on the sheets to bring her round and tack off into the wind, were losing the battle. Only the set of the tide stopped her drift to the rocks and allowed the crew to haul her around and into Spring Cove, in the lee of the North Head. It was a heart-stopping finale to her voyage across the world.

The men were still coming down from the rigging when Watkin Tench and a handful of Sydney Cove officers came swarming over the sides of the ship like the urchins of Rio, slapping the seamen on the back, shaking hands with the officers, all speaking at once. They knew nothing of the upheavals in France, nor the terrible illness and recovery of His Majesty, nor the wreck of the *Guardian*: "News burst upon us like meridian splendour on a blind man," wrote Tench. They stayed until dark.

The night of 3 June was the first in two months that the women had not slept through heavy seas but they were exhausted and apprehensive. Few can have slept well. Rumor and supposition raged. The officers who had rowed out to meet them had been dressed in tatters, with holes in their boots and skinny limbs, faces pockmarked and drawn with hunger. The women had taken a distant second place in their inquiries to the number of flour barrels and cattle on board. Perhaps already the news that they were a disappointment rather than a relief had gone around the orlop. The women could not see the camp from their anchorage in Spring Cove but the harbor of Port Jackson was unwelcoming in the worst of the June weather. A mass of low dripping green lay across the headlands; the coves were deserted. For any who had heard the sailors' tales of south sea islands and expected palm belts and smiling natives in canoes, Port Jackson in June was a rude shock. Dark came suddenly. Lieutenant Tench and his comrades had gone back to their huts in Sydney Cove. Anyone on deck would notice flickering pinpoints of light from first on the beaches where the unknown savages of Botany Bay were watching them.

The fourth of June was another blustery day; the *Lady Julian* would not be able to move downriver. The usual morning rituals of eating, cleaning and airing were observed amid tension and uncertainty. The distant firing of small arms shocked the company before they realized the camp was honoring His Majesty's birthday. Midmorning, longboats started to appear from Sydney Cove with convict men aboard, sent to unload the first provisions. Hunger was too immediate to wait for the ship to come alongside the wharf in Sydney Cove which had been built to receive a mighty store ship.

The workers who came aboard were not officers who gazed past the women and asked after the cows, but convicts like themselves. Two Maidstone men, John Jeffries and Robert Abel, were among them and, with ten Maidstone women on board, unloading must have come second to the exchange of news: who was dead, who still alive, who in prison, who had had babies, with whom, which partners left behind had struck up new relationships in England, which partners sent overseas had done the same here. And Sydney Cove? The Indians, the hard labor in plantations, the overseers? Any lingering expectation that a new America had been planted in the Sydney soil was finally dispelled. The colony was newly excited because a whole four fields of corn were predicted from the Rose Hill harvest later that year and the potatoes were promising on Garden Island. It was not the bounty of Virginia.

As to the "Indians," if Robert Abel and John Jeffries believed the rumors current in the camp, their answers were scary. A few had been tamed; two orphaned children actually lived in the camp and one fellow was a frequent guest at the house of the governor. His hospitality to this black was viewed with suspicion. The rest were savages, with bones through their noses and white clay markings on their faces, animals' teeth and lobster claws glued into their hair with gum, vicious and accurate with their spears, dangerous to any white settler in the bush. Twelve men had already gone missing, thought speared; one convict who had lost himself in the sinister hinterland of Sydney Cove came back with reports of a human body burning in a native bonfire.

The reunion was brief, because the men had orders to obey, and tainted when John Nicol discovered that records of sugar landed on the Sydney wharves did not match those of sugar disembarked in Spring Cove. He would have to give evidence against them. It was not until 6 June that the wind abated sufficiently to tow the *Lady Julian* into Sydney Cove. They passed Clark Island. Its lettuce and bean plots had been sown by Lieutenant Clark—or, rather, convicts lent him for the work—before he was posted up to Norfolk Island and had to leave his greens to the public store. Rounding Bennelong Point, where the Opera House now stands, the women had their first view of Sydney Cove. Jubilant officers had reported in more optimistic times that Port Jackson could hold a hundred ship of the line, supplied from the wharves of Sydney Cove, but in June 1790, the wharves were unbuilt and the harbor empty. The *Supply* was on her way to Batavia. The *Sirius* was wrecked on the coral of Norfolk Island. The *Lady Julian* was the only ship there.

She moored in a narrow bay between two muddy headlands dotted here and there with huts sodden from recent rain. At the head of the harbor, the water narrowed to a snake of silvery water beneath a

The governor's house in Sydney Cove as it looked when the *Lady Julian* arrived in 1790. (William Bradley, Mitchell Library, State Library of New South Wales/Bridgeman Art Library)

trestle bridge. To one side stood a bunkhouse. This was the barracks, from which more skinny men with holes in their uniforms watched them and cheered. Next to it, strategically placed, was the thatched barn which served as the public store. On their right was a hospital, a cookhouse and more tatty soldiers guarding more tatty cabbage patches. Further back were little rows of wet huts, the rushes on their roofs sagging beneath the weight of rain. Rivulets of dirty red water ran between them down to discolored pools in the waters of the cove.

On the other side of the bridge, at the top of a slight slope, was the only decent-looking house in the place: two stories, double fronted, an attempt at a porch but with an eccentric kitchen garden running from the front steps to the water's edge, patrolled by barefoot sentinels with muskets over their shoulders. Could this truly be the residence of the governor? More sad huts spread between his gardens, the river and the shoreline. At the water's edge, gaunt men and women stood among the rocks to see the *Lady Julian* warped in. Relentless rain on water drowned any noise from the shore. They had arrived.

14

A CARGO SO UNNECESSARY

$\mathcal{D}$espite the scurvy on the far side of Rio and the cold and wet since Cape Town, most of the women aboard the *Lady Julian* were healthier when they arrived in Sydney Cove than they had been when they left England. Their diet had on the whole been decent and their alcohol intake restricted. Fresh air and clean linen had improved skin, hair and breath. On 4 or 5 June, with the ship still stormbound in Spring Cove, they had brought their trunks up from the hold where John Nicol had stowed them in the Thames and shaken out their best dresses. They had given each other whatever haircuts they could manage, cleaned their nails and teeth, plucked, squeezed, tweezed and sluiced.

Fear of savages was one expectation of New South Wales, but not the only one. The expectations of the wiser women were informed less by lurid tales of cannibalism than by a century's experience of convict and indentured labor in America and the Indies. This was played by tough rules but had been far from uniformly negative. Women had returned from America, and returned richer, with New World fortunes. There had been opportunities in that colony and there would be opportunities in this one. There had also been rough rituals, one of which notoriously followed the arrival of female blood, which would now presumably be carried over to the new colony. The captain would make his arrangements with dealers on the docks and women would be put up for sale, sometimes at open auction, standing on bales of newly landed cloth on the quayside, sometimes by the agreement of gentlemen behind closed doors. Surely this was what the kinder matrons were preparing the little ones for as they dressed themselves to look their best sailing into Sydney Cove.

Too little is available on Captain Aitken's past to tell us if he had previously been involved in the transportation of convicts or slaves. His appointment to the *Lady Julian* implies relevant experience. He may, like Lieutenant Edgar, have sailed in the South Pacific or the Southern Ocean in the 1770s, or he may have worked in some connected branch of maritime trade. Given his rank, he was certainly old enough to have been sailing before the American wars cut off the plantations; he could have been making delivery runs to the Indies well into the 1780s. Certainly, he had demonstrated familiarity with the traditions of the transportation industry: he had accepted the cohabitation of convicts and seamen and he had connived at the sale of sex in their ports of call. In Sydney Cove, Captain Aitken also observed another ritual of his profession—the sale for private profit of articles he had bought on speculation in England or on the voyage out. He had his fresh linen shirts, sewn by the convicts, he had a private supply of wine and liquor and he had either held back from government supplies or had bought on his own account a large quantity of sugar.

Within years, the traditional model of distributing incoming females was well established in Sydney Cove. A marine arriving in 1792 on another female transport saw his ship overrun by male colonists thrusting each other out of the way in order to claim their prize. "The women," he wrote, "were no less objects of desire than the animals." This arrival ritual would continue for thirty years, until changing ideas of decency put a stop to it.

However, the *Lady Julian* arrived at a unique moment in the colony's history and the apprehensive women in their best dresses

were only one of two cargoes aboard her. Governor Phillip had petitioned for more skilled men, more food and more women to remedy
the imbalance of the sexes. London seemed to have answered his petitions in the wrong order. The colony had been expecting a store ship,
with a few skilled men aboard to take charge of the building and agricultural projects. What it got in June 1790 was 222 females with their
brats to be housed and fed. True, it brought the immediate relief that
Britain had not forgotten them but "it was not a little mortifying to
find," wrote the normally gallant Judge Advocate Collins, ". . . a
cargo so unnecessary and so unprofitable as 222 females, instead of a
cargo of provisions . . ." Of all receptions the women of the *Lady
Julian* had hoped or feared, it was surely not this one.

Distribution of women took second place to distribution of stores
in Sydney Cove, Rose Hill and Norfolk Island. It took five days to get
all the provisions off the *Lady Julian*'s decks and out of her holds.
Cask after cask went down the wooden wharf at the foot of the governor's garden, into carts which convict gangs in yokes hauled around
the head of the cove and into the store, where they were kept under
armed guard. Sheep, cattle and stallions were swum ashore through
the rain and given into the charge of convict herdsmen. Recent experience of hunger showed in the colonists' reverence for food. All
remaining hay and fodder was taken off the ship to save the settlement's own supplies. Surgical materials, remnants of linen, spoons,
pots, plates, needles, patched blankets, reels of twine, oil, vinegar,
wine, flour and every last wet piece of biscuit which the seamen
would not eat between Sydney Cove and China was handed ashore,
itemized and stowed away in the store by the creek. When the final
sums were done at the end of the week, it was calculated that the
colony could increase its weekly ration from 4 to 5.5 pounds of flour
per week (male ration) for three months. The relief the *Lady Julian*
had brought would make almost no difference at all.

There were no salutes from weather-worn batteries to mark the
Lady Julian's entry into this colonial port or candle-lit Government
House dinners. The colony had run out of candles and anyone

invited to dine with Governor Phillip was expected to bring his own bread. Edgar's reception was a barrage of questions: How far behind were the other ships of the Second Fleet? what supplies might be expected from them? was a relief corps of marines on board? how many women, men, superintendents, convicts skilled in building and farming? Edgar knew only that the transport vessels were still in Deptford in mid-September 1789, when the *Guardian* left England. The mystery of the sail sighted the day before the *Lady Julian* arrived was discussed. The only conclusions they could draw were that another stray European explorer had passed by—or that one of the transports had made a rapid passage before the gales and another shipload of convicts would shortly arrive with more mouths to feed and bodies to shelter. Consensus was quickly reached that Sydney Cove could not support the *Lady Julian* women. They would have to go to Norfolk Island. The only ship available to carry them over was the one they had arrived in but the *Lady Julian* would once again require substantial repairs to her hull. In the meantime, the women would be accommodated in the camp.

Throughout Friday, women squelched up paths between the rocks to the convict huts, red mud oozing between their toes and clinging to the hems of their skirts. They brought their bedding with them, for there were no spare blankets in the colony, nor even enough to go around the people already there. They may also have taken crockery and cooking pots off the ship, on official loan or quietly hidden when no one was looking. Some women were accommodated temporarily in the hospital, a low brick building which occupied the plot bounded by present-day Argyle and George Streets. Others squeezed into the existing women's districts in huts made from Sydney wattle and daub: cabbage tree fronds worked into a pine frame and fixed with mud and lime, whitewashed with clay, standing in uneven lines which would later become Cumberland and Gloucester Streets. Their rush roofs were disfigured by the bushes piled on top to keep out the cold. Those last off the ship and those who had no connections in the colony probably curled like the spokes of a wheel into the giant roots of the trees later named Moreton Bay figs or on ledges sheltered by overhangs in the rock faces behind what is now Glouces-ter Walk. By five o'clock, it was dark. Surrounded by hungry strangers who had been wearing the same clothes for over a year, they did not let go of their bundles and boxes.

When the convicts of the First Fleet embarked in January 1787, the sexual frustrations of the voyage were worked off in an orgy among the rocks, carried on with the usual half knowledge, half col-lusion, half condemnation of those in charge. The marines had requested—and been given by the officers—"rum to make merry with the women upon landing." Perhaps Governor Phillip thought he might pick out the inhabitants of his whores' ghetto as soon as possible. No officer's diary records a similar party when the *Lady Julian* women arrived on 11 June but a few marines surely went knocking at a few doors where lanterns were lit and voices raised into the small hours, and men from the labor gangs in camps inland, for-bidden to enter Sydney Cove after dark, surely did so to greet the arrivals from home.

The smaller of the women's districts stood to the west of the gov-ernor's house. The other was way down the eastern arm of the cove toward Dawes Point, far from any intervention by officers. Many newcomers were friends or acquaintances of women already in the colony and their arrival was surely celebrated, Bristol with Bristol, Ratcliff with Ratcliff, Seven Dials with Seven Dials. Most had liquor, bought at Rio and the Cape. In huts a few yards away, there were men—unmarried men and convicts nearing the end of their sen-tences who knew their governor was more anxious to keep them in the camp than they were to stay. The borrowing of bedding, cooking pots, food and lantern oil for new hut mates meant any person mak-ing trips back and forth among the huts had a ready excuse for break-ing the curfew. Judge Advocate Collins may have thought the women useless mouths, but he returned each day to the convict embraces of First Fleeter Nancy Yates. Those who did not enjoy the same privileged access to a female saw possibilities in the cargo of the *Lady Julian* which Collins could afford to disdain.

Whatever unrecorded license prevailed on Friday night, during the weekend the women were reintroduced to the tired old world of expiation—first the rod, then the Bible. On Saturday, Robert Abel and John Jeffries were marched to the whipping tree at the head of the creek and given 200 lashes each, in public, for their theft of sugar from the *Lady Julian*. On Sunday, all women were assembled by the tree which had become the spot for divine service, there being no building in the colony large enough to hold its congregation, to hear a sermon from the Reverend Richard Johnson, which, he recorded with satisfaction, brought home to them so sharply their new situation that several were moved to tears. That Sunday, the first of the *Lady Julian* ship babies was baptized. The pagan waters of Sydney creek burbled Christian into the reverend's hands and Edward Dorset Powell was sprinkled and handed back. It was the first Sunday in a month of baptisms, burials and holy matrimony.

Richard Johnson had come out with the First Fleet and was an old hand at baptizing illegitimate babies and blessing unusual unions. What he could not do, however, was legitimize the *Lady Julian* couplings. For some of the seamen, parting from mistress and baby was just part of the seafaring life, but John Nicol wanted to marry Sarah Whitelam and, finally, here was a reverend, authorized by God and George III to pronounce them man and wife. Nicol begged to be allowed to stay in New South Wales, to work as a free man until Sarah's sentence expired and then bring her home. Skilled and experienced workers were desperately needed there; men like Nicol were what Governor Phillip had had in mind when he petitioned for artificers and superintendents. Agent Edgar and Surgeon Alley were both staying. Their contract was with the Admiralty only; they had not signed on for the East India tea run. One of the seamen was also to remain in Sydney Cove. This was Sam Braiden, forecastle husband of Mary Warren and Rio father of baby Sam, more probably because he was sick or injured than because of an attachment to Mary. He did not marry her, he showed no interest in becoming a settler and he left the colony alone a year later.

Captain Aitken would not release John from his contract. The ship was already three men down, with one sick in Rio, the carpenter lost overboard in the Southern Ocean and now Sam Braiden ashore in Sydney Cove. If Nicol were allowed to stay, how many other men would want to do the same? Certainly Edward Powell, to stay with Sarah Dorset—and they would then be five down on a thirty-six-man ship, sailing a winter passage to Canton. The captain's East India tea contract was conditional on his arriving there by 15 January 1791 and on the *Lady Julian*'s being in a fit state to take on the cargo. Undermanned, and without cooper or carpenter, he would stand to lose a lucrative commission.

By the end of June, Captain Aitken was not the only force to prevent seamen from jumping ship and becoming colonists. The "useless mouths" had been a sore disappointment on 3 June but, by the time the first of the *Lady Julian* wharf brides signed her cross on 28 June, the potential of her shipmates had been reassessed.

On 20 June, another sail had been sighted by the lookout at the South Head and, on 21 June, the store ship *Justinian* was warped into Sydney Cove. Her arrival saved the colony. The *Justinian* had made a remarkable five-month dash from London, bypassing both Rio and Cape Town, and had run into adventures just at the entrance to the colony. The gales which kept the *Lady Julian* in Spring Cove had sent the *Justinian* hurtling up the coast of New South Wales and nearly driven her onto the rocks around Black Head.[26] Had she gone down, the New South Wales colony might have gone down with her, one more colonial experiment ending in dry bones on a beach. The *Justinian*'s arrival tipped the balance from probable starvation to probable survival. The stores aboard her would keep the colony going for some months—and by then, the rest of the Second Fleet would have

---

[26] Port Stephens.

arrived, the *Supply* would have returned with grain from Batavia and the sullen Australian soil might have started to yield. The women of the *Lady Julian* could now be assessed not as unnecessary consumers of food but as providers of the services London had sent them over to deliver: sexual comfort and a breeding bank.

The colony had only one week of relief between the blessed arrival of the *Justinian* and the joy of taking off the stores she had brought, and the horrors which came up from the holds of the next three ships in. At the end of the month, a signal went up at the South Head that a sail had been sighted. This time, there was no mystery. It could only belong to the *Neptune*, the *Scarborough* or the *Surprize* with cell mates, lovers, pimps, receivers and husbands among the convicts aboard. Again, the colonists of Sydney Cove headed for Dawes Point to gaze seaward. Elizabeth Barnsley would be reunited with a husband she had last lived with in 1785. If Ann Wheeler had survived the gaol fever, she might also be on board. Sarah Carter awaited the arrival of William Pimlott; Charlotte Simpson alias Hall would have to tell George Simpson of her arrangement with Superintendent Doidge; Sarah Young did not know if her husband, whom she had left petitioning Lord Sydney to join her, was among the convicts at the far end of the river. They had a night to prepare themselves. Like the *Lady Julian*, the newly arrived ships lodged in a cove at the mouth of the harbor overnight and were warped into Sydney Cove the following day to join the *Justinian*. It would become clear later in the week that their crews spent much of the night bringing on deck the bodies of the convicts who had died in the hold since Cape Town and throwing them over the side. For days, bodies washed up onto the beaches around Sydney Cove, bloodless hands still fettered.

At the beginning of the month, the waters of the cove had been deserted. By the end, they lapped at the hulls of five large merchant-men riding to anchor. Men rowed back and forth, water casks floated across, there were shouts, the splash of oars and the smell of boiling pitch—all the cheerful activity of an international port of call. The optimistic picture in the river was deceptive because on land the scene was one of horror. One thousand seventeen convicts had embarked on the *Neptune*, *Scarborough* and *Surprize*: 759 survived, 273 were buried at sea or thrown over the side in Spring Cove and 486 of the survivors were now unloaded too sick to feed or care for themselves. More would die during their first days in the colony. The First Fleet convicts, with all their sufferings in an inhospitable and infertile country, had been treated with fairness and stern humanity by Arthur Phillip. The convicts of the *Lady Julian* had lost only five of their comrades on the voyage out, none of them to neglect. When the first boats put out from the transport vessels just in with the first heaps of stinking, dying humans in irons, the colonists in Sydney Cove stood unbelieving at the water's edge. "What a difference between us and them," a *Lady Julian* convict wrote home. "God bless our good Agent."

Dying men and women were heaved from the decks like bales of cotton, one on top of another into the boats below. The lighters rowed to wading distance of the shore and the oarsmen stood, levered the convicts over the side and went back for more. A few drowned in the shallow waters of their destination. Those that could crawl ashore collapsed there in mewing heaps. The governor's fury galvanized rescue teams. People plunged in to pull their comrades up the shore. Blacksmiths knocked off fetters on the beach but many could not walk on muscles atrophied from months in shackles. The healthy carried the sick on their backs and in their arms through the rocks to the hospital. Boats plowed back and forth, dumping more of the helpless onto the shoreline from where they were ferried to makeshift tents. It seemed to go on for hours—boatload after lousy boatload of men and women blinking at the light, so filthy, drawn and disfigured that even lovers and brothers were unrecognizable.

Women from the *Lady Julian* pushed across the beach, turning over bodies and demanding information from people who could not answer them. Forty-six-year-old Elizabeth Dell from Reading was searching for her son John, who had sailed as a marine aboard the *Surprize* to stay with his mother and brother, transported on the First

Fleet. Elizabeth Barnsley, Sarah Gregory and Sarah Young were looking for their husbands, Sarah Carter was trying to find William Pimlott, Grace Maddox was searching for her accomplice, Thomas
Higgins. No one could help—the convicts themselves did not know
who had come out of the holds alive and who had gone over the side
in a sack. It would be days before it became clear who had survived
and who had not.

The eighty beds of the camp hospital had been swamped and its
dispensary drained by the smallpox in May. At the beginning of
June, it had had to house some of the women just off the *Lady Julian*.
It could not cope with the casualties of the *Neptune*, the *Scarborough*
and the *Surprize*. One of these three ships had on board a prefabri-
cated timber frame designed in Deptford as a "portable hospital."
When the scale of sickness aboard became clear, disembarkation was
halted until this was put up on the Argyle Street plot. Most of the
Lady Julian women had their first employment here, tending the
sick. Bonfires burned at a careful distance from thatched huts, fed by
serge rags stiff with human filth. Fleas leapt in the flames. The naked
sick were wrapped in blankets until clothes could be made for them.
Bales of cloth brought by the *Neptune* were issued to *Lady Julian*
seamstresses to run up a wardrobe for eight hundred convicts. Men
were sent into the bush, guarded by marines against unfriendly
blacks, to replenish supplies of myrtle against the dysentery which
swept the camp.

Reverend Johnson was stretched. On 2 July, he buried four
men; the following day, he buried another four, then two, then
five. On 6 July, five men and one woman went into the sod. The
woman was 26-year-old Ann Hardiman, who had pawned Nimrod
Blampin's clothes along Fleet Street two years before, after he had
been robbed and left naked by Rachel Hoddy. The cause of her
death was unrecorded: it could have been infection from the lingering smallpox of May, or typhus brought by the newest arrivals
or dysentery, fever, childbirth—the list of possibilities is long.

Within the chaos caused by the arrival of over 400 sick, some of the *Lady Julian* women were quietly sorting out their own futures. Word had crept out that most were to be sent to Norfolk Island, a colony even more isolated than the one in which they had just arrived. Those who stayed on the mainland would be the ones who had someone to plead their cause for them—an employer or patron, a husband whose work or prospects kept him in Sydney Cove, a marine whose officers would look sympathetically on a request to maintain a mistress. Thomas Barnsley was now reunited with his wife, Elizabeth. The Reverend Johnson had been complaining for months of over-work. If a literate, plausible assistant presented himself and his capable wife at a moment like this, when graveyard duty was on the rise and more ship babies had just arrived requiring salvation, such an aide would have been gratefully employed. It seems Thomas swiftly found his feet as clerk to the Reverend Johnson and Elizabeth became the colony's midwife. The Barnsleys had arrived.

A network of persuasion and protection, favors granted and with-held, had bound the women and ship's company of the *Lady Julian*. This was beginning to dissolve and another to emerge between the women and the men of the colony. Some had been taken, or had taken themselves, off the availability list. Jane Forbes, Sarah White-lam, Sarah Dorset, Elizabeth Griffin, Ann Bryant and Margaret Wood were all nursing babies. Mary Flannegan was pregnant; so were Hannah Teesdale Gee, Susannah Mortimore and Elizabeth Gale, all presumably to *Lady Julian* seamen. Charlotte Simpson and Margaret Smith were living with two of the superintendents who came aboard in Cape Town. Ann Mash was with Surgeon Alley. Mary Warren may or may not have continued her liaison with Sam Braiden. But in a colony "in great want of women," bigamy, imminent childbirth and the maintenance of other men's seaborn offspring did not have the same impact on a woman's marriage prospects as they might have back home.

There is little evidence among the emerging relationships to reveal how they were initiated, by whom organized, by whom approved. The men in charge had a utilitarian view of camp women, if one often tinged with compassion: basically, they were an undifferentiated mass of mouths and wombs. The people attached to these fundamental body parts would be moved from place to place according to what the mouths required and the wombs offered; it was unnecessary to know them as individuals to determine their colonial future as a group. They had been brought over from Britain to sleep with the camp guards and bear children to male settlers and this is largely what they did.

In one case, there is clear evidence of an arranged marriage. John Nicol was quite sure that the story of Mary Rose had had a happy ending in Sydney Cove. According to him, after the departure of the *Lady Julian*, her relations had discovered the fate of their lost and ruined Mary. "By their exertions, the whole scene of the landlady's villainy was exposed" and the landlady stood in the pillory of Lincoln for her perjury. "Upon our arrival," he continued, "we found a pardon lying at Port Jackson and a chest of excellent clothes sent by the magistrates for her use in the voyage home." In John's memory, Mary spent the rest of her time in Sydney living in the governor's house, restored to her status of lady, a gentle heroine with her wrongs righted. Some version of this story had presumably gone around the camp. It is true that Governor Phillip took a personal interest in Mary Rose's case. Probably a rare summons from the convict huts to the big house and the rumor that Mary Rose had important connections at home contributed to the story of her pardon. Perhaps the magistrates who had collected pocket money for her in Lincoln sent out some articles for her use on one of the later transports. We do know that among the letters brought for Phillip aboard the last three ships of the Second Fleet was one from Sir Joseph Banks, requesting he keep an eye on her. Phillip assured him he had fixed Mary up with "one of the best men in the colony." This was John Trace, a Devon man who seems to have had some agricultural knowledge and was therefore a colonist to woo. With two years of his sentence left to serve, he was a promising future emancipist and over twenty years older than the bride the governor picked out for him.

Evidence for Mary Rose's arrangements survives because she had
an important patron. It is possible to infer from the background and
occupations of the men who married the wharf brides of June and
July that men whom the governor wanted to keep in the colony were
granted favors from among the cargo of the *Lady Julian*. Of the
twenty-four women who were married by the end of September,
some married convicts who had risen to positions of some responsibility in the colony and others married men with agricultural knowledge. The first of the wharf brides, Mary Williams, married William
Whiting on 28 June. Whiting was storekeeper, one of the first men to
get a look at the women while the stores were being taken off the ship
and, given his employment in the most important public institution,
a man esteemed by the governor. Elizabeth Ayres married John Cuss
two weeks later. He was twenty-two years older than she and a trusty.
Isabella Manson married literate Cornishman John Rowe, like John
Trace a man with agricultural knowledge and little time left to serve
of his sentence. The next round of weddings saw the colony's chief
game killer, Patrick Burn, married to Mary Newton. However, the
granting of favors to men is not the only possible inference. Another,
equally likely, is that the *Lady Julian* women were setting up the most
advantageous unions for themselves. Elizabeth Ayres, Isabella Manson, Mary Williams, Elizabeth Cook and Mary Newton may have
married their men because they had made a swift assessment of who
would succeed and who would not. The vows taken under the marriage tree in June and July were a considered gamble. The privileges
of marriage worked both ways; if a woman had judged her man cor-
rectly and he turned out to be a humane keeper and steady provider,
her life in the colony would be more comfortable than if she
remained single.

To see them only as a lump contingent of comfort women handed
out to the men denies them any individuality. Throughout the rest of
the year in Sydney Cove, a picture emerged of women silently pairing
up with colonists and reproducing; silent, because no woman's voice
speaks from the records. But there are too many glimpses of individ-

ual decision, the stamp of personality emerges too often in records of marriage, baptism and land grants, and there are too many stories which circumvented—perhaps subverted—any orderly plan for social engineering to believe the women were simple building blocks in the colonial edifice. Officialdom clearly entered the private life of Mary Rose and may have entered that of the wharf brides signed up to approved men. However, if the women for whom scraps of information still exist are typical of the rest, there was a vital stream of personal choice flowing beneath the formation of breeding pairs in the colony.

What emerges clearly is that many of the men and women signing up for life together in New South Wales had either known each other in England or had some English connection in common. Everything else was alien. People sought the comfort of familiarity and attempted to re-create something of their former lives in this unfriendly country. Within the structure of a penal colony where so much of a convict's life was public property, the women and men in the huts and the labor gangs clung to their personal history.

On 30 July, two *Lady Julian* women stood beneath the marriage tree with two men who had arrived on the *Scarborough*. Mary Winsfield had been convicted in April 1788 of stealing three pairs of shoes from a house in Whitechapel and selling them on in Rosemary Lane market. Her husband, John Young, was a market dealer who had been convicted the following month of stealing twenty-three pairs of shoes in Cable Street, 200 yards from Rosemary Lane. Their witness was Mary Davis, who had snatched three pairs of leather shoes from a shop in east London. Next in line under the tree were Mary Winsfield's 19-year-old shipmate Esther Thornton and her bridegroom William Sherberd, in his previous life a Whitechapel shoemaker and dealer in secondhand clothes in Rosemary Lane market. You could take the convicts out of Rosemary Lane, it seems, but you could not take Rosemary Lane out of the convicts.

The following week, Mary Kymes alias Potten married William Ayres, West Country highwayman. Here was a couple whose con-

nections extended even further back than those of the Rosemary
Lane gang. Six years earlier, they had both embarked on the Amer-
ica-bound *Mercury*, which had gone no further than Devonshire.
William was one of seventy-seven ex-*Mercury* convicts now in Syd-
ney Cove. His partner in highway robbery was also in the colony,
Patrick Burn, now game killer and husband of *Lady Julian* shoplifter
Mary Newton. Connections which might have been tenuous back in
England were revived in the tiny colony.

By the time the *Lady Julian* left Sydney Cove at the end of July,
five of her women were married. Four more would marry the day
after she left. The rest were still bunking up in the huts of the female
districts, working in the hospital, sewing clothes, waiting to hear who
would stay in Sydney Cove, who would go to Rose Hill, who to Norfolk Island. The *Lady Julian* had been patched up on the north shore
to get her first to Norfolk and then Canton. Now she came back
across the river for her last few days in the colony and the seamen and
their wives were reunited. When John Nicol had signed up for the
voyage at the end of 1788, he had done so to see New South Wales;
once there, he scarcely left the huts of Sydney Cove. "Any moments I
could spare, I gave them to Sarah," he recalled, misty eyed at a distance of thirty years. "The days flew on eagles' wings. We dreaded the
hour of separation." It seems the wives were permitted to return on
board for the last few nights in port and that the men were allowed
ashore by day. The officers may have thought this would defuse the
situation but it did not. There were couples on the *Lady Julian* who
had been living together for over a year, some of whom had become
parents. Temporary sexual partners had become lovers. If Aitken's
intention back in London had been to keep his men contented by letting them sleep with convicts, the strategy backfired when the women
had to be left in Sydney Cove.

There were two ways these couples could stay together: either the
men jumped ship or the women stowed away. Requests that the men
be allowed to stay in Sydney Cove threatened to become demands.
Captain Aitken had had the story of the *Bounty* firsthand from Mas-

ter Fryer only three months ago at the Cape. Fryer's men had turned mutineer to stay with their women in Tahiti and, as far as anyone knew in July 1790, had done what they set out to do. The exploits of the *Bounty*'s company were known to seamen as well as officers. Wild plans were made during the *Lady Julian*'s last days in Sydney Cove to steal the women away and hide them in the ship until they were too far north to turn back. There seemed no possibility of the women's getting back to England by themselves. Both Sarah Whitelam and Sarah Dorset had been sentenced to seven years, like most of the *Lady Julian* women, but, as one of their shipmates wrote dolefully home that month, "I do not think I will ever get away from this place." Not only were the practical difficulties of earning the price of a passage home almost insuperable for single women, but the letters from Sydney's office which listed each woman's term of transportation had been left behind. "I do not suppose the women will give us any trouble on that head," wrote Governor Phillip. For him, clearly, they were there for life.

With hotheaded talk reported from the forecastle and surly glances and resentment spreading among his men, Captain Aitken called on Governor Phillip for help. It was decided that the women and stores going north to Norfolk Island would sail aboard the *Surprize*. The *Lady Julian* would not even touch at Norfolk; extra stores would be sent up on the *Justinian*. In January of that year, some of the Norfolk Islanders had attempted a mutiny of their own. Their plan had been to overpower the camp guards and make a break for Tahiti, every sailor's fantasy island. The Norfolk insurrection had been put down easily enough by the marines but it would be folly to send up a ship whose men might feel sympathy for a Tahiti dash. The *Lady Julian* would sail for Canton on 25 July; the *Surprize*, with women from the *Lady Julian* aboard, would follow north at a safe distance of a week's sailing.

Despite these precautions, as the day planned for the *Lady Julian*'s departure approached, the officers realized they had a serious problem on their hands. On the night of 24 July, either the women would not leave the ship or the men refused to go on board and the marines were sent in. There was a scrum, as marines laid hold of the women and passed them down to the boats, the seamen came down the ladders after them and carried the fight to the shore, the women tried to splash back out and the camp turned out to watch. Amid the shoves and taunts of the marines and the crying of bewildered babies, John took leave of his wife and son. "We exchanged faith—she promised to remain true and I promised to return when her time expired, and bring her back to England." He gave her his Bible. He wrote his name, hers and the baby's on the frontispiece and then he was pushed into a boat and they were separated by the crowd at the waterline.

On 25 July 1790, John Nicol left Sarah Whitelam in the dirt camp at Sydney Cove. Six days later, the colonists of Norfolk Island sighted the sails of the *Lady Julian* on the horizon. The excitement which had stirred the inhabitants of Sydney Cove when the *Lady Julian* appeared off the Heads in June now gripped this frightened outpost, which had not had contact with its fellow colony in over a year and feared itself abandoned once by London and again by Sydney. News of a sighting brought the island to a standstill. Tools were downed, people from every camp on the island were called to Cascade Bay to see the tiny squares of canvas on the horizon. Even those in the hospital huts heaved themselves out of bed and limped to a vantage point. When darkness fell, fires were lit on the beach at Cascade to guide the ship in. She was within 2 miles of shore when the men ankle deep in the surf realized that her crew was not reducing sail but adding. "All the harm I wish [the captain] is that I hope that he will goe to Hell for not calling when he could with so little trouble to himself," wrote Ralph Clark that night. He expressed the feelings of all—sick of their posts, longing for news of home, they loathed the barbaric backwater to which they had been sent. The resentment of a year was aimed at the ship which failed to call on 31 July. The islanders did not know that there were men on board more desperate to stay than they were to leave.

The day the *Lady Julian* sailed past Norfolk Island, the *Surprize* left Sydney Cove for the same destination. She carried aboard about 150 of the *Lady Julian* women with their children. The great majority was still unspoken for but some were already part of a couple or pregnant. Sarah and Thomas Gregory were there, reunited and accompanied by their little daughter Elizabeth. So was the newer couple of Charlotte Simpson and Superintendent Doidge. There was a clutch of *Lady Julian* wives: Sarah Dorset and baby Edward, Mary Barlow and baby Ann; Mary Flannegan and Elizabeth Gale, pregnant to *Lady Julian* seamen. Susannah Mortimore, already accompanied by one small daughter, bore another one on the voyage from Sydney Cove to Norfolk Island, fathered by a *Lady Julian* seaman, name unknown, heading for Canton a week's sailing north. Some of the early wharf brides sailed with their men: Mary Winsfield and John Young, Esther Thornton and William Sherberd were aboard; so was Nelly Kerwin and her new husband Henry Palmer. One of the last aboard was Mrs. John Coen Walsh, formerly Sarah Whitelam, who had married another man the day after John Nicol sailed out of Sydney Cove.

15

LOVE PILGRIMAGES

The *Lady Julian*'s departure from New South Wales accelerated the collapse of the relationships which had arisen within her little self-contained world. Vows had been taken by John Nicol, Edward Powell and perhaps other lovesick seamen that they would come back; vows had been returned by their wives that they would wait. But neither those leaving nor those staying could predict events in the small world of Sydney Cove or the larger one of the British Empire. Development of the relationships initiated aboard the *Lady Julian* would not only be governed by the decisions of the men and women involved but by events outside their control and by the subtle effects of absence.

The women of the *Lady Julian*, snatched from the anonymity of city streets and thrown into sudden, unwilling relief would now relapse into anonymity on the other side of the world. From maidens in distress, teenage mothers or hardened street criminals, some would evolve into the mistresses of wealthy households and founders of dynasties, others would sink without trace and the majority would settle somewhere in between. The aftermath of life on the *Lady Julian* would continue to shape the lives of a few but for most the voyage was simply the first of many eventful years spent adapting to new circumstances and new faces. As aboard the *Lady Julian*, the development or decline of their relationships with men and with each other are caught in snatches and seen in glimpses, raising more questions than can ever conclusively be answered. The lives and decisions of each individual who left the *Lady Julian* in June 1790 have become obscured, hidden behind the lowest common denominators of convict experience.

The colonial lives of a few women are reasonably well illuminated, often because of their association with a man of consequence, sometimes because of their own achievements. Sarah Whitelam—now Sarah Coen Walsh—was one, because of her appearance in John Nicol's memoirs. Sarah Dorset is another, because of her liaison with Edward Powell, who became a man of some influence in the colony. Elizabeth Barnsley, Nelly Kerwin and a handful of others continue to raise their heads above the mass. The very fact these women were exceptional enough to have left a dent in the records may mean their experiences differed from those of the average woman. Nevertheless, this is the only material we have from which to draw inferences, however approximate, about life for the rest of their shipmates. One thing the records do show is that these women became neither the undifferentiated breeders and consumers of colonial planning nor the uniformly oppressed victims of convict folklore. Rather, they remained individuals; personality and accident continued to stamp their life in the colony as they had done life in Britain and life afloat.

Two of the most enduring labels to cling to the female convict experience are those of victimization and abandonment. Both victimization and abandonment, however, were intricate, practiced by women on men as well as by men on women. More men passed through the colony than women ever did, so the number of men leaving and women staying is skewed toward a suggestion of base male treachery. Individual stories suggest a different truth lurks.

When Sarah Whitelam signed her cross to John Coen Walsh on 26 July 1790, John Nicol was working the first day of a miserable passage to Canton on a ship full of ghosts. He took down his hammock and went to sleep in another part of the ship where he would not be haunted by Sarah. It did not work. Everything on board reminded him of her, everything "brought her endearing manners to my recollection." Nicol and his disconsolate comrades arrived in Canton in October 1790. He had sailed from here to London two years before, alone and looking forward to retirement from the sea and a reunion with his father and brothers in Scotland. That plan had not worked and instead he had sailed from London to New South Wales with his hopes vested in a new life with Sarah Whitelam. Forced to leave Sarah in Sydney Cove, he had come full circle and was once more alone.

It seems John Nicol and Edward Powell, who had left his own Sarah and their baby back in the colony, spent their time in Canton laying plans for their return to Sydney. They had been brought away from Sydney Cove by force but Nicol, at least, was still rebelliously considering the possibility of jumping ship in Canton. If he could find a ship to Rio or the African cape, he would at least be on his way back south and would take a chance on picking up a ship for New South Wales. What dissuaded him from this plan was not the practical difficulty of escaping the *Lady Julian*. It was the fact that neither he nor Powell could afford to forfeit the wages waiting for them in London at the end of the trip. If they were to bring their wives away from the colony, it would be at heavy expense, as neither woman would have the money to pay her own passage. The wages due at the end of an eighteen-month voyage were considerable and passion gave way to prudence. The *Lady Julian* left Canton with both men still aboard, their plans for rescue deferred but not defeated.

While John Nicol and Edward Powell brooded over their lost loves in Canton, Sarah Dorset, Sarah Coen Walsh, their babies and 150 of the other *Lady Julian* women were settling into life on Norfolk Island. Norfolk was run by Major Ross, who had his own idea of colonial development based on the pig. Pigs, he thought, would get convicts involved in the production of their own food and off the public store as quickly as possible. Unfortunately, there were not enough pigs for the convicts to have one each, nor even one per couple. A pig per three people was all that could be managed and, when the beasts were issued at the end of the year, Norfolk arranged itself into a bizarre society of ménages à trois, each based around the household pig. There was no clergyman on the island until November 1791, when Richard Johnson came over from the mainland to perform a mass marriage fest for upward of thirty couples, baptizing an estimated hundred babies at the same time. Only after Johnson's visit did more conventional family units emerge from the three-per-pig tangle. The lack of records on Norfolk and the particular difficulty of distinguishing couples amid the pig keepers make it difficult to tell who was cohabiting with whom, and how soon these relationships started.

The Coen Walshes successfully reared their pig. Sarah Dorset, who had arrived alone on the island with baby Edward, was issued her pig in company with two male convicts. She did not marry but became pregnant again in March 1792, presumably by one of her two fellow pig keepers. Among the people she would have known in the community of 550 souls on Norfolk Island was Thomas Webb, a First Fleet seaman who had remained behind as part of the company of the *Sirius* or *Supply*. Webb's contract ended shortly before Sarah Dorset's baby was born. He returned to England smitten with the new colony and its possibilities and found a berth straight back, this time as a settler.

Among his shipmates on the return journey was Edward Powell, Sarah Dorset's *Lady Julian* lover. Unlike John Nicol, still trying to work his passage back aboard a series of vessels, Powell had saved and paid for a passage back out as a free settler. His plan was no longer to bring his wife and baby back to England, but to stay in the colony. The 1792 voyage aboard the *Bellona* was substantially different for Edward Powell than that aboard the *Lady Julian* in 1789. Then, he had been an ordinary seaman who spent his off-duty hours canoodling with a convict before the mast. The 13,000 miles which the *Lady Julian* covered in twelve months the *Bellona* managed in five and a half, sailing with thirteen settlers and seventeen female convicts aboard. Presumably

Powell's intention in returning to Sydney Cove in 1792 was still to find and marry Sarah Dorset. Certainly John Nicol, when he wrote his memoirs, was under the impression that this was what he had done: "when her time expired," he wrote, "[Powell] brought her home, and married her." John never heard the real end to the story.

Edward Powell may have learned from Thomas Webb that Sarah Dorset had last been seen pregnant with someone else's baby. For whatever reason, his plans changed. Also aboard the *Bellona* was a large farming family from Blandford in Dorset. Thomas and Jane Rose were emigrating with their four children, their 18-year-old niece Elizabeth Fish and her 1-year-old daughter, who died in the first weeks of the voyage. There was plenty of time for the settlers to get to know each other well aboard ship. They shared ambition and were thrown together by proximity and events. Edward Powell's knowledge of the colony and his financial status as a man who could set himself up in New South Wales made him an attractive addition to the Rose family circle: a manly arm for Mrs. Rose to cling to when she took a tottering constitutional; a drinking companion for Mr. Rose; a comfort to their bereaved niece. Somewhere between the Port of London and New South Wales, the tales which had seduced Sarah Dorset were recycled to seduce Elizabeth Fish. The *Bellona* arrived in Sydney Cove on 16 January 1793. By now, it was a town of decent appearance, unlike the collection of dirty huts Powell had seen last time around. There was even a small church instead of the tree beneath which the congregation had gathered in the early days, and here, on 21 January, Edward Powell and Elizabeth Fish were married.

What had changed his plans? Either Powell already knew that Sarah was living with another man or he had decided to reject her anyway. Insidious doubt could have entered his mind, creeping disloyal thoughts of the advantages offered by a free bride, possibly with dowry, over a convict, penniless and likely to be a different woman from the sweet girl he had left three years before. Edward Powell would display great ambition later in his colonial life, becoming a prosperous landowner and a respected voice in local politics. A convict bride did not necessarily hold a man back, but she did not help him advance either.

In February 1793, Mr. and Mrs. Edward Powell went to seek out land from the allotments on offer in the Homebush area. Powell was granted 80 acres and their homestead was given the uneasy name of Dorset Green. Here they began a life which revolved around the homestead, the stores of Rose Hill (now renamed Parramatta), the settlement's church and markets and the company of settlers whose land adjoined theirs. They were given use of the labor of convicts, possibly even of women Powell had known aboard the *Lady Julian*, although this is impossible to know for certain. Certainly, Powell would soon have come across familiar faces at Divine Service, or doing business at the Commissariat, or selling produce on the Kissing Point wharves. Women who recognized the latest settler as Sarah Dorset's lover might have asked him a few pointed questions and turned their backs on his bride in loyalty to their old shipmate. Equally, they might have shrugged and displayed indifference. Sarah Sabolah Lyons would shortly turn up nearby, back from Norfolk Island. She might have had a caustic comment or two. Ann Mash, another *Lady Julian* wife, was a couple of miles down the track. Surgeon Alley had gone back to England and Ann had moved in with John Irvine, a Lincolnshire quack transported for the theft of a silver cup who, as there were not enough free surgeons to go around, had been appointed surgeon of Parramatta. Mary Stewart, Sarah Varriner, Mary Williams and Ann Young were all *Lady Julian* women living close to Edward Powell's 80 acres in the early 1790s, ready to remind him of his early days should his settler status go to his, or his wife's, head. By 1793, when Edward and Elizabeth Powell were claiming their land, many of the *Lady Julian* women were nearing the end of their seven-year sentences. Those who had wed emancipists had already become free on marriage, in an automatic calculation of a woman's status according to her husband's, and a few were living on plots as large as Dorset Green and were already important within the colonial economy. Any acquaintanceship rekindled with the seaman they remembered from their days of sleeping on the orlop would be colored by their new position as respected and productive settlers whose stake in the colony predated his own.

Sarah Dorset herself came back from Norfolk in 1794. She had two children but no husband and settled in Sydney. It may have been only on her return that she learned Edward Powell had come back—and that he had married another woman. A broken heart, a vow of revenge, so much water under the bridge? We know what she had done by about 1800—she had settled with a Sydney butcher by whom she had three more children—but not what happened in the intervening years. The colony was still small enough in the 1790s that a man living in Homebush and coming downriver to the wharves of Sydney Cove every so often stood a good chance of bumping into a woman he knew who lived around the Rocks. Edward and Elizabeth Powell's first child, a daughter, was born in April 1794 and baptized Sarah. Maybe the relationship between Sarah Dorset and Edward Powell had not ended with his marriage to Elizabeth Fish. However, two years after baby Sarah's birth, the Powells baptized their second child Edward and this effectively annulled Powell's relationship with his first son, the Edward born five years earlier in Rio de Janeiro.

Another of the notions which cling to the "thieves' colony" is that no one escaped it. Antitransportation rhetoric of nineteenth-century British reformers would refer to Sydney Cove as "the bourne from which no traveller returns," and the phrase "for the term of his natural life" became the title of the classic Australian saga of convict life. Although the document certifying the *Lady Julian* women's terms of exile had been left behind in London in 1789, either it turned up later or the women somehow forced acknowledgment from the colonial government that their terms of exile had expired.

Governor Phillip's reaction to not receiving this document was that the women were unlikely "to give any trouble on that head," suggesting he considered them to be there, meekly, for life. Many people could not conceive of a woman's finding a way to leave the colony, other than by selling herself to someone aboard a passing ship who would smuggle her away. Emancipated convicts who wanted to leave the colony were obliged to pay their own passage back to Britain and, if they could not raise the money, had no choice but to remain and make the best of it. Clearly, it was more difficult for a woman to raise the substantial sum of money required than it was for a man; women earned less and, if they were married or in a relationship which had produced children and domestic duties, owned neither their own money nor the time necessary to earn it. Nevertheless, about twenty-five of the *Lady Julian* women did eventually leave New South Wales. Not all went legitimately.

The women who got out early and on their own initiative were, almost without exception, those who did not contract some alliance with a male mate. London thief Ann Bone alias Smith, literate, 19 and single, maintained herself on land granted to her in her own right on Norfolk Island. She returned to Sydney on the first possible ship and left the colony. Maidservant Amelia Harding, also young and literate, also given a plot of land to cultivate in her own right as she had not entered a relationship with a male "head of the household," had no children and left for Sydney, thence England, in 1794.

Other women who, unlike Ann Bone and Amelia Harding, did not manage to elude domesticity had to wait until later in life to free themselves from their responsibilities. Grace Brown, London shoplifter, now 38 and mother of five children, walked out on a de facto colonial marriage of nearly twenty years' duration when she sailed from the colony in 1809, her sentence long since expired. Two other wives of colonial marriages were sailing on the same ship. Elizabeth Gosling dumped her husband Daniel Brewer when they failed to make a go of their land grant on the Northern Boundary Farms, just outside Parramatta, and went home in 1799, aged 42. Elizabeth Gale, superior maidservant—and literate, like Elizabeth Gosling—also left her colonial partner in 1809 and returned to England; it is unclear how many of her children she took with her.

Other women paid their passage home from sums of money given them by lovers or partners. Sarah Young's husband had petitioned

Lord Sydney from his Portsmouth hulk to join his "beloved 18-year-old wife" in 1789. Shortly after he arrived in Sydney Cove on the *Scarborough*, Sarah seems to have ditched him in favor of a marine lieutenant. She later paid her passage home, apparently from the money the lieutenant left her when his corps sailed from the colony. This unnamed lieutenant was not alone in his generosity. Surgeon General John White, who arrived on the First Fleet, spent four years in domesticity with *Lady Julian* maidservant Rachel Turner. He left her a generous settlement when he departed. Unlike Sarah Young, Rachel did not leave New South Wales, and her allowance from White continued even after she had married an up-and-coming boat-builder in Sydney.

Not all the *Lady Julian* women who departed the colony did so legitimately. In 1796, Mary Kymes alias Potten, now Mrs. William Ayres, quietly departed the records when her husband completed his sentence and returned to England. It seems likely she went with him, despite the fact that she had been sentenced to transportation for life. However, it was Nelly Kerwin who most neatly turned on its head Governor Phillip's satisfaction at not receiving details of the women's sentences. Nelly's capital conviction, like Mary Kymes', had been respited to transportation for the term of her natural life after George III recovered from his madness. Her life on Norfolk Island had been eventful. The husband she had married shortly after arrival in Sydney Cove was killed on the island by a falling tree and she bore a stillborn baby during her three years there. Even these experiences did not defeat her. In 1793, seven years after she was sentenced, and three years after she arrived in the colony, Nelly Kerwin sailed triumphantly and alone for England as a free woman. The government in New South Wales had been bamboozled.

The woman whose perfidy, or pragmatism, is most poignantly recorded is Sarah Whitelam, mistress of the hapless ship's steward John Nicol. Nicol had arrived back in London just after the next fleet of transports sailed for Sydney Cove at the beginning of 1791 and all agents he visited inquiring for a ship to the colony told him the same—that "there was none, nor likely to be soon." He took the next best option—a cooper's berth on the *Amelia*, a South Sea whaler, which he was assured would touch at Rio. His plan was this: to sign on as though he intended to complete the round journey, then to feign sickness at Rio, be left behind and find his way however he could to New South Wales. He got no further than the Kentish coast, where the *Amelia* was blown upon the sands, threatened by the wreckers, and had to be towed back up to the Port of London.

Nicol's memories of the voyages he made over the early 1790s were confused by the time he came to dictate his memoirs in 1822. What emerges from his tangled recollection of these years is a telescoping of ships and contracts which had him back off Cape Town in about 1792 or 1793, biding his time for a ship heading for the colony. In fact, this Cape Town voyage must have been undertaken in 1796 or 1797 and it was then that his hopes of ever seeing Sarah again reached their highest and lowest points. Sarah was at the end of her sentence and he was two months' sailing away. His ship wallowed in the Cape waters, harpoons whistled, decks ran with whale oil and John Nicol packed his trunks below. And then the sails of the *Venus* were sighted to the east. Signals were exchanged, the ships hove to and longboats were hoisted for the captains to exchange news. Captain Coffin of the *Venus* was returning to Britain having left a cargo of convicts in Sydney Cove.

The two ships remained in company for some time in and out of Cape Town and Nicol became friendly with several of the *Venus'* company. At some point, he confided his Sydney Cove love affair and the next time they appeared, the sailors brought along a stowaway convict who had popped up in the Southern Ocean. The stowaway had news not only of progress in the settlement but of Sarah White-lam personally. She was in good health, she had a fine son—and she had left the colony some months previously, bound for Bombay. The pain this news caused the other ship's eager cooper must have persuaded the stowaway to withhold the details he suspected would be most hurtful: "how she got away, he could not inform me."

Sarah Whitelam had done well in the colony. She and her husband farmed successfully on Norfolk and had two sons together. Six years after their wedding, they paid passage for themselves and the three boys aboard the *Marquis Cornwallis,* which left Sydney Cove for Bombay in June 1796. This was how she got away.

Where many men would have given up on the chase, John Nicol seemed almost revitalized at this point: "my love for her revived stronger at this time than at any other since I left her. I even gave her praise for leaving it. She did so to be out of bad company, my mind would whisper, and I resolved to get to Bombay as soon as possible." It might have been better if the convict stowaway aboard the *Venus* had told him the whole truth: that she left the colony a prosperous young matron with a family, in the care of a faithful husband. Had John known this, he might have resigned himself to her loss. Instead, his imagination conjured up pictures of a single, young and pretty woman, the Sarah he remembered, reduced to using whatever means she could to escape the colony because she believed her lover had forgotten her.

The hunt for Sarah Whitelam now became an obsession. From the Cape, he crossed the Atlantic to Rio and jumped ship to sail for Europe aboard a Portuguese merchantman. He went from Lisbon to Portsmouth hiding from the press gangs which were searching for men to fight the French, and took a coach to Lincoln to visit Sarah's parents. They had no more news of her than he—or so they said; the last they had heard of her was John's own letter, posted before he left on his last voyage, announcing he would soon be bringing her back. If they were withholding something from Nicol from kindness, they, too, did him a disservice.

In London, once more he trudged about the docks looking for a suitable berth. Nearly a decade had passed since he had left for New South Wales. Years of service at sea, with the usual variety of seaman's accidents and diseases, meant he was not the catch he had once been to a recruiting captain. The Indiamen turned him down; the whalers had no berths. At length, he accepted a berth on a ship bound for China, "depending on Providence if we were ever to meet again." It

A portrait of John Nicol, aged 67, which appeared in the first edition of his memoirs in 1822. (National Maritime Museum, London)

was a dreary voyage. After China, the *Nottingham* sailed toward the fever-struck Dutch at Batavia and John Nicol was nearer the colony than at any point during his long quest.

He considered jumping ship and finding a passage south to ask after Sarah in the colony. However, the fever in Batavia, the "Europeans' grave" was so virulent that he stood a real risk of illness if he stayed to wait for a ship south. And if he did not catch the fever, the Dutch press gangs would get him. John found he was no longer prepared to take such risks to find Sarah again. He was hurt by "her leaving [the colony] so soon, without waiting for me," which "showed she cared less about me than I cared for her." Rather than continue chasing a ghost from port to foreign port, he would return to Britain, visit Sarah's family again, and "be ruled by the information I there obtained." But fate remained against John Nicol to the last, for it was several years before even this more modest plan could be realized. He did return to Britain from Batavia, but the press gangs caught him and he was swept into the maelstrom of the French wars, the blockades at Malta and Cadiz, the siege of Gibraltar, the battle off Cape St. Vincent. At the turn of the century, he finally limped off his last man-of-war in Portsmouth. Even now, Sarah was still on his mind, although he accepted the search was over: "I was now too old to undertake love pilgrimages after an individual as I knew not in what quarter of the globe she was, or whether she was dead or alive."

When John Nicol dictated his memoirs to an Edinburgh bookbinder in 1822, he was living pathetically off scraps and charity on the streets, an old man whose memory for dates, names and the sequence of events was growing cloudy, but whose memory of Sarah Whitelam was still glowing and tender. "Old as I am," he said, "my heart is still unchanged." He never forgot the elusive convict lover he left in Sydney Cove.

PRINCIPAL CHARACTERS

AITKEN, CAPTAIN	Captain of the *Lady Julian*.
ALLEY, SURGEON RICHARD	Ship's surgeon aboard the *Lady Julian*, lover of convict Ann Mash by whom he had a son in Rio de Janeiro.
BANKS, SIR JOSEPH	Lincolnshire landlord, botanist, President of the Royal Society, gentleman traveler with Captain Cook and promoter of New South Wales as a penal colony, sponsor to botanical missions all over the globe, he took a special interest in the case of Mary Rose.
BARNSLEY, ELIZABETH	31-year-old convict, highwayman's sister, shoplifter of distinction and grande dame of the *Lady Julian*. She was sentenced to seven years' transportation, left behind her infant children in England, and was reunited in the colony with her husband, Thomas, also a convict. She was reported to have become a

successful midwife and remained in the colony.

BLIGH, CAPTAIN WILLIAM
Previously an officer of Captain Cook's and a colleague of Lieutenant Edgar's on Cook's last voyage of exploration and discovery; 1788–89 captain of HMS *Bounty*, whose crew famously mutinied in the South Pacific.

COOK, CAPTAIN JAMES
British explorer and navigator who commanded the 1770 expedition which named and claimed New South Wales; the greatest seaman of the age.

DORSET, SARAH
20-year-old convict, found guilty at the Old Bailey, London, of attempting to steal a cloak and sentenced to seven years' transportation, she bore a baby son in Rio to seaman Edward Powell. She remained in the colony and married a butcher in Sydney.

EDGAR, LIEUTENANT THOMAS
Government agent and master of the *Lady Julian*, previously an officer of Captain Cook's.

GORDON, LORD GEORGE
Aristocratic troublemaker in Newgate Gaol at the same time as many of the *Lady Julian* women; died of gaol fever in 1793.

KERWIN, NELLY (AKA ELEANOR KIRWIN ALIAS KARAVAN)
29-year-old convict, forger, fraudster and businesswoman from Portsmouth, widowed with two small children she left in England.

Sentenced to death, then pardoned on condition of transportation for the term of her natural life, she left the colony in 1793 and returned to England.

NICOL, JOHN

Ship's steward and cooper aboard the *Lady Julian*, lover of convict Sarah Whitelam, by whom he had a son in Rio de Janeiro. His memoirs, written in 1822, are the only known firsthand account of the *Lady Julian's* voyage.

PHILLIP, GOVERNOR/
COMMODORE
ARTHUR

British naval officer who commanded the eleven ships of the First Fleet to Botany Bay and became the first governor of the new colony of New South Wales.

PITT, WILLIAM

Prime Minister of Britain and cousin of one of the junior officers on HMS *Guardian.*

POWELL, EDWARD

Seaman on the *Lady Julian*, originally from Lancashire. Fathered a son on convict Sarah Dorset, who was born in Rio; returned to New South Wales in 1793 and married another woman.

RIOU, LIEUTENANT
EDWARD

26-year-old commanding officer of HMS *Guardian*, store ship which followed the *Lady Julian* out toward Sydney Cove.

ROSE, MARY

16- or 20-year-old convict, daughter of a Lincolnshire farmer found guilty of stealing from her landlady and sentenced to seven years' transportation. She became best friend to Sarah Whitelam on the voyage out, married convict John Trace, farmer from Devonshire, and remained in the colony.

SYDNEY, LORD

British Secretary of State for Home and Colonial Affairs. Sydney, Australia, was named in his honor.

WHITELAM, SARAH

19-year-old convict thief from Lincolnshire sentenced to seven years' transportation; bore a son to John Nicol in Rio de Janeiro. She left the colony in 1796 with her ex-convict husband and their sons.

SELECT BIBLIOGRAPHY

Aitken, Dr. John. *Priniciples of Midwifery; or, Puerperal Medicine* (Edinburgh, 1785).

Anderson, C.L. *Lincolnshire Convicts to Australia, Bermuda and Gibralter* (Lincoln, 1993).

Archenholz, Baron Johann Wilhelm von. *A Picture of England: containing a description of the laws, customs and manners of England* (London, 1789).

Austen, Jane. *Pride and Prejudice* (London, 1813).

Banks, Sir Joseph. *Journal of the Right Hon. Sir Joseph Banks . . . during Captain Cook's first voyage,* (ed.) Sir J.D. Hooker (London, 1896).

Barrington, George. *A sequel to Barrington's Voyage to New South Wales* (London, 1800); and *A Voyage to Botany Bay* (Philadelphia, 1793).

Bateson, Charles. *The Convict Ships*, 1787–1868 (Sydney, 1974).

Beaglehole, C.J. *The life of Captain James Cook* (London, 1974).

Beattie, J.M. *Crime and the Courts of England*, 1660–1800 (Oxford, 1986).

Bland, Dr. Robert. *Some Calculations of the Number of Accidents or Deaths which happen in consequence of Parturition* (London, 1781).

Bligh, Captain William. *A Voyage to the South Seas, undertaken by command of His Majesty . . . including an account of the mutiny on board the said ship, etc.* (London, 1792).

Bloxhame, Marion. Unpublished research.

Bradley, Lt. William. *A Voyage to New South Wales . . . with a portfolio of charts* (Sydney, 1969).

Buchan, Dr. William. *Advice to Mothers, on the subject of their own health; and on the means of promoting the health, strength, and beauty of their offspring* (London, 1803).

Carpenter, Kenneth J. *The History of Scurvy and Vitamin C* (Cambridge, 1986).

Cioranescu, Alejandro. *Historia de Santa Cruz de Tenerife* 1494–1803 (Santa Cruz de Tenerife, 1976).

Clark, Lt. Ralph. *The Journal and letters of Lt Ralph Clark, 1787–1792*, (ed.) Paul G. Fidlon and R.J. Ryan (Sydney, 1981).

Cobley, John. *Sydney Cove in 1788* (London, 1962) and *Sydney Cove in 1789–90* (Sydney, 1963).

Collins, Judge-Advocate David. *An Account of the English Colony in New South Wales* (London, 1798).

Colquhoun, Patrick L. L. D. *A Treatise on the Functions and Duties of a Constable, etc.* (London 1803); *A Treatise on the Police of the Metropolis* (London, 1797); *The State of Indigence, and the Situation of the Casual Poor in the Metropolis* (London, 1799); and *Observations and Facts relative to Public Houses; interesting to Magistrates, the Clergy and Parochial Officers* (London, 1794).

Cook, Captain James. *A Voyage to the Pacific Ocean* (London, 1784); *The Journals of Captain James Cook on his Voyages of Discovery with Charts and Views,* (ed.) J.C. Beaglehole; and *The Voyage of the Endeavour 1768–1771* (Cambridge, 1955).

Cuppage, Frances E. *James Cook and the conquest of scurvy* (Cambridge, 1994).

Dos Santos, Lucio José. *A Inconfidencia mineira. Papel de Tiradentes* (Sao Paulo, 1927).

Easty, Private James. *Journal of a First Fleet marine.* Dixon Papers (Mitchell Library, Sydney).

Finch, Bernard and Green, Hugh. *Contraception through the ages* (London, 1963).

Flynn, Michael. *The Second Fleet: Britain's Grim Convict Armada of 1790* (Sydney, 1993).

Fowkes, Francis. Collection of maps and drawings in Mitchell Library, Sydney.

Freund, Bill. *The Making of Contemporary Africa* (London, 1984).

Gardner, James Anthony. *Above and Under Hatches,* (ed.) Christopher Lloyd (London, 1955).

Gentleman's Magazine

George, Mary Dorothy. *England in Transition: Life and Work in the eighteenth century* (London, 1931); and *London Life in the eighteenth century* (London, 1925).

Gillen, Mollie. *The Founders of Australia – a Biographical Dictionary of the First Fleet* (Sydney, 1989).

Golding, William. *Rites of Passage* (New York, 1980).

Green, Shirley. *The Curious History of Contraception* (London, 1971).

Hamilton, Dr. Alexander. *A Treatise of Midwifery, comprehending the management of female complaints* (London, 1781).

Hickey, William. *Memoirs of William Hickey 1749–1809,* (ed.) Peter Quennel (London, 1960).

Historical Records of Australia (Mitchell Library, Sydney).

Holford, George P. *Letter to the Rt Hon. The Secretary of State of the Home Department . . . on the propriety of taking other measures for the supply of women to the settlements in New South Wales, than that of sending thither all the female convicts sentenced to . . .* (London, 1827).

Hughes, Robert. *The Fatal Shore* (London, 1987).

Hunter, Captain John. *An Historical journal of events at Sydney and at sea, 1787–1792* (Sydney, 1968); and *An Historical Journal of the Transactions at Port Jackson and Norfolk Island* (London, 1793).

Jackson, Stanley. *The Old Bailey* (London, 1978).

Kelley, Hugh. *Memoirs of a Magdalen, The History of Louisa Mildmay* (London, 1767).

Levy, M. C. I. *History of Ryde and its Districts* 1792–1945.

Lincolnshire, Rutland and Stamford Mercury

Lind, Dr. James. *A Treatise of the Scurvy* (Edinburgh, 1753).

Maitland, William. *The History of London from its foundation to the present time* (London, 1775).

Nash, M.D. *The Last Voyage of the Guardian, Lieutenant Riou, Commander, 1789–1791* (Cape Town, 1990).

New South Wales Historical Records (Mitchell Library, Sydney).

Newgate Prison Books (PRO, London).

Nicol, John. *The Life and Adventures of John Nicol, Mariner,* (ed.) John Howell (Edinburgh, 1822).

Nihell, Elizabeth. *A Treatise on the art of midwifery* (London, 1760).

Noah, William. *Voyage to Sydney aboard the Hillsborough*, 1798 (see Frank Clune, *Bound for Botany Bay*, London, 1965).

O'Brian, Patrick. The Jack Aubrey/Stephen Maturin series.

Old Bailey Sessions Papers (Corporation of London Records Office).

Pardons and judges' correspondence–unpublished (PRO, London).

Place, Francis. *Autobiography of Francis Place,* (ed.) Mary Thale (London, 1972); and *Illustrations and Proofs of the Principle of Population . . . Together with unpublished letters of Place on birth control,* (ed.) Norman E. Himes (London, 1930).

Portlock, Captain Nathaniel. *A Voyage Round the World . . . in 1785–1788* (London, 1789).

Poultry Charge Books (Corporation of London Records Office).

Rodger, N.A.M. *The wooden world, an anatomy of the Georgian navy* (London, 1986).

Rumbelow, Donald. *The Triple Tree, Newgate, Tyburn and the Old Bailey* (London, 1982).

Ryan, R. I. *The Third Fleet Convicts* (Cammeray, 1983).

Scott, Sergeant James. *Diary*, Dixon Papers (Mitchell Library, Sydney).

Searing, James F. *West African Slavery and Atlantic commerce the Senegal River Valley 1700–1860* (Cambridge, 1993).

Smith, Dr. William. *State of the Gaols in London, Westminster and the Borough of Southwark* (London, 1776).

Stone, Lawrence. *Road to Divorce* (Oxford, 1990).

Tench, Lt. Watkin. *A Narrative of the Expedition to Botany Bay, with an account of New South Wales* (London, 1789).

The Times

Thompson, George. *Slavery and Famine, punishments for sedition; or, an account of the miseries and starvation at Botany Bay* (London, 1794).

Watling, Thomas. Collection of drawings (Mitchell Library, Sydney); and *Letters from an exile at Botany Bay to his aunt in Dumfries* (Perinth, 1792).

Watson, Robert. *The Life of Lord George Gordon* (London, 1795).

Welch, Saunders. *Proposal to render effectual a plan to remove the nuisance of common prostitutes from the streets of this metropolis* (London, 1758).

West, Peter. *A History of Parramatta* (Kenthurst, 1990).

White, Surgeon-General John. *Journal of a Voyage to New South Wales* (London, 1790).

Yarwood, A. T. *Marsden of Parramatta* (Kenthurst, 1986).

INDEX

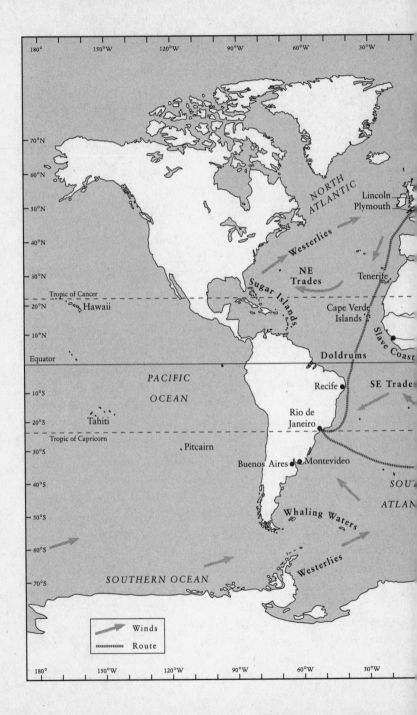

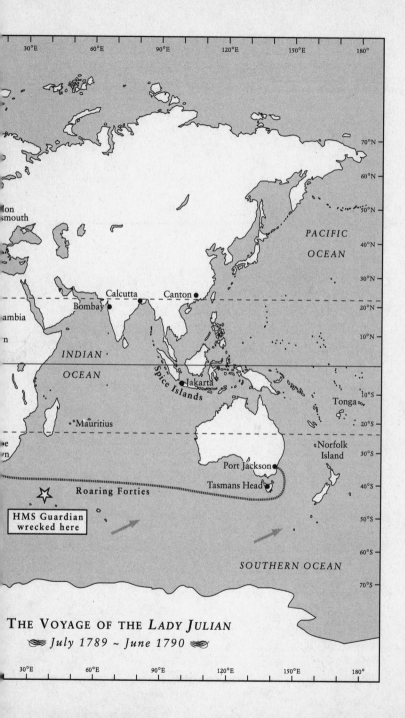

THE VOYAGE OF THE *LADY JULIAN*
≈ *July 1789 ~ June 1790* ≈